Offbeat Golf

Offbeat Golf

A Swingin' Guide To A Worldwide Obsession

By Bob Loeffelbein

Santa Monica Press

SANTA
MONICA
PRESS

Copyright © 1998 by Robert L. Loeffelbein

All rights reserved. This book may not be reproduced in whole or in part or in any form or format without written permission of the publisher.

Published by:
SANTA MONICA PRESS LLC
1-800-784-9553
P.O. Box 1076
Santa Monica, CA 90406-1076
www.santamonicapress.com
email: smpress@pacificnet.net

Printed in the United States

Library of Congress Cataloging-in-Publication Data

Loeffelbein, Robert L. 1924-
Offbeat golf: a swingin' guide to a worldwide obsession / Bob Loeffelbein

p.   cm.

ISBN 1-891661-02-7 (pbk.)
1. Golf—Humor.
2. Golf—History.
I. Title.
GV967.352 1998
796.352–DC21   98–1158
                                CIP

10 9 8 7 6 5 4 3 2 1

Book design by Ken Niles/Ad Infinitum, Santa Monica, CA
"Mr. Golf" front cover illustration by Ken Niles

Contents

Introduction **vii**

1 An Eccentric History of the Oldest Form of Self-Torture **9**

2 Golf Rules Are Made to Be ~~Broken~~ Bent! **19**

3 Let's Ditch The Rules Altogether **33**

4 Trick Shot Artists **59**

5 Curious Courses **67**

6 Automated Golf **81**

7 Groovy Gadgets to Improve Your Game **95**

8 It Don't Mean A Thing, If It Ain't Got That Swing **123**

9 Putt 'er There, Pardner! **137**

10 Having a Ball! **147**

11 Golf á la Cart **161**

12 Hole in One Helter-Skelter **171**

Resources **181**

Acknowledgments **184**

Permissions **187**

Introduction

Golf is a funny game! It isn't supposed to be, of course. It's just that truth is stranger than fiction. And nowhere is this more aptly demonstrated than in golf. Consider the following: The game is played on carefully cultivated sod with as many clubs as a player can afford and tiny balls of varied hues. It is possible to support a family of five on the money represented by the number of these balls lost in a single afternoon.

The course has 18 holes, 17 of which are only put in to make the game more impossible. A hole is a tin cup in the green, cunningly hidden between sandpits and ponds of water. A green is a small parcel of grass, costing about $1.98 a blade, usually located in the most inaccessible spot of the landscape, surrounded by "unfinished excavations."

The idea of the game is to get the ball from a given point into each of the 18 holes in the fewest number of strokes, golf or cranial. To do this, the ball must be propelled by about $1,500 worth of curiously shaped gardening tools, especially designed to provoke their user. Each implement is supposed to have a specific purpose and, ultimately, some golfers learn what they are. But these players are the exceptions.

We spend well over $200 million annually in the U.S. alone on golfing equipment. This includes gadgets and gimmicks for every real hitch or imagined quirk in our games. For, no matter what type of help a golfer needs, someone has innovated or invented a sure cure. And we, the physically pffft, may resist any advice or aid for reducing our girth or tightening our buns through exercising, but we will listen avidly, go to almost any lengths, and buy almost anything that is purported to add five yards to our tee shots or cut a couple of strokes off of our scores.

Throughout this book, I try to demonstrate that, when it comes to golf, funny can also be fun. And like the game of golf, I hope that Offbeat Golf provides a good time for all.

Bob Loeffelbein

An Eccentric History of the Oldest Form of Self-Torture

chapter 1

The origin of golf is as doubtful as the average amateur's handicap. The oldest known activity resembling modern or ancient golf was a Roman game called "paganica." This was played in an open field with a bent stick and a leather ball stuffed with wool. Historians have theorized that the Romans took the game with them when Julius Caesar invaded Britain in 55 B.C.

A description of sports played at the coronation of Alfred the Great in 871 mentions players "driving balls wide over the field," and another early reference occurs in "Roman de Brut," a rhyming-verse chronicle of British history written by a Norman poet about 1155.

Yet another report states the game goes back to 13th century Holland. It originally may have been called "het kolven," reportedly quite similar to the later "kolf." It is said to have contributed many terms to today's game. The word "golf" closely resembles the Low Dutch word "kolf," which is thought to derive, in turn, from the German word "kolbe," meaning "club."

Dick Anderson, writing in *Golf Magazine,* reported that kolf originated on December 26 (Boxing Day in Holland), 1297 in north Holland. Two teams, four on a side, used wooden clubs and balls. "Each team hit the ball in turn— a two-ball eightsome" over a 4500-meter course, with each of its four "holes" ending at the portcullis of a neighboring castle. Four clubheads used in this game were discovered in the 1970s when Robert Stenuit was excavating the *Lastrager,* a 17th century Dutch trading ship bound for the East Indies that sank off Scotland's Shetland Islands. This seems to show that kolf was exported by the Dutch to Scotland.

If you believe the Scots, however, the

chapter one

game of golf started with the antics of idle Scottish shepherd boys knocking small stones into crude holes in the ground with their shepherd's crooks. Back in 1887 Sir Walter Simpson, in his book *The Art of Golf,*

THIS PAINTING BY CLINTON PETTEE SHOWS SHOEMAKER JOHN PATTERSONE AND ENGLAND'S FUTURE KING JAMES II DEFEATING TWO ENGLISH NOBLES ON LEITH LINKS, SCOTLAND, IN 1682.

wrote: "A shepherd tending his sheep would often chance upon a round pebble and, having his crook in his hand, he would strike it away; for it is inevitable that a man with a stick in his hand should aim a blow at any loose object in his path as that he should breathe." From there the story has been told that one shepherd accidentally knocked a stone into a rabbit hole, which broke up the boredom enough for him to challenge other shepherds at the newfound pastime.

In the 14th century, several similar games have been chronicled. A game called "chole" was played in the Flanders section of Belgium, with a rule variation. Opposing teams bid to become the "scoring team," with the lowest number of strokes bid to hit a distant target earning the opportunity to score. This team got three strokes, then the opponents got a stroke to knock the ball as far out of position as possible. (On one occasion, this action, as reported in French legal documents dated 1353, resulted in a quarrel in which one player hit another over the head with his club.) This sequence continued until the scoring team reached the goal in the number of strokes bid or the opposing team thwarted them.

Another game, called "cambuca," was played in England about the same time. It was described in public documents dated 1363 as "the game of the crooked stick or curved club or playing mallet with which a small wooden ball is propelled forward." Other evidence that something akin to golf was played in England at this time is the stained glass window dating from the mid-14th century in Gloucester Cathedral, wherein a figure is depicted in a golferlike pose. The player is halfway into his backswing, the club horizontal to the ground.

Regardless of who invented golf, the unusual thing about the game is that it became popular more as a result of legislation *against* its play than it did from development and promotion *for* it. By 1457, golf had become so popular that Scotland's King James I passed an edict that no one could play "golfe" because it used up the leisure time of the people when they should be practicing archery, the main skill of the warrior of that period.

The actual proclamation, of the XIV Parliament of March 6, 1457, read: "Item, it is statute an ordinit that in na place of the Realm be usit fut-bawls, gouff or uthir sik unprofitable sportis bot for common goode and defence

> IF YOU BELIEVE THE SCOTS, THE GAME OF GOLF STARTED WITH THE ANTICS OF IDLE SCOTTISH SHEPHERD BOYS KNOCKING SMALL STONES INTO CRUDE HOLES IN THE GROUND WITH THEIR SHEPHERD'S CROOKS.

Golf Fashion

Bright plumage has always been the order for the day in linkage wear. When John Reid established the New St. Andrews Golf Club in the U.S., the official uniform for all players, even on the hottest days, consisted of a red jacket, white shirt, and club tie. Trousers, while not specified, were, presumably, mandatory. Most early clubs introduced uniform coats to be worn on the links. They had rigid rules requiring members to wear the uniform at all club meetings and dinners, under penalty. This was a tradition carried over from the Scots and Brits, where an example is taken from the Edinburgh club's meeting minutes of 1837: "John Wood was reported fined 'two tappit hens' for appearing on the links without his red coat."

In the 1870s, ladies wore bustles and large hats, tied or pinned on. Their play was thereby restricted pretty much to putting, especially since it was considered against social decorum for them to swing a club above shoulder height. Twenty years later they were still dressed in long skirts, buttoned-up boots, blouses with leg-o-mutton sleeves, and straw boaters (hats). They were forbidden to show even an ankle during play.

Among the men over the years, the top Beau Brummel may have been Adam Green. He played during the early 1900s, regularly golfing in patent leather shoes, wing-tip spats, knickers, checkered jacket, celluloid collar and cuffs, and red gloves. To complete his resplendent attire, he wore goggles while driving off the tee, then switched to a monocle for his approach shots.

Dressing the part of a golfer *is* important in playing a good game, according to psychologists. Anything that relaxes the player, or gives him a mental lift, can be worth strokes.

TYPICAL WOMAN'S GOLFING ATTIRE AS SEEN IN THE LATE 19TH CENTURY.

MARY, QUEEN OF SCOTS, SHOWING FINE FORM DURING A ROUND OF "SUDDEN DEATH" AT ST. ANDREWS IN 1563.

of the realm be hantit bowes shutting and markis yrfore ordinit. In ilk yere guhare it beis fundin yat bow markis be not maid na shutting hantit as said is." The Parliaments of three successive Scottish Kings then prohibited golf, until the bug bit King James IV and he became a golfer.

Mary, King James IV's granddaughter, learned the game as a child and became quite proficient. When she was in France attending school, she called the young boys who chased her golf balls "cadets." Through gradual usage and natural change "cadets" became "caddies," possibly through a French mistranslation.

When Mary became Queen of Scotland, the game was played openly and had advanced considerably. She became so addicted,

chapter one

• MARY QUEEN OF SCOTLAND, BECAME SO ADDICTED, THAT, WHILE PLAYING GOLF IN 1567 AND INFORMED THAT HER HUSBAND, LORD DARNLEY, HAD BEEN MURDERED, SHE FINISHED THE ROUND BEFORE GOING TO HIM. •

according to one history, that, while playing golf in 1567 and informed that her husband, Lord Darnley, had been murdered, she finished the round before going to him.

Mary's son, Britain's King James I, was such a big fan of the game that he established an honored position of Royal Clubmaker, a title first held by a bower (bow maker) from Perth. Then, in 1618, unhappy as any golfer over rising prices of good golf balls, he created another post, Royal Ballmaker, to try to keep the price at four shillings each.

St. Andrews

During Mary's reign, in 1552, the most famous of all golf courses was founded—St. Andrews (though Scots are actually reported to have started clubbing a wooden ball there about 1100 A.D.). Mary, while queen, is reported to have played this course.

It wasn't until two centuries later, in 1754, that the first semblance of organization came when 22 "Noblemen and Gentlemen, being Admirers of the Anicient (sic) and Healthful Exercise of the Golf" formed the Society of St. Andrews Golfers, the second club in Britain. With the approval of William IV, the name was changed in 1834 to The Royal and Ancient Golf Club of St. Andrews. Today the R&A, as it is called by familiars, is a worldwide club of 1,800 members, of which no more than 1,050 may live in Britain and Ireland, and 700 in other lands, including 275 in the United States and 95 in Canada. Six continents are often represented at the club's annual autumn meeting.

An anomaly is that the R&A—which cut the Old Course from 22 holes to the now universal standard of 18 in 1764—is a private club and does not own a golf course. It helps support and, thus, has privileges at the five St. Andrews courses, which are also open to the public. The heart and soul of St. Andrews is Pilmuir Links, a 400-acre spit of sandy linksland left behind by the receding sea. It consists of four abutting 18-hole spreads—the Old Course, the New (opened in 1895), Jubilee (1897) and Eden (1914).

The 6,933 yard, par-72 Old Course is by far the most deceptive and difficult. It has been sculpted more by nature's whimsies than any architect's plan. Even the bunkers' names are intimidating: Hell, Coffin, Lion's Mouth and Grave. Those who

A DRAMATIC FINISH TO A MID-19TH CENTURY MATCH AT ST. ANDREWS.

an eccentric history

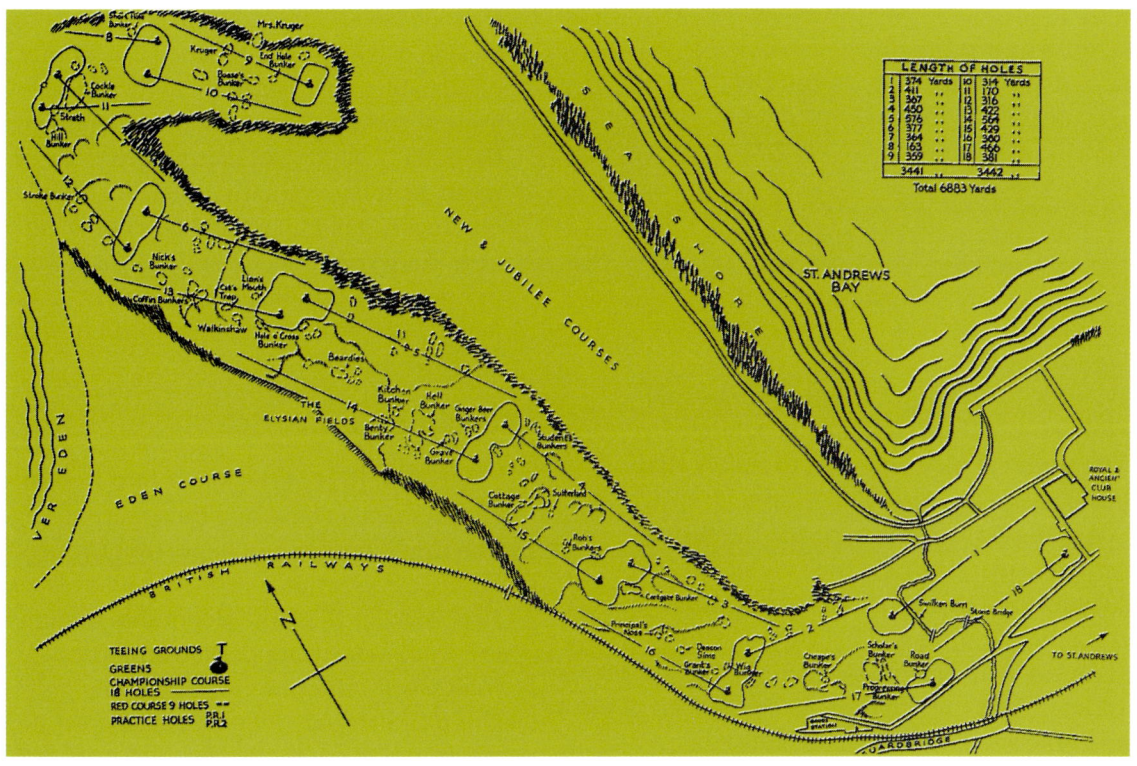

A DETAILED MAP SHOWING THE VARIOUS HOLES OF TORTURE AT ST. ANDREWS OLD COURSE. COMPARE THIS MAP WITH A PHOTO OF THE COURSE ON PAGE 68.

would like to see what the original Old Course looked like may see a 12-by-5 foot scale model of it at the James River Golf Club Museum near Newport News, Virginia. It was reproduced from Dr. A. McKenzie's map, considered the most authentic in existence.

The Old Course now has six double greens, 74 to 100 bunkers (changeable), and is at the mercy of wild winds off the Firth of Tay. The pivotal hole is probably the 17th, nicknamed the "Road Hole" and labeled "the world's most famous/infamous hole," because its tabletop green tolerates only the most accurate of putts.

It was here, in 1876, that Lord Gormley Whiffle didn't just miss his four-inch putt, but completely missed the ball, costing him a Silver Medal. Spectators remarked, repeatedly, "Did you see that Whiffle?" And it gave us our term for the air swing, eventually shortened to "whiff."

The Old Course is subject to wildly perverse weather, from sunny and calm one day to a downpour that floods the links or a 60 mph gusting gale the next. One time, as the

•

IN 1876, LORD GORMLEY WHIFFLE DIDN'T JUST MISS HIS FOUR-INCH PUTT, BUT COMPLETELY MISSED THE BALL, COSTING HIM A SILVER MEDAL. SPECTATORS REMARKED, REPEATEDLY, "DID YOU SEE THAT WHIFFLE?" AND IT GAVE US OUR TERM FOR THE AIR SWING, EVENTUALLY SHORTENED TO "WHIFF."

•

crowd applauded a 40-yard chip shot by Scottish ace Eric Brown, the ball was suddenly blown back and rolled to a stop *behind* him. Another Scottish pro damned it as "a dirt track," while an American pro, wishing to remain unnamed, stated he doubted 20 bulldozers could make it fit for golf. One Canadian visitor, flubbing shot after shot, and trapped finally in Deacon Sime Bunker on the 16th, wistfully asked his caddy,

chapter one

> WHEN BOBBY JONES FIRST COMPETED AT ST. ANDREWS IN 1921, HE SWORE IT WAS "THE WORST COURSE ON EARTH," AND EVEN QUIT IN DISGUST MIDWAY THROUGH HIS ROUND. JACK NICKLAUS, IN 1964, LABELED IT "A CATTLE PASTURE."

"What should I do now?" "Well," he was told, "ye'd best take the first plane back home."

The weirdest play here was probably that of Lee Trevino and Seve Ballesteros in 1984, the day after Ballesteros had won the British Open. They played a nine-hole match on the Old Course for British TV *using only one club*—a nine-iron—each. Ballesteros shot a 38, Trevino a 40. Trevino's comment afterward was, "You can't play St. Andrews with your whole set, much less one club!"

When Bobby Jones first competed there in 1921, he swore it was "the worst course on earth," and even quit in disgust midway through his round. Jack Nicklaus, in 1964, labeled it "a cattle pasture." "But, if a golfer is to be remembered," he said later, on winning the 1970 British Open there, "he must win at St. Andrews."

GOLF LOGIC

THE SCOTS INVENTED GOLF. THAT COULD ALSO EXPLAIN WHY THEY INVENTED SCOTCH WHISKEY.

Nonetheless, the Old & Ancient has become an icon of sorts to the addicted. Ian McLachlan of Adelaide, Australia, frequently flew halfway around the world to play there. And Zenya Hamada, a Japanese industrialist, was so taken with its charm that he went home intending to build a multi-million dollar replica near Tokyo (with membership fees of $10,000 per year). Groundskeepers even note that many players keep carting off their divots as mementos!

Coming to America

Introduction of the sport into America shares many claims, and thus remains vague. The first mention of it reportedly appears in records of what is now the city of Albany, New York. In 1659, the Honorable Commissary and Magistrate passed an ordinance prohibiting "the practice of playing golf along the streets, which causes great damage to the windows of the houses, and also exposes people to the danger of being injured, and is contrary to the freedom of the public streets . . . under the penalty of forfeiture of Fl. 25 for each person who shall be found doing so."

According to one old police report, het kolven was also discouraged by the Albany authorities. In the year 1657, Claes Hendericksan, Meeuwess Hoogenboom and Gystert van Loenen were brought before the local courts of Fort Orange and Beverwyck "for playing het kolven on the ice on the 7th of March, being the day of prayer." Since no one appeared against them the following day, however, the charges were dismissed.

Probably the first reference to the word "golf" appearing in any American publication is in a little volume entitled "Sermones to Gentlemen on Temperence and Exercise," published in 1772 by Dr. Benjamin Rush of Philadelphia. "Golf," he wrote, "is an exercise which is much used by gentlemen in Scotland. A large common in which there are several little holes is chosen for the purpose. It is played with little leather balls stuffed with feathers and with sticks made somewhat in the form of a bandy wick. He who puts a ball into a given number of holes with the fewest strokes gets the game."

an eccentric history

A Philadelphian named Joseph Fox, who learned about golf while on a trip to Scotland, introduced the organized game to Americans upon his return in 1885. By then, or shortly afterward (according to the *Golfing Annual #2* of 1888) there were already 73 golf courses in Scotland, 57 in England, six in Ireland and two in Wales. The list was 183 pages long. In the volume for 1896-97, the list had grown considerably, taking up 477 pages.

Fox founded Foxburg Golf Club, which is "probably" the oldest club in the U.S. However, the Golf Club of Savannah, Georgia also made that claim at one time. A 1796 issue of the *Georgia Gazette* reportedly includes an invitation to a ball given by the club that year, ostensibly proving its existence at that time. It didn't prove, however, that there was a golf course there or that golf was actually played.

The Homestead at Virginia Hot Springs claims another esoteric title—the country's oldest continually operating golf *tee*. According to other claims that have surfaced, 1) "Our first recorded golf club and clubhouse was Harleston's Green in Charleston, South

AMERICA'S OLDEST TEE AT THE HOMESTEAD AT VIRGINIA HOT SPRINGS. ALSO, THE OLDEST UMBRELLA.

Olympic Sport

Golf was played in both the 1900 Paris and 1904 St. Louis Olympic Games. Only three nations—Great Britain, France and the U.S.—competed in 1900. American Charles Sands won by a shot over Briton Walter Rutherford, and American art student Margaret Abbott defeated nine opponents for the women's gold medal. In 1904, the women's event was discontinued and 74 of the 75 men's entrants were American. The only non-American, Canadian George Lyon, 46, won. He was a former champion pole-vaulter and baseball player. He attended the 1908 London Games to defend his title, but became the only competitor when British golfers boycotted the

1904 Olympic Golf Medal

Games because of a domestic dispute. So Lyon refused the gold medal and golf disappeared as an Olympic sport.

However, the IOC has been talking with major golf organizations again about returning the sport to the Games, though it almost certainly won't happen before 2004. International Olympic chairman Juan Antonio Samaranch met with IOC sports director Gilbert Felli and representatives of the World Amateur Golf Council, the Royal & Ancient Golf Club of St. Andrews, the European Golf Association, the U.S. Golf Association, the PGA of America, the U.S. PGA Tour, and the PGA European Tour, in Sotogrande, Spain during the 1997 Ryder Cup matches. The problem is that golf must compete with dozens of other sports also seeking to join the hallowed Olympic program. Rugby, surfing and ballroom dancing —as of 1997—were the most recent sports to gain full recognition.

chapter one

ACCEPT NO SUBSTITUTE — THE SPALDING TRADE-MARK GUARANTEES QUALITY

Carolina, dating from 1795"; 2) a one-man course was laid out at the Merchanstan Ranch in Nance County, Nebraska, with the first game played in April 1887; and 3) America's first 18-hole course was built in 1893 by the Chicago Golf Club in Wheaton, Illinois.

Of these, the Merchanstan Ranch claim is the most intriguing. It was reported a few years back by Norman E.J. Findlay of Norristown, Pennsylvania, who claimed his father, Alexander H. Findlay, played alone on it "because there was no one else around who knew how to play."

One of the most well-known claims of "first" is that of the St. Andrews Golf Club, founded in 1888 in Yonkers or Hastings-on-the-Hudson, New York (depending on which report one reads). One of its instigators and charter members was Robert Lockhart, who had been arrested a short time before for hitting a golf ball about a sheep pasture located in Central Park. The St. Andrews course started with only six holes, and it had numerous apple trees located on it. Regular players were jokingly dubbed the "Apple Tree Gang." It may also be where the term "apple knockers" originated, though even that is disputed by some baseball researchers.

It was also on this course, in 1889, that the first mixed foursome on record was played. Miss Carrie Low, complete with cinch belt, flowing skirts, bonnet and veil, teamed with Mr. John Reid against Mrs. Reid and a Mr. Upham. The event was chronicled because the original golf clubs barred women members.

One of the first Scots to teach their game to the Americans was Willie Dunn, imported in 1891 to construct the Shinnecock Hills Club in Southampton, Long Island, New York. The club bought 80 acres for $2,500 and, with the help of 150 Indians recruited from the nearby Shinnecock Reservation, Dunn laid out 12 holes in time for late summer play that same year. By the following spring a white-shingled clubhouse, complete with locker room, showers and a grill room, had been added. The clubhouse was designed by Stanford White, the most celebrated architect of the day, which was a factor in getting 70 members signed up by the summer of 1892. Annual dues were $25, with $1 per day greens fees for guests.

PROMPT ATTENTION GIVEN TO ANY COMMUNICATIONS ADDRESSED TO US — A. G. SPALDING & BROS. STORES IN ALL LARGE CITIES — FOR COMPLETE LIST OF STORES SEE INSIDE FRONT COVER OF THIS BOOK

Prices in effect January 5, 1915. Subject to change without notice. For Canadian prices see special Canadian Catalogue.

an eccentric history

By the turn of the century, there were 1,000 golf courses in the U.S. Ten years earlier there had been only 16.

FORE

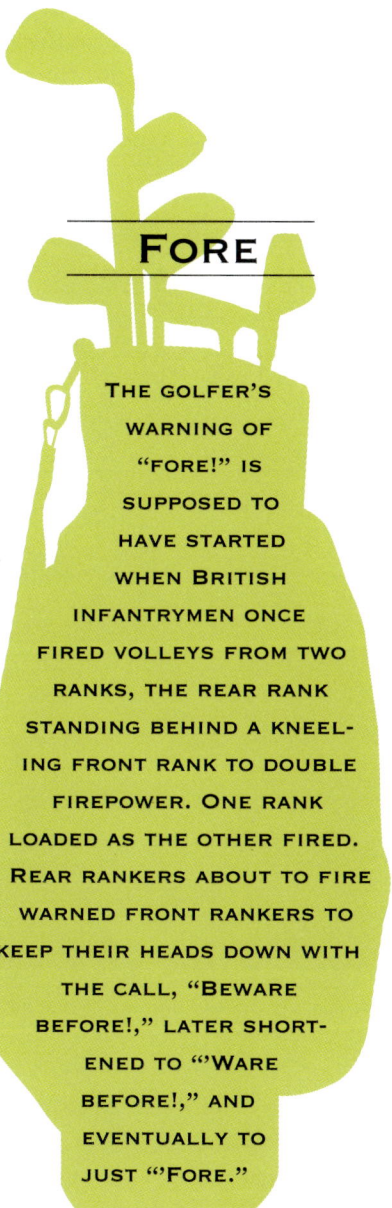

The golfer's warning of "fore!" is supposed to have started when British infantrymen once fired volleys from two ranks, the rear rank standing behind a kneeling front rank to double firepower. One rank loaded as the other fired. Rear rankers about to fire warned front rankers to keep their heads down with the call, "Beware before!," later shortened to "'Ware before!," and eventually to just "'Fore."

An avid duffer, Babe Ruth consistently shot in the high 70s and sometimes reached the low 70s. He often displayed his Ruthian power with 250 to 300 yard drives off of the tee.

A complete set of woods or irons at this time cost about $24, with a carryall canvas bag adding $6, and balls selling for 50 to 60 cents each. A ball cleaner cost $1, rubber golf tees were 25 cents each, and the caddie fee for a full round was 20 to 35 cents.

Also in 1892, an employee of A. C. Spalding & Bros. named Julian Curtiss went to Europe to buy golf merchandise. He came home with $500 worth of golf clubs and balls. Considering there were only two or three courses in existence at the time, company managers considered firing him on the spot. But Curtiss built a five-hole course on his own estate, and sold out Spalding's stock in no time.

With Spalding thus promoting the sport, albeit unwillingly, other clubs were quickly formed—in Newport, Tuxedo Park, and Philadelphia. This, in turn, increased demand for equipment, until Spalding was virtually forced to manufacture its own line. The first clubs made in this country rolled off the production line in 1895.

To further promote sales, Harry Vardon, the

17

chapter one

MRS. CHARLES S. BROWN, THE FIRST WOMEN'S NATIONAL AMATEUR CHAMPION.

British professional, was imported to play a series of exhibitions. Spalding honored him by naming their first ball after him, the Vardon Flyer, and brought out a new line of Vardon woods, which featured an insert of leather in the faces to soften the impact of the hard ball.

Other eventual Spalding firsts included a shoe especially adapted to golf, the dimpled ball cover for truer flight, and the matched club set.

In order to adopt rules of play and regulate the question of amateur status, several clubs met in 1894 and formed what is known as the United States Golf Association. The next year the new association held its first amateur men's championship, at the Newport, Rhode Island Golf Club, with a lineup of one amateur and 10 professionals. A 19-year old English professional named Horace Rawlings (or Harry Rawlins, depending upon which historic report one reads) became the first U.S. Amateur champion, with a score of 173 for the 36 holes.

In 1893, Shinnecock Hills built a nine-hole course exclusively for women. Shortly thereafter, a group of female entrepreneurs formed a seven-hole club in Morris County, New Jersey, with each hole being a drive and an iron shot, "suitable for driver, cleek, mashie and gutta-percha ball." This daring venture was hugely successful, and the course was eventually expanded to 18 holes and Morris county became the site of the second Women's National Championship in 1896. (The first Women's National Amateur champion was Mrs. Charles S. Brown of Shinnecock Hills, who shot a 69 and a 63—132—at the old Meadow Brook Club on Long Island in 1895 in a field of 13 ladies.) It was also the site of the Men's National in 1898 and the first championship of the Women's Metropolitan Golf Association in June 1900.

IN ANOTHER ERA, LIZ CURRAN SHOWS OFF HER FINE FORM.

Golf Rules Are Made To Be ~~Broken~~ Bent!

chapter 2

The Royal & Ancient Golf Club of St. Andrews (which doesn't even own a golf course) and the U.S. Golf Association (comprised of 5,000-plus clubs) jointly make rules for the entire world of golfdom. Today, besides organizing all British Opens, the R&A administers the rules of golf on every continent—except North America and the Philippines, where the USGA holds the reins—including, apparently, outer space. In 1971, the R&A Rules Committee sent a curt reminder to Alan Shepard, the Apollo 14 crew commander who hit a couple golf shots on the moon: "Before leaving a bunker, a player should carefully fill up all holes made by him herein."

These two have been at it a long time, trying to get the rules right to make sure everybody plays the same game. In 1990, the rules became uniform, except for the R&A espousing a smaller ball (1.62 inches to the USGA's 1.68 inches). For years, golfers were forced to contend with a two-volume 900-page rules collection. Then, in 1988, a 450-page paperback titled "Decisions on the Rules of Golf" was published (with a 136-page condensation in pamphlet form). This is all sort of surprising when you consider there are actually only 34 rules!

13 Original Rules

The original 13 rules of golf were drawn up by the Company of Gentlemen Golfers in 1744 under the title "Articles and Laws in Playing at Golf":

1. You must Tee your Ball, within a Clubs length of the Hole.

2. Your Tee must be upon the Ground.

3. You are not to change the Ball which you Stroke off the Tee.

4. You are not to remove Stones, Bones or any Break Club, for the sake of playing your Ball, Except upon the fair Green & that only within a Club's length of your Ball.

5. If your ball come among Watter or any wattery filth, you are at liberty to take out your Ball & Bringing it behind the hazard and Teeing it, you may play it with any Club and allow your Adversary a Stroke, for so getting out your Ball. ("or any wattery filth" was later deleted as unseemly.)

6. If your Balls be found any where touching one another, you are to lift the first Ball till you play the last.

7. At Holling, you are to play your Ball honestly for the Hole, and, not to play upon your Adversary's Ball, noy lying in your way to the Hole.

8. If you should lose your Ball, by it's being taken up, or any other way, you are to go back to the Spot where you struck last, & drop another Ball, and allow your Adversary a Stroke for the misfortune.

9. No man at Holling his Ball, is to be allowed to mark his way to the Hole with his Club or anything else.

10. If a Ball be stopp'd by any person, Horse, Dog, or anything else, the Ball as stop'd must be played where it lyes.

11. If you draw your Club, in order to Strike and proceed so far in the Stroke as to be bringing down your Club; If then, your Club shall break in any way, it is to be accounted a Stroke.

12. He whose Ball lyes farthest from the Hole is obliged to play first.

13. Neither French, Ditch or Dyke, made for the preservation of the Links, nor the Scholar's Holes or the Soldier's Lines, Shall be accounted a Hazard, But the Ball is to be taken out Teed and played with any Iron Club.

As shown by C.B. Clapcott in his "Rules of the Ten Oldest Golf Clubs" (1935), these 13 rules weren't universally used for some time. Various clubs made up their own, or modified these. At some a tee area was noted—tee for next hole is within a club length from last hole. It was 1875 before a formal teeing ground was first mentioned and 1893 before it was finally defined as "two marks placed in a line at right angles to the course." Fairways were originally called "fair greens," and greens were called "hole greens." The term "bunker" came into use in 1812. The size of the hole was not mentioned until the code of 1893, when it was recorded as 4½ inches diameter and less than 4 inches deep.

In 1996, of course, Frank Hannigan, senior executive director of the USGA, and Tom Watson wrote *The Rules of Golf: Through 1999*, which is currently the standard by which all golfers play.

Can We Have a Ruling, Please?

USGA rulings can be rather harsh at times. Even at the national championship level, there have been some questionable decisions. For instance, during the final round of the 1940 U.S. Open at the Canterbury Golf Club in Cleveland, Ed "Porky" Oliver—one of the best liked tournament pros of the era—had to be disqualified after finishing the 72 holes tied with Gene Sarazen and Lawson Little. The group with which Oliver had been playing began its afternoon round 32 minutes ahead of its official starting time in order to beat a threatening storm, and the USGA ruled that this had given the players an unfair advantage.

Jerry Barber made a worse mistake once when he wrote in the number 36—his back nine score—in the space for the 18th hole. It dropped him from the lead to the bottom of the board.

At the 1957 Women's Open at Winged Foot, Mrs. Jackie Pung, the portly, genial Hawaiian matron, brought home the winning score of 298. But, in the excitement of her victory, she signed a scorecard where her playing partner had mistakenly marked a 5 on a hole where Mrs. Pung had taken a 6. Though the final score of 72 was correctly entered, the Rules called for a disqualification.

Even more damaging was when Dave Hill, at the 18th hole of a tournament he doesn't want to remember—very unhappy with his game—scribbled a 108 on his card and signed it, making the 108 official *for the 18th hole*! It remains the highest score ever posted by a pro for one hole.

At the 1987 Andy Williams Open, Craig Stadler knelt on a towel to hit a shot from under low-hanging branches and was disqualified for turning in an incorrect score. A rule had been passed two weeks before, to resolve a question raised in the 1982 NCAA championship. Neither Stadler nor the tournament judges knew of the rule, but a golf nut watching a video replay noted that he should be assessed a penalty for "building a stance."

Lloyd Mangrum was once assessed a penalty for blowing a bug off his ball in a tournament.

During the 1987 Women's Mid-America Amateur Championship, in a seeming about-face, the Committee awarded relief to a player whose ball came to rest against a dead squirrel. Though a natural object, it was feared the dead animal might carry disease. At another tourney, however, a ball coming to rest in a bunker beside some dead land crabs was declared playable.

In other situations involving natural objects, though, committees haven't been so enlightened. One golfer's ball was embedded in an overripe orange and he was offered only options of "playing it as it lies" or declaring it unplayable and taking the penalty stroke. Another's ball landed in a half-eaten pear. The fact that it was bitten into and there was no tree in the vicinity didn't sway the judgment. Same ruling.

> LLOYD MANGRUM WAS ONCE ASSESSED A PENALTY FOR BLOWING A BUG OFF HIS BALL IN A TOURNAMENT.

chapter two

THE CURRENT STANDARD RULE BOOK FOR GOLF, WHICH, DESPITE THE PHOTO, IS NOT AN "ABRIDGED" VERSION!

that common sense alone can't decide or can't be allowed to decide. See if you can solve the following tricky questions (answers below):

1. A caddie has fallen into a bunker, with his player's golf bag and clubs, before the player has hit his ball out of the bunker. Should the player be penalized the two strokes for grounding a club in a hazard?

2. A club championship has reached a semi-final round with only three players. What should be done?

3. A tee shot comes to rest six inches from the cup. As the player and the

It was during qualifying rounds for a British Open that the toughest penalty ever was assessed for moving one's ball to a better lie. A Scot, David Robertson, was slapped with a 20-year ban. It was noted he had done this repeatedly, however.

You Make the Call!

The USGA claims the system for decision-making is "surprisingly democratic," with a 12-member committee deciding questions referred both by amateurs and professionals. It includes five members from the USGA board and seven consulting members, including representatives from the PGA, PGA Tour, and LPGA, plus "distinguished elders."

Still, sometimes, they don't seem to have made enough rules to tie down all the loose ends that keep popping up. In the course of a year the USGA alone receives more than 1,000 formal inquiries (and double that via phone) for rulings on sticky technicalities

FOR YOUR FURTHER READING PLEASURE . . .

22

bending the rules

rest of the foursome approaches the green, a crow lands beside the ball, picks it up in its beak and drops it into the hole. Is this a hole in one?

4. A player has made a hole in one, but doesn't want to buy drinks for a crowded barroom. Can he declare his ball unplayable (harking back to an old rule in Britain, the so-called "lost-in-the-hole" rule, which stated that if a golfer thought his ball was lost and so played another, it did him no good to later find his first one in the cup) and take the resultant penalty?

5. Nigel Denham of Leeds, England, playing the 18th hole of the Moortown course, drove into the clubhouse through an open door, scattering bar patrons willy-nilly. Coolly appraising his situation, Denham asked for quiet in the room and chipped flawlessly back out through an open window onto the green. Is this a legal shot?

6. A player hits a ball so hard it breaks in two. What can be done, and how is this scored?

7. With rain coming down, while playing on an already soaked course, can a player play barefoot?

8. A lady hit her ball out of the rough, saw it strike a tree trunk and carom straight back at her. She took a baseball-type swing and belted it all the way to the green. What's the stroke count?

9. Two players hit from the fairway successively toward a hidden green. At the green they find one ball in the cup and the other two feet away. Then they discover they have both shot the exact same kind of balls. Who gets the hole ball?

10. A drive stops in a deep rut, which has been made overnight by some misguided juvenile hot-rodding over the fairways, so the ball is almost unplayable. Is the player stuck with this lie?

ONE WAY TO SNEAK A SECOND DROP.

Bonus Question: Arbitrate this reported inquiry. Player #1 finds Player #2's ball in the rough and puts it in his pocket. After a few minutes search, Player #2 pops his head out of the bushes, holds a ball aloft and says, 'Ah, here it is!' What should Player #1 do?

Answers

1. He should not.

2. Decide a fourth player by stroke play, or hold a round robin playoff.

23

3. No. It can't count as one because an "outside agency" was involved. A slightly different situation involved Sam Snead one time in Chattanooga. He hit an iron to the green and, in his words, "danged if my ball didn't hit a bobwhite in the air and knock it dead. My ball stopped about a foot from the cup and I tapped it in. Only time I ever made two birdies on the same hole."

A topper for the above crow story involved one Robert W. Kneebone. A consulting VP of the Texas National Bank of Commerce, he was golfing in 1966 at Jasper Park Lodge in Canada. About to take his fourth shot on the par-5 13th, he paused to watch three large black bears come out of bordering woods to frolic on his green. Growing impatient after awhile, however, he went ahead and chipped to the green. The ball rolled within a yard of the cup. But it attracted one of the bears, which ambled over and picked it up in its mouth. Affronted, Kneebone shouted at it. The bear reared up onto its hind legs, turned its head to locate the shouter and dropped the ball directly into the cup, before lumbering off. (Considering it a gimme putt anyhow, Kneebone handled his rules decision differently. He gave himself a par 5 and blithely headed for the next tee.)

4. He cannot. The hole has been completed.

5. His shot was ruled legal since the clubhouse is officially part of the course. Lee Trevino had a barroom tale to add here. Says he saw a ball land neatly in a mug of beer. Didn't say how it was ruled, though, or how it was played.

6. In this unlikely eventuality with modern balls, the player would drop a new ball near the larger piece of the old one, add a penalty stroke, and proceed. Actually, it was Jack Nicklaus who, at age 13, exploded a Maxfli-3 ball (at the 5th hole in York Temple). He was using an 8-iron, and the ball went about 40 yards. It was squashed!

7. Not in USGA-sanctioned play.

8. Ball in play is stopped by outside agency, the player taking the second swing. Add penalty stroke and return ball to point of second contact. Incidentally, the world record rebound of a ball hitting a person's head is 75 yards, with a Colonel brand ball. Edward W. Sladward, on Sept. 28, 1913, at the 7th hole of the Premier Mine Golf Course in South Africa, drove a ball 150 yards and hit a caddy on the forehead. It rebounded on a direct line and was actually measured! It caused only a small abrasion and the caddy continued on.

9. If it is impossible to differentiate the balls, both balls must be regarded as lost, so there is no unfairness to either player.

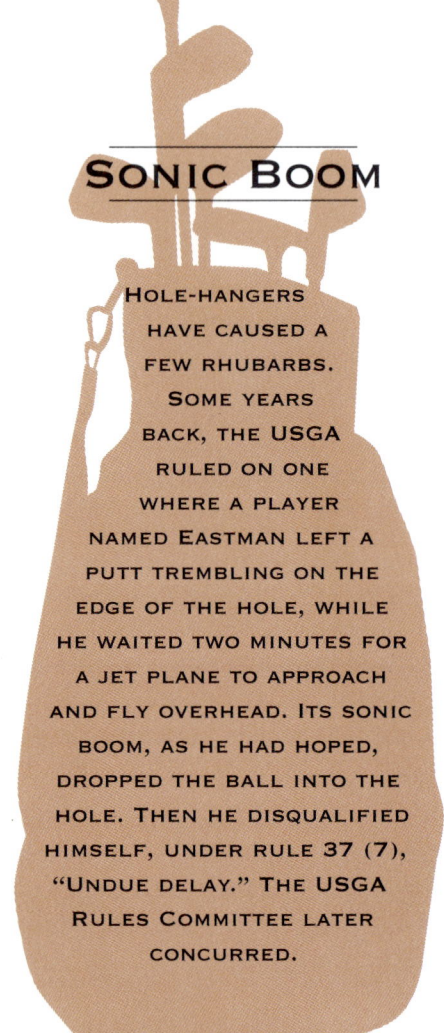

SONIC BOOM

HOLE-HANGERS HAVE CAUSED A FEW RHUBARBS. SOME YEARS BACK, THE USGA RULED ON ONE WHERE A PLAYER NAMED EASTMAN LEFT A PUTT TREMBLING ON THE EDGE OF THE HOLE, WHILE HE WAITED TWO MINUTES FOR A JET PLANE TO APPROACH AND FLY OVERHEAD. ITS SONIC BOOM, AS HE HAD HOPED, DROPPED THE BALL INTO THE HOLE. THEN HE DISQUALIFIED HIMSELF, UNDER RULE 37 (7), "UNDUE DELAY." THE USGA RULES COMMITTEE LATER CONCURRED.

bending the rules

10. Ground "under repair" should be marked in advance, but, in such an emergency situation as this, a referee or committee appeal may classify such fresh damage as "ground under repair," defined as any portion of the course so marked by the committee or "so declared by its authorized representative."

Bonus Question: You make the call!

> AN ALLIGATOR ONCE SHOWED UP ON THE 6TH FAIRWAY AT ARNOLD PALMER'S TOURNAMENT IN ORLANDO. A PLAYER WHOSE BALL LAY NEAR THE ALLIGATOR CALLED FOR A RULING. HE WAS TOLD HE HAD TO PLAY IT.

The unplayable ball situation is a common uncommon query. Balls have encountered worms poking out of the ground (removed without penalty), ant hills (player gets relief if they are the home of fire ants), rattlesnakes (ball removed beyond fang's range), and bird nests (moved, out of environmental consideration, without penalty). An alligator once showed up on the 6th fairway at Arnold Palmer's tournament in Orlando. A player whose ball lay near the alligator called for a ruling. He was told he had to play it. But he wouldn't go near the sun-basking gator. The marshall finally solved the situation by driving a cart at the beast until it slid back into the water.

War-Time Rules

In England, during World War II, according to a document titled "Temporary Rules—1940—Richmond Golf Club, Sudbrook Park, England," the following were in force:

"Players are asked to collect the bomb and shrapnel splinters to avoid damage to the mowing machines.

"In competition, during gunfire or while bombs are falling, players may take shelter without penalty for ceasing play.

"The positions of known delayed-action bombs are marked by red flags at a reasonable, but not guaranteed, safe distance therefrom.

"Shrapnel and/or bomb splinters on the fairways or in bunkers, within a club's length of a ball, may be removed without penalty, and no penalty shall be incurred if a ball is thereby caused to move accidentally.

"A ball moved by enemy action may be replaced, or if destroyed, a ball may be dropped not nearer the hole without penalty.

"A player whose stroke is affected by the simultaneous explosion of a bomb may play another ball. Penalty, one stroke."

chapter two

THIS POOR DUFFER HAS BEEN WAITING FOR A RULING SINCE 1937.

Larry Mancour, playing in one of the early Bob Hope Chrysler Classics at Rancho Mirage, California, impaled his ball on a thorn-like extrusion high in a date palm tree. The resulting penalty was like adding insult to injury.

Knowing what to do until the rules decision arrives stood Sam Snead in good stead on one occasion. In the 1955 Open, he hooked into the rough on the 12th hole and found his ball lying in the cast thrown up in all probability by "a burrowing animal" (covered under rule 32-1). Sam summoned an official for corroboration. During the five minutes he waited for the official to arrive, Sam paced nervously back and forth through the rough, so that, whether through coincidence or perspicacity, the stubbly grass was nice and trampled down when Sam received official word that he could lift and drop without penalty.

Gary Player's first trip to Britain in 1955 was for a tournament in Leeds. On the last hole, needing a birdie to win, he hooked his second shot right up against a stone wall. There was no ruling to help him. The only way to play it was to carom it off the wall. But, when he hit it, the ball came back and hit him on the jaw, knocking him out. When he recovered, he chipped onto the green and putted in for a probable tie for the lead. But the Rules Committee stepped in and assessed a two-stroke penalty for allowing the ball to touch him. He lost the tourney by a single stroke.

On the other hand, some players have been their own worst enemies by not recognizing a minor defeat and taking a penalty. At the 1919 U.S. Open at Brae Burn Country Club in West Newton, Massachusetts, a ball Willie Chisholm hit from a tee became lodged in a rock just off the fairway. Chisholm began hacking away at the ball, taking 16 strokes to dislodge it. His 18 on the hole is probably still a U.S. Open record for a par-3 hole.

Surprisingly, that isn't even close, though, for the most-strokes-for-a-hole record. In 1912, a women's tournament was held at Shawnee-on-Delaware, Pennsylvania. One contestant, whose name has been graciously obscured, topped her drive on a hole to send the ball rolling into the swift-flowing Binniekill River. She could have taken the customary penalty, but she wouldn't. So her husband obligingly rowed her downstream after the ball. With a 5-iron, she swung vigorously at the ball whenever it showed

RHETORICAL

"How come you never play golf with Harry any more?" queried the golf widow. "Well, would you play with a guy who strokes six and writes five on his card, who tees up his ball in the rough, and who kicks it inbounds when no one is looking?" returned the husband. "Of course not!" "Neither will Harry."

up in the shallow, swift and foamy water. For a mile and a half, goes the story, she chased that ball downstream until she finally managed to hit it onto land. Then, swinging away with renewed vigor, she started the long trek back to the distant green. Her score for the hole was 166.

Lee Trevino also has a water story. At Augusta one year—not in a tourney—he bet a guy he could skip his ball five times across the lake at 16 and put it on the green. He was on, whereupon he took a 1-iron, skipped the ball about six times right up onto the bank and two-putted for par.

Carl Fricki, at Del Monte, California in 1938, hit a brassie shot into the pocket of a spectator *without the spectator even realizing it!* Likewise, Jim Smith sent a 9-iron shot on the 6th at Ft. Dodge, Iowa, Country Club into Jim Van Gurdy's left-hand back pocket, while Van Gurdy was waiting to tee off over on the 7th hole (June 30, 1991). Van Gurdy also didn't realize it until he reached into his pocket for his ball and found an extra one.

chapter two

> A MINI-SUBMARINE BROKE LOOSE FROM A SLING BENEATH A GIANT HELICOPTER AND PLUNGED SEVERAL HUNDRED FEET INTO THE TURF . . . UNNERVING A FEW GOLFERS, BOTH THEN AND THEREAFTER, UNTIL REMOVED.

Gary Player had a somewhat similar occurrence in 1968 at The World Series of Golf. On the par-3 12th he hit a 5-iron and the ball landed on the back of the green, then hit a lady (who turned out to be his manager's wife) in the chest and dropped down onto her folded arms. He got a ball drop and made a par.

The *Scottish Sunday Express* once reported that a Father Morton and two companions of Chessington, England, saw a clump of bushes suddenly burst into flames at the 16th tee at Carnoustie. They didn't worry about a rule on an unplayable lie due to fire hazard, which probably didn't exist anyway. Since it was too hot to putt from the burning side of the green, they moved their balls to like distances on the opposite side and putted out, while a groundsman tackled the blaze and someone else called the fire department.

At the Eagle Haven Golf Course at the Norfolk (Virginia) Naval Amphibious Base, a mini-submarine broke loose from a sling beneath a giant helicopter and plunged several hundred feet into the turf . . . unnerving a few golfers, both then and thereafter, until removed.

Another so-called "natural hazard" introduced unnaturally onto a course was a tree. The USGA planted a 25-foot scraggled Black Hills Spruce to the left of the 8th tee *after* the first round of the Arbor Day Open in July 1979 to prevent Lou Hinkle from taking a short cut. No tree, of course, had ever been planted on a golf course after a championship had begun, so players and press protested the integrity of the hole. But it stayed.

The fact of the matter was that Hinkle had outsmarted the rules-makers by finding an opening on the 8th tee that allowed a player to drive down the adjacent 17th fairway and, from there, with a difficult but not impossible shot, hit the 8th green. He thus shortened the 528-yard par-5 hole by about 75 yards. On the first day Hinkle drove with a 1-iron, played a 2-iron approach and got a two-putt birdie. His discovery filtered back to others and eight players tried the shortcut, six of them making birdies. Hinkle's 70 gave him a tie with four other players for the first-round lead.

Next day, when Hinkle and Chi Chi Rodriguez, in the same threesome, reached the 7th green, they started laughing. Chi Chi teed up his ball on a pencil, six inches high, and went over the top of the new tree, while Hinkle cut a low driver around to its left, after carefully first removing gallery ropes and stakes and shooing spectators out of the line of fire. Hinkle then hit a 7-iron over some more trees toward the 8th green, but fell short into a bunker. Still, he got down for another birdie! Later the USGA discovered it wouldn't have had to plant a tree if it had only just moved the tee markers forward.

Emergency rules are definitely called for when much more surprising situations than those mentioned above occur. At the New Delhi Golf Club in India, for instance, the ground rules used to specify that if a monkey picked up a ball, it had to be played . . . . But now there are no more monkeys on the course, according to Col. R.S. Brar (Ret), club secretary. Instead, peacocks, which infest the course, now have right of safe passage across all fairways. And fairways are lined on both sides with thick, thorny jungle, so one doesn't dare go around them. The course also has nine ancient monuments, dating back to the 14th century, that serve as both art and hazards.

Tommy Thorne, 72, was playing Kiawah

bending the rules

CHI CHI RODRIGUEZ HAS BEEN KNOWN TO GO OVER THE TOPS OF TREES IN ORDER TO SHAVE SOME YARDS OFF OF A HOLE.

Island's Osprey Point when his tee shot flew into the marsh, coming to rest on an alligator's tail. Thorne, unperturbed, prodded the gator with a club until it wriggled away, leaving the ball behind. Thorne then holed out the 60-yard shot for an eagle 2.

Occasionally outside forces seek to usurp the regulating powers of the USGA and the R&A. Such was the case of the sheriff of Honolulu, Hawaii, when he blew his cool upon finding that his golf ball had been trampled into the Ala Wai turf. He located the offending foot, handcuffed and arrested its owner and took him off to jail.

Palma Ceia Golf Club in Tampa, Florida once issued a formal warning that dogs

Golfer-Friendly Rules

In 1976, the Union Printers Golf Club in Baltimore came out with some appealing provisos for the Rules of Golf. Under the expressive heading of "The Rules of Golf for Good Players Whose Scores Would Reflect Their True Ability if Only They Got an Even Break Once in a While," the club suggested:

"A ball sliced or hooked into the rough shall be lifted and placed in the fairway at a point equal to the distance it carried or rolled in the rough. Such veering right or left frequently results from friction between the face of the club and the cover of the ball, and the player should not be penalized for erratic behavior of the ball resulting from such uncontrollable mechanical phenomena.

"A ball hitting a tree shall be deemed not to have hit the tree. Hitting a tree is simply bad luck and has no place in a scientific game. The player should estimate the distance the ball would have traveled if it had not hit the tree and play the ball from there, preferably from atop a nice firm tuft of grass.

"There shall be no such thing as a lost ball. The missing ball is on or near the course somewhere and eventually will be found and pocketed by someone else. It thus becomes a stolen ball, and the player should not compound the felony by charging himself with a penalty stroke.

"In or near a bunker or sand trap, a ball rolling back toward the player may be hit again on the roll without counting an extra stroke or strokes. In any case, no more than two strokes are to be counted in playing from a bunker, since it is reasonable to assume that if the player had time to concentrate on his shot, instead of hurrying it so as not to delay his playing partners, he would be out in two.

"If a putt passes over a hole without dropping, it is deemed to have dropped. The law of gravity holds that any object attempting to maintain a position in the atmosphere without something to support it must drop. The law of gravity supersedes the law of golf.

"Same thing goes for a ball that stops at the brink of the hole and hangs there, defying the law of gravity. You cannot defy the law.

"Same thing goes for a ball that rims the cup. A ball should not go sideways. This violates the laws of physics.

"A putt that stops close enough to the cup to inspire such comments as 'You could blow it in' may be blown in. This rule does not apply if the ball is more than three inches from the hole, because no one wants to make a travesty of the game."

caught on the course would be captured and held for the dog catcher. Immediately a dog-owning resident of a home facing a fairway responded with a letter to the club's management, giving notice that any golfers caught searching for lost balls in his yard would be bound to the garage, with police notified of the trespass. Furthermore, he warned, if a golfer bit a yardman during the struggle, he would be confined for five days awaiting the results of a rabies test.

But the ultimate "extra" ruling comes from the Netherlands. There, to play golf on any of the 56 full-sized

BASEBALL VS. GOLF

"SLAMMIN'" SAMMY SNEAD, WHO WAS A CLOSE FRIEND OF TED WILLIAMS, PREMIER HITTER FOR THE BOSTON RED SOX, SHARED THE BENCH ONE DAY DURING A GAME BETWEEN THE SOX AND THE NEW YORK YANKEES. WILLIAMS, AN INVETERATE NEEDLER, GOT THE REST OF THE HORSEHIDERS RAGGING SNEAD. "BASEBALL," THEY TOLD HIM, "IS A MAN'S GAME—TOUGH AND COMPLEX. WHO COULDN'T SWAT A DEFENSELESS SITTING-STILL GOLF BALL? IT'S DIFFERENT TRYING TO HIT A BASEBALL PROPELLED TOWARD A BATTER BY A DETERMINED STRONG-ARMED PITCHER." SNEAD TOOK THE RIBBING GOOD-NATUREDLY, BUT HAD THE LAST WORD. "MAYBE WHAT ALL YOU BOYS SAY IS TRUE," HE DRAWLED, "BUT THERE'S ONE THING IN GOLF. WHEN YOU HIT A FOUL BALL, YOU GOTTA GET OUT THERE AND PLAY IT!"

DOES BEING LOWERED BY A ROPE ATTACHED TO YOUR HORSE CONSTITUTE A PENALTY?

courses, a report states, everyone needs a "Golf Ability Card." You get one by passing a skills test. Aspiring golfers must hit five reasonably straight drives of at least 130 yards, five approach shots to within 4½ yards of the cup, and five putts from 11 yards to within three to six feet from the hole.

chapter two

"I DON'T REALLY CHEAT," EXPLAINED THE CLINICALLY DEPRESSED DUFFER, "BUT I'VE BEEN TOLD TO PLAY GOLF FOR MY HEALTH, AND A GOOD SCORE MAKES ME FEEL SO MUCH BETTER."

Let's Ditch The Rules Altogether

c h a p t e r **3**

Have you ever played the game so badly that you told yourself you could *throw* the ball around the course and come up with a lower score? Well, some people have actually done it. The world record for throwing a ball around an 18-hole course is 84, set by Douglas V. Shipe at the University of Misssouri course in 1971.

But throwing a ball around a course is hardly the only way to subvert the rules. Throughout the 20th century, specialty tournaments in which the traditional rules of golf are turned inside-out have been held around the country. The Duffer's Tournament, for some 12,000 members of the U.S. Duffers Association headquartered in Newport, Kentucky, is a good example. A duffer who shanks his drive out of bounds, for instance, can take another shot with only one penalty stroke added, instead of two, or he can improve his lie as much as six inches, smooth out spike prints on the green, and clean or replace his ball at any time without penalty. He is allowed to whiff without counting the stroke. If he hits into the water, he can drop on the far side of the hazard for only one added stroke. In short, they still play for fun.

The Interdenominational Churchmen Tournament in Grand Rapids, Michigan installed four special rules: "Thou shalt not use profanity," "Thou shalt not covet thy neighbor's putter," "Thou shalt not steal thy neighbor's ball," and "Thou shalt not bear false witness in the final tally." What

> THE WORLD RECORD FOR THROWING A BALL AROUND AN 18-HOLE COURSE IS 84.

might have been deemed unseemly, however, was that the rules, according to one of the organizers, were swiped from another preachers' tournament. "I'm afraid we'll be accused of plagiarizing," said one white-collared official.

The National Association of Left-Handed Golfers was born in Chicago, Illinois in 1935. It sponsors about 30 tournaments a year, including an annual championship. Their main rule is that "all but trouble shots must be played lefty." They now have a women's division, as well as a newsletter called "Southpaw Activities."

Bald-Headed Men Need Only Apply

Specialty tournaments are not always about unique rules; sometimes, simply the entry requirements are enough to raise some eyebrows. Tournaments have been held for: bald-headed men (Clarkston, Washington); public links players (Hershey, Pennsylvania); Vietnam POW-MIA bracelet wearers (Corpus Christi, Texas); hoboes (Shawnee, Oklahoma); obese men (Baton Rouge, Louisiana); maitre d's (Las Vegas, Nevada, played in tuxedos with scarcely-clad showgirls for caddies); workers for companies having a gross revenue in excess of $1 million, or more than 100 employees (the USA Company Golf Challenge, which varies venues); handicapped persons, including one for blind players; men named Bob Jones (Bob Jones Open in Fenton, Michigan, honoring the great l920's golfer who won 13 national championships in eight years); and penitentiary inmates with touring professionals (the Pros & Cons Invitational).

The George Gobel Duffers Classic (named for the popular comedian), had rather a rocky start. The "first annual," for 18-handicappers and over, was held in 1975. When word got out that they were offering a $50,000 winner's prize—$10,000 more than Nicklaus won at the Masters—the USGA tried to stop them, reminding them that "any prize over $200 would cost a player his amateur standing." The duffers counterattacked by filing a lawsuit to cease interfering. "It's ludicrous to say a guy who shoots 95 to 100 is going to make his living playing golf," said Duffer's Association President Tom Drennan.

The National Tournament for Public Linkers is for those golfers not connected with any private club. It was originated in 1922 by James Standish, Jr., in Toledo, Ohio. At that first tourney, one spectator—possibly unnerved by the general level of play—shot himself in the head and play had to be temporarily suspended while his lifeless body was carried out.

In June 1985, at the Tournament Players course in Ponte Vedra Beach, Florida, (one of the country's most difficult), *Golf Digest* magazine sponsored the "America's Worst Avid Golfer Tournament." Angelo Spagnolo, a 3l-year old grocery salesman, took 257 strokes to win the dubious title of "America's Worst Recreational Golfer." He lost "about 60 balls," 27 of them on the 17th water-surrounded hole, before he was forced by course officials to walk around the green and putt down a narrow cart path to the flag.

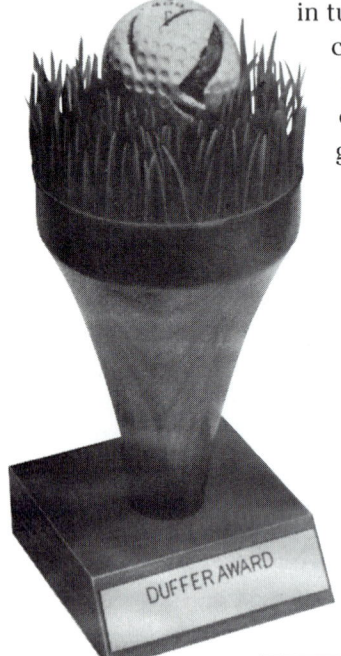

THE HALLOWED "DUFFER'S AWARD."

ditch the rules!

Golf Nuts Society of America

The Golf Nuts Society of America (GNSA) was founded by Ron Garland on July 4, 1986 to provide an affinity group for people who are "nuts" about golf. "It is open," according to their membership kit, "to men and women, boys and girls, high and low handicappers . . . anyone who wants to add a little fun to their golf." With a membership of over 2,500 and a Board of Directors that boasts Michael Jordan and Bob Hope, as well as professional golfers Peter Jacobsen, Calvin Peete and Amy Alcott, the Golf Nuts Society of America is truly one of a kind.

Members are ranked into four classes—"Class A Nut," "Class B Nut," etc.— according to how nuts they are about golf. Their nuttiness is determined by their score on the mandatory Entrance Examination. Divided into three parts— Commitment, Attitude and Mechanics—the exam features questions in the form of statements, the answers to which determine one's points. For instance, in the Commitment section, question number 8 states: "I have played golf on New Year's Day (100 points), Easter (100 points), Mother's Day (men—200 points), Father's Day (women— 200 points), Thanksgiving (100 points), Christmas (200 points), Spouse's Birthday (100 points)." A 1,000 point bonus is given to anybody who has achieved the "Golf Nut Slam" by playing in all of the above in a single year. Upon reaching the 10,000 point level, a member is automatically promoted from "Registered Golf Nut" to "Certified Golf Nut." The golfer with the most Nut Points at the end of any year is named "Golf Nut of the Year." Garland, of course, is the official Head Nut of the Society, and as such he doles out bonus points throughout the year to members who drop him a note detailing their latest accomplishments.

While the GNSA's Hall of Fame includes such luminaries as Jack Lemmon, John Havilcek, Julius Erving, Clint Eastwood, Dave Pelz, Phil Mickelson and The Golfing Gorilla, their regular membership is made up of a host of "nut cases," each of whom have earned bonus points for golf-related actions that were beyond the call of duty. For example, Don Rose has a dozen putters hanging from a noose in his garage (120 points); Marshall Gleason was married— and divorced—on the third tee at Mauna Kea (300 points); Pete Schenk went camping to get away from the game for a few days, and ended up building a makeshift nine-hole course in the woods (500 points); Mark Howard claims he was playing golf during the conception of his son (his wife denies this—500 points); Mike Brands was arrested by a State of Arizona Park Ranger, and threatened with attempted manslaughter charges, for hitting golf shots off the South Rim of the Grand Canyon (515 points); Howdy Giles, Arnold Palmer's personal dentist, has a gold ballmarker made from the gold in Arnie's fillings (2,000 points).

Among the many benefits touted by the GNSA are a personal membership card, bag tag and membership certificate; discounts on travel, merchandise and events; and copies of their monthly newsletter, "Golf Nuts Report." A Golf Nuts counseling service is also available for those members who are being driven nuts by the game.

chapter three

SPEED GOLFER JAY LARSON, SHOWN HERE IN TOP FORM AFTER LEARNING THAT GERALD FORD WAS TEEING OFF NEARBY.

Spagnolo was awarded a crystal trophy and a tacky green-plaid jacket—parodying the green coats given winners of the Masters. *Golf Digest* editors said that they put on the event "to show that average players can have fun even while ending up with scores that look more like four-round totals."

The senior citizen's Shoot-Your-Age event was first tried out as a tournament on a par-3 course in Los Angeles. A great many elders have recorded this feat both before and after the tournament, the most notable being perhaps Jimmy Drake, life member of the Miramar Golf Club in Wellington, New Zealand. At age 86 he had bettered his age 191 times and lost count of the number of times he had equaled it. His first attempt was at age 70, when he went around in 69. At age 86 his handicap was 13 and he was shooting for 200 better-than-age scores.

Bill Diddel, at age 88 in 1972, had 83 rounds under his age *in one year*. He shot a 74 when he was 86, 12 strokes under his age, which was a record. Diddel was a five-time Indiana state amateur champ, winning the first title in 1905.

Best-Ball Turkey Shoots, where low gross scores, holes in one, etc., win turkeys, are popular as Thanksgiving tournaments. Players often dress in Pilgrim garb and Indian costumes, or in old-time golfing fashions—celluloid collars, boaters and jackets for the men and bustles, bonnets and button shoes for the ladies.

Another less-than-serious tournament is the occasional April Foolish Open at a course near Mims, Florida. Temporary April Fools hazards—such as a clothesline of laundry in front of a tee, coat trees in the fairway, and ceramic croaking frogs—are scattered about the course.

The nuttiest golf tournament of all was probably the Hawaiian Holiday Masters in Honokaa, Hawaii. They used macadamia nuts for balls, padding clubs with rubber from old zori sandals so that they wouldn't break or scuff them. Nuts were coated with latex and went about 150 yards (unless one cracked, in which case it hardly moved). Entries for this unique tournament came from as far away as New Zealand.

> **THE NUTTIEST GOLF TOURNAMENT OF ALL WAS PROBABLY THE HAWAIIAN HOLIDAY MASTERS IN HONOKAA, HAWAII. THEY USED MACADAMIA NUTS FOR BALLS**

Golf on the Run

Another interesting variation on the way golf is traditionally played involves the time in which it takes to complete a round. Stop-Watch Golf began in Walla Walla, Washington in 1949. 20 golfers played nine holes (relay style) and achieved a score of 41 in just 7 minutes, 24 seconds.

Members of two other golf clubs heard about it and set out to beat their record. The Roebuck Club of Birmingham, Alabama used 25 players and negotiated the 9 holes in only 5 minutes, 56.6 seconds. But the team stroke score was a 49. The second group, consisting of 18 players in Amarillo, Texas, ran off nine holes in only 40 strokes, but took 6 minutes, 31 seconds. The *Amarillo News-Globe* published a hole-by-hole account, probably the first such report of this eccentric spinoff.

The nine-hole record is probably the 5 minutes, 14 seconds it took 34 players to go a round on the Monroe Golf Club in Michigan. The 18-hole record goes way back to 1939 when a team of players at the Tam O'Shanter course in Chicago got the ball properly holed out 18 times in 17 minutes, 20 seconds.

> **WITH SPEED GOLF, ATHLETES CAN RELY UPON THEIR INSTINCTS AND ACTUALLY IMPROVE THEIR SCORE. AS LARSON SAYS, "INSTEAD OF TAKING FIVE BEAUTIFUL PRACTICE SWINGS BEFORE HITTING THE BALL CROOKED, LET'S TAKE ONE SWING AND HIT IT STRAIGHT."**

A slight variation of Stop-Watch Golf is Speed Golf. The first Annual Speed Golf Tournament was held in Raleigh, North Carolina in 1966. According to its "official" rules, the time used to play each hole was counted rather than the number of strokes (but no times from greens to tees). Fitness buffs espoused it because it eliminated golf cart use. Players *had* to run behind their shots to make a decent showing. The inventor of Speed Golf was Edwin H. Paget, a professor at North Carolina State University, who was actually better known for his penchant for climbing Pike's Peak, which he had done 313 times in 47 years.

Presently, a new form of Speed Golf is being touted by Jay Larson and Bob Babbitt of Solana Beach, California. Larson was the perennial champion of the sport until August 21, 1997, when Rick Gladfelter of San Diego, California knocked him out of the top slot by shooting a 70 in 43 minutes, 52 seconds. In the current version of the game, the speed golfer's score for 18 holes is added to his overall time to determine his final total. On this day, Gladfelter narrowly defeated Larson 113.52 to 113.54.

Larson, a world class triathlete, insists that Speed Golf offers a great alternative for someone who can't spare four to six hours to play a round, or for those who would like to incorporate a more intense cardiovascular workout into their golf game. He suggests that "over-thinking and the indecision it breeds keeps us all from tapping into our talent resources. Most of us grew up playing sports where we reacted to the ball or object in our sport. We were usually in motion while we were reacting, and didn't have much time to consider consequences such as failure or success." With Speed Golf, athletes can rely upon their instincts and actually improve their score. As Larson says,

BAD LIE

THE GOLFER WHO PLAYED EVERY WEDNESDAY ALWAYS GOT HOME ABOUT TWO IN THE AFTERNOON, UNTIL ONE DAY HE RUSHED BREATHLESSLY INTO THE HOUSE AT 7:30 P.M. MET BY HIS WORRIED WIFE, HE BLURTED, "I LEFT THE COURSE AT THE USUAL TIME, BUT ON THE WAY HOME I HAD TO STOP AND CHANGE A FLAT TIRE FOR A YOUNG WOMAN. IN GRATITUDE SHE OFFERED TO BUY ME A DRINK, THEN ONE THING LED TO ANOTHER AND, BEFORE I KNEW IT WE HAD SPENT THE ENTIRE AFTERNOON IN A MOTEL. I'M SORRY. I'LL NEVER DO IT AGAIN." HIS WIFE LOOKED INTO HIS EYES. "DON'T HAND ME THAT MALARKEY," SHE SAID, NOW ANGRY. "YOU PLAYED 36 HOLES, DIDN'T YOU?"

chapter three

"Instead of taking five beautiful practice swings before hitting the ball crooked, let's take one swing and hit it straight."

The most bizarre method for trying to speed up play probably comes courtesy of Hall of Fame football player Deacon Jones. He and Merlin Olson, another Hall of Famer, were playing golf in the NFL Players Tournament at Canyon CC in Palm Springs in the late '60s. Jones admittedly liked a nip or two while playing and he was very happy out on the course. When two girls came along on horseback he talked one into letting him ride along (ostensibly so he could golf a la polo style). He put his foot into the stirrup while carrying his golf bag on his back. The rattling of the clubs evidently startled the horse and it took off through the mesquite, dragging the six-foot, five-inch, 280-pound Jones by one foot, clubs scattering everywhere. Fortunately, only Jones's pride was hurt.

IN NITELITE® GOLF TOURNAMENTS, PLAYERS USE GLOW-IN-THE-DARK BALLS, TEES, PUTTERS, NECKLACES AND BRACELETS.

Golf-Till-You-Drop

Still another spinoff of Stop-Watch Golf was the "most holes played in one day" hit-and-run marathon. The record for this event was first held by James J. Johnson, Jr..

Johnson, 42, a welder by trade and a Texan by birth, went on a Conan-like training regimen in preparation for his assault. He bounced on a trampoline in his backyard nightly for three and a half months, and trotted through 54 holes of golf four evenings a week for the same time period. Periodically he added 12-mile jogs through city streets, in the dark.

Then, with 14 clubs in his bag and accompanied by two golf carts equipped with spotlights, he tried for the record. 30 assistants worked several shifts to hand him clubs and find errant balls. He lost nine balls and five pounds (despite drinking four gallons of milk and orange juice). His 328 consecutive holes—played in 23 hours, 58 minutes—broke the old record by 4. He averaged 90 strokes per round on the par-70 course.

He was at work the next morning and back at the golf course in the afternoon. "I was a little sore," he admitted, "but I got in 18 holes, parring the last five. I haven't done that well in a long time. Maybe I worked some of the kinks out of my swing."

Arthur Smith, a 38-year old factory worker from Meriden, Connecticut, broke Johnson's record by three strokes. He used luminous balls and had six cars follow him to provide light in the late hours. Smith's record was in turn broken by Harry Graham of Pomona, California. Graham finished 433 holes in 22 hours, 3 minutes on the Sam Snead

ditch the rules!

All-American course. He used five balls, 22 caddies and five golf carts (though only the caddies rode in the carts). A 10-handicap golfer, Graham averaged 61.75 strokes per 18 holes on the par-57 course. During play, he kept up his strength by eating high-protein liver, beef, chicken and clam chowder.

Ralph A. Kennedy, a sales executive from Hopkinton, Massachusetts, claims two interesting world records. He once played on six different courses in one day, completing 18 holes on two courses and nine on the other four, all located in Springfield, Illinois. Between 1910 and 1957 he also played full rounds on 3,150 different courses, including a course in Guayqull, Ecuador, where fissures in the hard-baked clay fairways sometimes swallowed the ball (no penalty other than loss of ball). He also played in Negritos, Peru, where the fairways and greens were sand, and the black-painted ball had to be dug out after each lofted shot.

One of the most famed marathons was a four-day coast-to-coast performance by a 31-year old Chicago stockbroker named J. Smith Ferebee in 1938. He won his partner's half of a Virginia plantation by playing 600 holes of golf in eight cities in four days. His itinerary started with 84 holes in Los Angeles, then—traveling by plane—81 holes in Phoenix, 72 in Kansas City, 72 in St. Louis (where he pulled a leg tendon that nearly made him give up the quest), 75 in Milwaukee, 72 in Chicago, 72 in Philadelphia, and the rest in Long Island by the light of flares. He actually walked 155 miles, and didn't lose a ball. Cost was estimated at $20,000.

The most recent variation of this coast-to-coast marathon was accomplished by Jeff Thorner, a retired school administrator from San Anselmo, California. On October 14, 1997

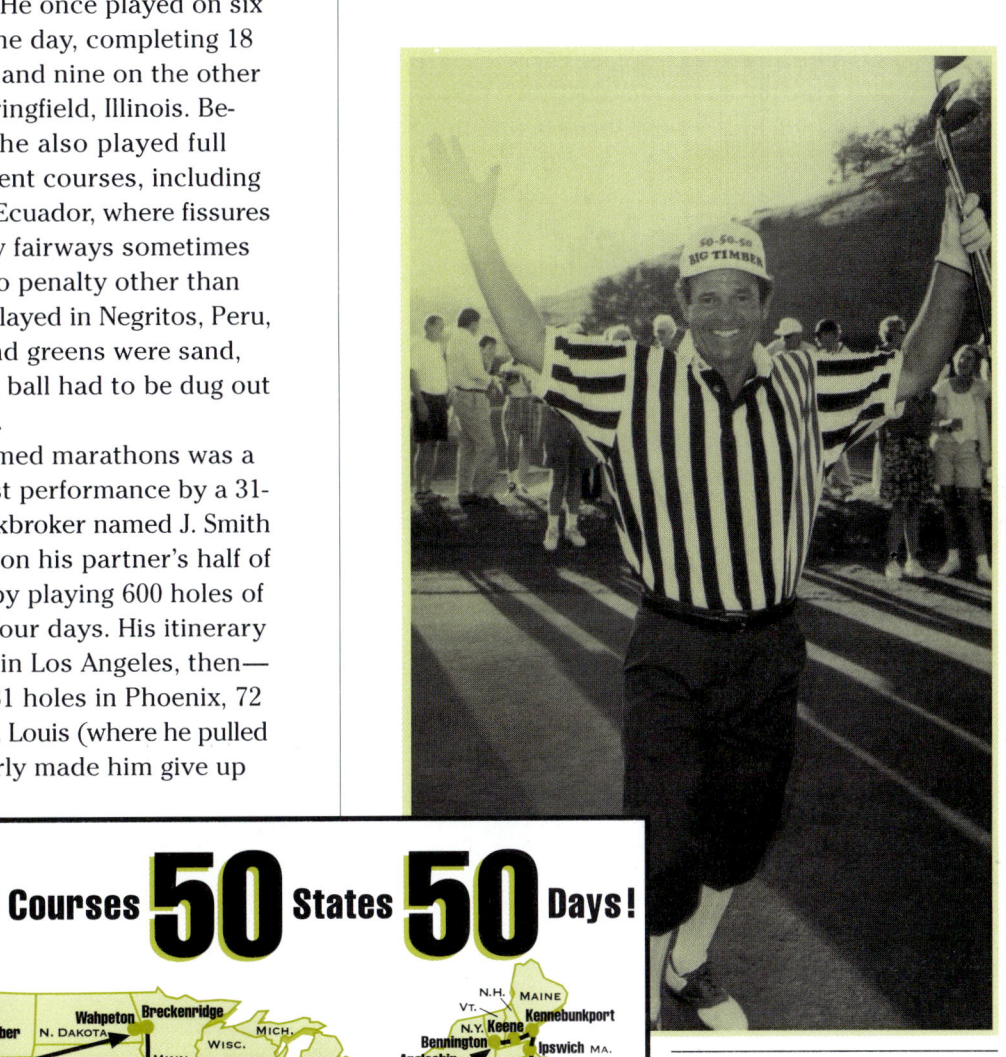

50-50-50 MAN JEFF THORNER SHOWN HERE IN BIG TIMBER, MONTANA.

50 Courses 50 States 50 Days!

chapter three

> THE MOST RECENT VARIATION OF THIS COAST-TO-COAST MARATHON WAS ACCOMPLISHED BY JEFF THORNER. HE COMPLETED A DREAM HE HAD NURTURED FOR SOME TIME, GOLFING 50 COURSES IN 50 STATES IN 50 DAYS!

he completed a dream he had nurtured for some time, golfing 50 courses in 50 states in 50 days! Starting on the Koolau course in Oahu, Hawaii, he then went to Alaska, south to Washington state, on across the northern United States to Kennebunkport, Maine, then through the others on a tight schedule, sharing driving chores with his daughter Shelby.

The trip was an estimated 11,000 miles long, and cost about $20,000. He finished with a stroke total of 4,474, for an 89.3 per round average. His worst score was the first, a 102, and his best a 79, in Rhode Island. His final round was played on his home course, San Geronimo, in Marin County, California.

He used the internet extensively in planning his itinerary and lining up playing partners. "My primary criterion for course selection was course proximity to the most direct route, and, then, to play as great a variety of courses as possible—municipals, resorts, historic, prestigious and cow pastures.

"The toughest problems I faced were lightning, bad food, long hours of driving, injury [his bad back flared up enroute], an angry daughter [who demanded separate sleeping arrangements because of his snoring], and finding the bathrooms at 50 different motels in the middle of the night."

**FIFTY ROUNDS
FIFTY STATES
FIFTY DAYS**

Thorner took up golfing in 1990 when bad knees forced him to give up tennis. He now plays at least four times a week, with a 19 handicap. He has played in 20 countries, including Scotland, Ireland, Somalia, South Africa, New Zealand, Spain, Brazil and Malaysia. In 1993, he played Alabama's seven Robert Trent Jones Tour courses in seven days, traveling with friends in a van; in 1996 he played 13 rounds in 12 days in Ireland, which motivated the 50-50-50 project. Next? An Irish friend has reminded him, "There are 32 counties in Ireland, you know!"

THORNER, SHOWN HERE WITH HIS DAUGHTER, SHELBY.

ditch the rules!

Other golfers have expanded the marathon concept as well. For instance, three West German businessmen—Uwe Siebald, Herbert Losing and Dieter Mager—played rounds of golf on three different continents in one day. They teed off in Tangier, Morocco on a Tuesday. Four hours later, they flew to London and played 18 holes. After a shower and change of clothes, they boarded a Concorde and headed for Kennedy Airport. After arriving in New York, they took a helicopter to the Plandome Country Club on Long Island, where a German band and a string of golf carts trailed the three of them on their final round before dark.

While these types of marathons are too expensive and too grueling to become bona-fide fads, variations of these events have occurred all over the world. One example is the hole in one marathon that was held by the Kildare Club in Ireland. One million pounds was the prize for a hole in one—but the hole was five miles from the tee! To make things even more difficult, hazards included a railway line, a race course, Army tank tracks, and one hundred telephone poles. The hole in one was, of course, a publicity gimmick, but the marathon was for real, and was conquered in a remarkably low 52 shots.

An even longer one-hole marathon was designed for the Pioneer Pass Golf Challenge—28 miles between Yucca Valley and Big Bear, California. The "fairway" was Pioneer Pass Road, an unpaved two-lane road that winds uphill through such unusual traps as the old Rose Mine and Rattlesnake Canyon. The tournament began with nine holes of regulation golf at the Yucca Valley Golf & Country Club. Then came the 19th hole, all 28 miles, for which the sponsors graciously allowed three days of playing time. Roving judges kept in touch with contestants along the route and official scorekeepers kept the tallies at nine checkpoints en route. The tourney ended with nine more regulation holes at Big Bear's Moonridge Golf & Country Club.

In spite of all these spates of lunacy, there will always be a place in golf history for Floyd Satterlie Rowe. He played golf across the entire United States, from the Pacific to the Atlantic. It took him 13 months. He needed 114,737 strokes and an average of one ball per mile.

The wildest marathon of all has to be the Great Canadian Race. Held over eight days in June 1976, it covered 320 miles between Toronto and Montreal. However, in this marathon, only Barry Smith drove golf balls the entire way. The rest of the participants were grouped into 36 different categories. Dale Powers, one of Canada's leading tennis players, bounced a tennis ball with his racquet. Mike Robertson hang-glided behind a power boat. A team of windsurfers sailed along a parallel route on Lake Ontario and the St. Lawrence River. Members of the Kiwanis Club of Belleville, Ontario swam the distance in relays—in a pool mounted on a

THERE WILL ALWAYS BE A PLACE IN GOLF HISTORY OR FLOYD SATTERLIE ROWE. HE PLAYED GOLF ACROSS THE ENTIRE UNITED STATES. IT TOOK HIM 13 MONTHS. HE NEEDED 114,737 STROKES AND AN AVERAGE OF ONE BALL PER MILE.

chapter three

flat bed truck. A team of 50-year olds jogged, another team roller-skated, a pilot flew his antique plane, a team of Huskies pulled a dog sled on wheels, beds on wheels were pushed, camels were ridden, and skateboarders abounded. Festivities were held each evening at checkpoints roughly 40 miles apart.

Proceeds from entry fees, distance pledges and a telethon all went to Muscular Dystrophy, Red Cross, Save the Children, and the Olympic Trust of Canada.

Iced Tee

Just to prove how crazy golfers *really* are, let's take a look at how some duffers pass the time during the winter months. The Chili Open, one of the country's oldest and most successful ice tournaments, was convened on Crystal Lake, Illinois in 1970. Fairways were plowed, rubber mats laid down for tees, and the greens carpeted for their 1,020-yard nine-hole layout. Discarded Christmas trees marked the fairways and added "natural" hazards to the snowy "roughs." Participants numbered 130, most using only a pair of irons and a putter, with balls painted black, red and green, (and a few polkadot striped or painted in plaids). Hot chili was served to help combat the below-zero wind-chill factor, which accounts for the amusing double meaning of the tournament's title. Jim Cowan, then president of the Northern Illinois Golf Association, won with a scratch 31 on the par-32 course.

Rules, of course, needed some revamping for this golfing innovation. The original nine were:

1 • Fairways will be marked with designated colors and markers. (Since all snow looked

THIS ICE DUFFER GLIDES THE PUCK, ER, BALL TOWARDS THE HOLE.

ditch the rules!

alike across the entire lake, painting different fairways with different colors kept players from getting lost.)

2 • Fairways extend to outer snow banks on each hole. (This was really an unnecessary reminder, since the snow banks indicated were composed of the detritus from the snow-blown fairway clearings. If a ball were lofted into them, the owner might be buried alive trying to burrow it out.)

3 • Everything not plowed is played as rough, literally.

4 • All shots must be played as inbounds, excepting soft ice and slush areas.

5 • Ball in soft ice or slush—no penalty, free drop from point of entry.

6 • Replace all divots. (Say what!?)

7 • Allow faster players to play through. (Some players wore spiked shoes.)

8 • Lost ball—one stroke penalty. New ball may be placed on fairway at point where ball left fairway.

OK, SO HOW COME SOME SMART INDIVIDUAL HASN'T INVENTED A WINTERTIME EQUIVALENT FOR BASEBALL? OR TENNIS? OR CROQUET? ARE GOLFERS REALLY MORE BALLSY THAN PEOPLE THINK?

9 • Ball in wrong fairway must be played as rough—no drop is allowed.

Another early ice tournament was the first Polar Ice Cap Open, conceived by Robert Scherer and Robert Twichell and held for 163 entrants in February 1970, in a wind-chill factor of minus 33 degrees. Now an annual event near Lake George, special rules allow teeing up anywhere on the course, and heating balls to keep them from freezing and cracking open. "Greens" may be swept clean of recent snow, so long as pathways aren't grooved to the cups. Separate competitions are held for men, women and children, since holes are short, ranging between 40 and 175 yards. And, since clubs are loaned from Scherer's par-3 course, he has insisted on one more special rule: "No banging clubs on the ice in frustration." He found that they freeze and snap rather easily.

Also in 1970, the small community of Grand Haven, Michigan held their own Polar Ice Cap Open on the frozen surface of Spring

chapter three

Tundra Golf Association

The Frozen Foursome—Jim "Ice" Berg, Tony "Dr. Storm" Smith, Paul Whitelaw "Winter Rules" Gorski, and Ron "Frozen Bear" Stierman—formed the Tundra Golf Association as a means of regulating golf played on frozen, often snow-covered, courses. As stated in the official rulebook of the Association, *Golf on the Tundra*, tundra golf "is a game that requires dedication. It is a game that requires passion. Above all, it is a game that requires warm clothes."

While Tundra Golf is traditionally played on golf courses which are closed for the winter, players are free to "establish their own courses on frozen rivers, lakes, or any open area as agreed upon by the players." In addition to traditional clubs, players are allowed to "carry up to three implements of snow removal such as a broom, a shovel, or a blowtorch." A fog-proof mirror is also recommended to help the golfer check for frostbite. At the end of a round, the winner is determined by a combination of the lowest score, the fewest number of lost balls, and the highest overall body temperature.

There are dozens of advantages to playing Tundra Golf, including: Built-in excuses for playing poorly; leafless trees are easier to see through; no tee times are necessary; and beverages stay cold so there is no need for a cooler!

JIM "ICE" BERG MAKES HIS WAY DOWN THE 14TH FAIRWAY OF THE LAKE MICHIGAN GOLF & ICE FISHING CLUB, STURGEON BAY, WISCONSIN.

A COMPLETE LINE OF LAKE-EFFECT GEAR AWAITS THE INTREPID WINTER DUFFER COURTESY OF TundraCo.

Don't be Intimidated by Frozen, Rock-Hard Tundra

Easy-Load Stainless Steel Teeminator Tees

NEW THIS YEAR! Easy Access Mitten-Grip Trigger

Drives Tees Into Ice, Frozen Tundra, even Solid Granite!

Drive Your Tees with a TEEMINATOR™ by TundraCo™

ditch the rules!

Lake. This event started out as a 9-hole par-3-type competition like Lake George's, but has blossomed over the years into both 9 and 18-hole tournaments. And the sponsoring Grand Haven area Jaycees and the Chamber of Commerce/Winterfest, Inc. has the huge advantage of having the Spring Lake Country Club being located just south of the lake. Contestants and spectators can thus use the club's parking, libation and warming facilities, which are ordinarily closed during the winter. Over 100 golfers turned out for that first icebound rap-around.

In succeeding years, this tournament suffered some rather unusual course maintenance problems. In 1971, they lost a pin from one of the greens when the sun warmed the metal pole enough so that it sank right through the ice. And one foursome lost one ball after another as they holed out, because the hole cup had thawed right through the ice as well. But the year before, in four degrees below zero weather, they had the opposite problem: The pins froze to the cups and it took several hours to free them.

Before the standard tournament version was formally incorporated here, there was a forerunner event, held only once on January 21, 1968. Initially called the BS Trophy Competition, its rules were reported "as originated and adapted by Raold Amundson and Cmdr. E.E. Peary, Artica N.N.P. (Near North Pole)." (The historical veracity of the claim, as well as correct spelling of names and places, was evidently never challenged!) Nevertheless, the event—ultimately named The Challenge Challenge—was conceived by a four-person team from the Challenge Stamping & Porcelain Company. They invented the rules, then challenged all comers.

The rules? Only one ball per foursome. Foursomes must contain four separate and individual players. Each player of a foursome must pre-designate which numbered golf club he will use (one club per player), and players must use only their registered club throughout the contest. (Selections were made by keeping in mind which club each player used best. Thus, one person might tee off, another handle long-iron work, a third take approach shots and the anchor person putt.) Before the event got started, this last rule prompted the addition of one more: "No fighting among the foursomes."

This last edict may have been helped immeasurably by the refreshment stand the Challengers constructed on a sled, with a tall flag so it could be easily located, a heater and lots of liquid refreshment and re-fortifier aboard.

The dippiest of the deep-freeze courses

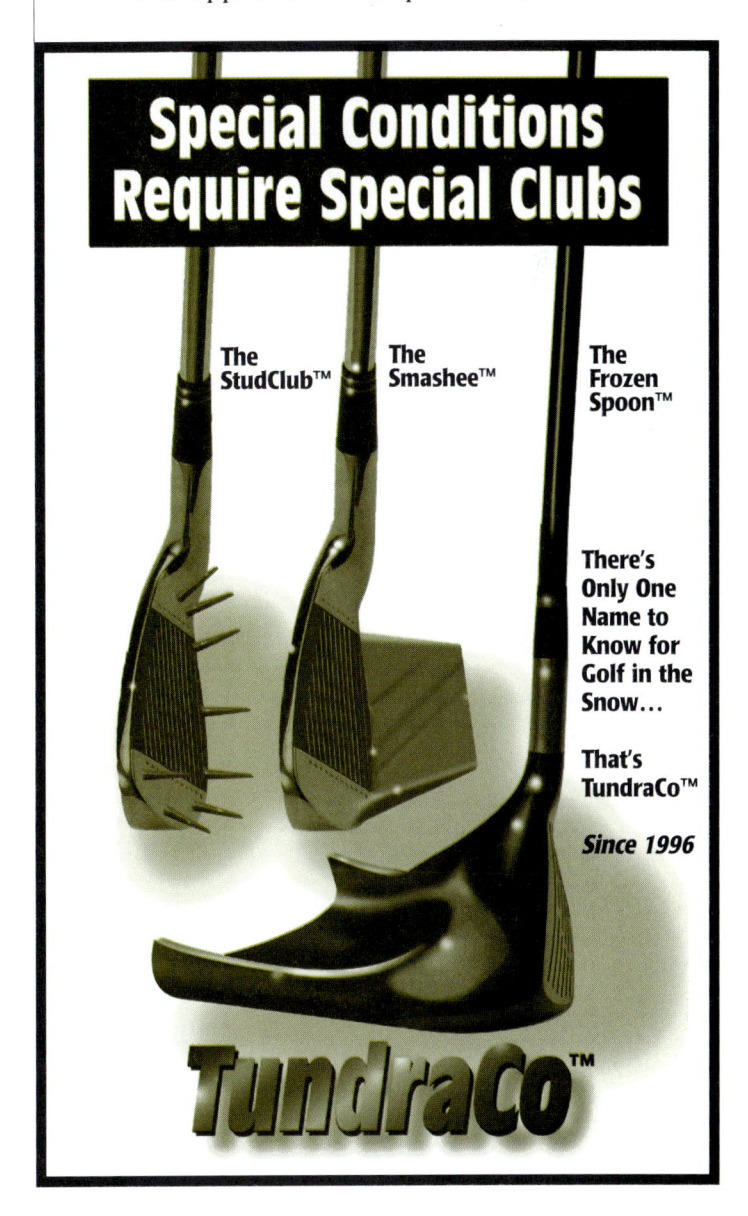

Special Conditions Require Special Clubs

The StudClub™   The Smashee™   The Frozen Spoon™

There's Only One Name to Know for Golf in the Snow...

That's TundraCo™

Since 1996

TundraCo™

45

chapter three

POWDERY SNOW MAY BE BRUSHED FROM THE PUTTING PATH WITH A WHISK BROOM. NOTE: PLAYERS MAY LEGALLY CARRY THREE SNOW REMOVAL IMPLEMENTS.

has to be Bill Joss's private one. Joss—a station manager for the Hudson's Bay Company at Holman in the Northwest Territories of Canada—used to lay out a course over ice each fall and play endless games by himself or with visiting bush pilots and Royal Canadian Mounted Policemen. Temperatures often dipped to 34 below zero and ice gusts blew in off the Beaufort Sea, but one rule always remained in force: All clubs had to be gripped with gloveless hands. He imported Jungle Glory nail polish to coat the balls, so that they could be seen in the snow. "Jungle Glory was selected because it brought back some fond memories," he once admitted, without offering any details.

Even more idiosyncratic is the Pillar Mountain Golf Classic, which started in 1985 and is Kodiak Island's Convention & Visitors Bureau-sponsored two-day, one-hole, par-70 golf tournament. Its four-mile fairway roughly follows an abandoned road up the backside of 1,400-foot Pillar Mountain through such natural hazards as steep-walled ravines, practically impenetrable alder thickets and lots of slate rock, thence into the higher reaches with snowbanks, extremely unpredictable weather and winds gusting up to 80 miles per hour.

Above the tree line is the one and only "green"—its cup being a five-gallon bucket frozen into a patch of ice. Putting, of necessity, becomes a series of chip shots, at the same time trying to keep the ball out of knee-deep footprints, since rules call for the ball being played "as is." In the case of a claimed, and approved, "unplayable lie," however, the ball may be moved three club lengths, but no closer to the hole, and the player must take a two-stroke penalty. A $5 penalty

•

TEMPERATURES OFTEN DIPPED TO 34 BELOW ZERO AND ICE GUSTS BLEW IN OFF THE BEAUFORT SEA, BUT ONE RULE ALWAYS REMAINED IN FORCE: ALL CLUBS HAD TO BE GRIPPED WITH GLOVELESS HANDS.

•

is levied against anyone cursing an official.

This bit of winter golf madness began with two local fishermen. "We were sitting around one February night, bemoaning the fact we had no real golf course," explained co-founder Glen Yngve. "One hundred books —reading is a main recreation here—were wagered. The winner would be whoever could make it to the top of Pillar Mountain in the least number of strokes. Before we knew it, 23 other people had signed up." Now it is an annual end-of-March event, attracting an average of 50 diehards, mostly local residents.

A story was going around Navy circles some years back about a two-hole course that had been constructed on the U.S. Naval Base in Anchorage, Alaska. The chaplain had constructed it for his own use, but he was soon inundated with requests from others to use it, so he had to find an equitable way to apportion use. His solution? He started giving out passes at his church services, good only for play *after* he had completed his sermon for the day. Attendance boomed.

Finally, for anyone thinking of starting up their own ice tournament, a note of caution: In February 1977, the Allegheny County Park Department decided to lay out a nine-hole Tom Thumb course on a Pittsburgh, Pennsylvania lake. Unfortunately, the four-ton bulldozer driven onto the frozen lake to scrape snow, along with its two passengers, went through the four-inch thick ice, canceling the event before it got started. Apparently, greenskeeping on ice can be a very hazardous task.

Golf for the Physically-Challenged

While the bulk of this chapter is made up of tournaments which feature inventive rules just for the fun of it, there are innovative ways to play the game designed especially for the physically-challenged. For instance, the Association of Disabled American Golfers, headquartered in Englewood, Colorado, was founded in 1992 by Greg Jones and is now represented in 43 states, Canada and Ireland. In 1997, it sponsored blind tourneys in Vero Beach, Florida and Nedlands, Australia, and amputee tourneys in nine states, as well as their fourth annual ADAG Championships and the first national tourney for integrated teams of able-bodied and disabled golfers. This latter idea is one they are pushing through their membership, which has now increased to include senior golfers, able-bodied players, owners and operators of facilities, municipalities with golf operations, and state, regional and national golf organizations.

The winners in their ADAG Championship were Scott D. Eisaman (a right hand amputee, blind in the right eye), Bryan Thurston (left hemiplegic with visual problems), Jeff Kjemhus (cerebral palsy), Janet Evans (cancer, heart attack survivor), and Eric Keller (hearing impaired).

Director Jones likes to point out that, "A good golf swing is highly overrated. Unorthodox swings produce some surprisingly effective golf shots," as has been shown in their tournaments. He also noted that "most of us put one too many hands on our putters." Disabled golfers are immune to the yips in putting, he pointed out. "When you have to concentrate on keeping your balance, you don't worry that you might miss the hole."

In Aiken, South Carolina, they have held a Bionic Invitational where, to qualify, you must have had a joint surgically replaced. "It's all about showing the world you can participate

> IN AIKEN, SOUTH CAROLINA, THEY HAVE HELD A BIONIC INVITATIONAL WHERE, TO QUALIFY, YOU MUST HAVE HAD A JOINT SURGICALLY REPLACED.

PHYSICALLY-DISABLED GOLFERS ARE NOW JOINING THE RANKS OF THEIR ALREADY MENTALLY-DISABLED BRETHREN.

chapter three

Comfortably insert your tee!

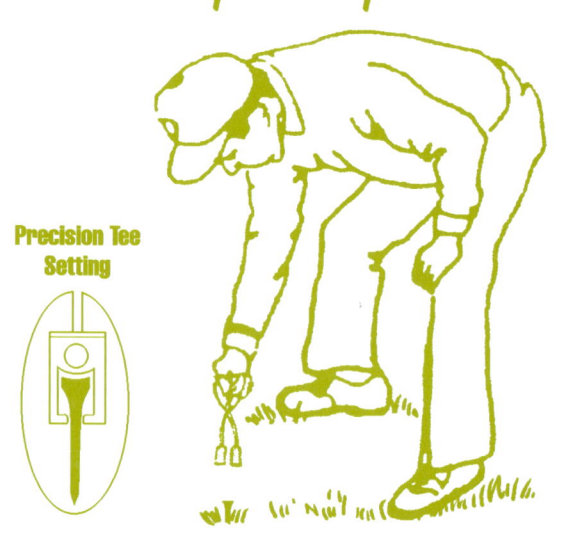

Precision Tee Setting

For the anal-retentive golfer (or those of us with bad backs).

and be just as good as anyone else," stated founder Hank Ford, who has had both knees replaced.

A blind golfer, Charles Boswell of Birmingham, Alabama, shot an 81 sometime after World War II, even though he had never played golf until after he was blinded by shellfire in that war!

Better yet is the story of Mrs. Margaret Waldon, 74, who is blind. On April 23, 1990, at Fernandina Beach, Florida, she aced the 7th hole, then came back the next day and aced it again!

Perhaps the most avid physically-challenged golfer has to be Bobbette Ranney, a 53-year old pediatrician from Brighton, Colorado. She was a skier and tennis player until 1986, when a drunk driver smashed a cement truck into her VW, rupturing her aorta and crushing her legs. So she wears braces on both legs and is unable to bend at the knees. She gets into position on her crutches, addresses the ball, drops the crutches and takes a full swing. When the follow-through gets belt high, she bends at the waist and falls forward onto her hands and elbows. She then hoists herself back up, hand over hand, on her clubshaft. And she shoots to a 17 handicap, even though she can't practice as much as she'd like. Wet grass, which makes her clubshafts slippery, is a problem. And hitting a bucket of balls can be tiring, since each swing and recovery may take as long as five minutes.

Some special equipment has made the game a bit easier for many disabled. Fabre woods, (from Fabre Golf Products, Baton Rouge, Louisiana), for example, have heads forged from aerospace-grade titanium so they produce no impact vibration. This is a godsend for golfers with arthritis or other problems where vibration and impact shock causes pain. RTS Golf, Inc. (Lorain, Ohio) markets bent titanium hosels for golfers playing from wheelchairs or single-rider carts. Tee Tongs were designed by Everett Engwall, a retired 90-year old golfer who couldn't bend over enough to set a tee or retrieve a ball. (Windmill Pointe Company, Romeo, Michigan). The No-Bend (Conco, Swanton, Ohio) gives much the same help, allowing golfers to tee a ball, pick up tees, retrieve balls from cups, set or retrieve a ball marker, and fix divots and ball marks.

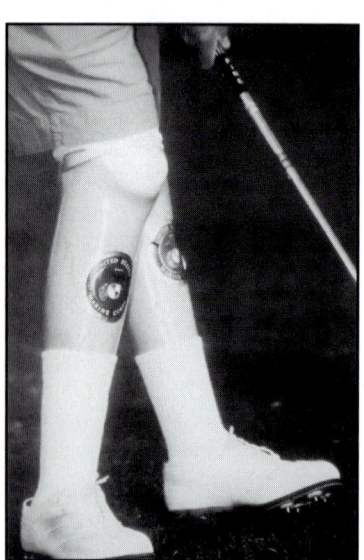

Some disabled golfers are truly able to say that they've got a leg up on the competition. (Groan)

The Power Glove (Powerglove Association, Princeton, New Jersey) has a loop on the back that hooks over the end of a clubshaft, for golfers without enough hand strength to control their swing.

Related to all of this is the Ben Hogan Trophy for handicapped players, which originated in the 1950s. It was named for Hogan because he had been injured so badly in a highway auto collision it was doubted he would ever walk again. But 16 months later he won another U.S. Open, and went on to win two more, as well as the British Open. The trophy does not demand victory, only that a nominee burdened with a physical handicap *tries*. Most of them did more than that. Winners included Babe Didrikson Zaharias, who underwent an operation for cancer in April 1953 and, 15 months later, won the Women's National Open, and Ed Furgol, who won the National Open in Balltusrol in spite of a withered left arm.

Golf for Fun and Profit

There are other methods of play invented for those for whom golf is not complete without a little wager. Perhaps the most unusual bet was made in 1935 by Eli Culbertson, then a renowned bridge game expert, who had never played golf. He got into a discussion with some golfing friends, vigorously arguing that any intelligent person could break 90 for nine holes without ever having played golf before. P. Hal Sims, another bridge authority, and Merlin H. Aylesworth, president of the National Broadcasting Co., bet Culbertson $300 he couldn't do it. Culbertson eagerly accepted. He would use only three clubs: putter, 2-iron and 5-iron. Legendary sportswriter Grantland Rice was selected to referee.

On his first swing he missed the ball completely. Then he whiffed three more times. On the fifth swing, the ball was tapped 30 yards down the fairway. 24 minutes later he finished the first hole, with a score of 15. As

chapter three

The Great Hustlers

Alvin "Titanic" Thomas, an Arkansas traveler type, may have been the last of the truly great golf hustlers. He could part a sucker from his gold with a set of golf sticks as slick as a riverboat gambler could with a deck of cards at a cotton farmers' convention. Born into the days of the fast-spieling medicine man in 1893, he became the epitome of the con man who would seek out the wise guy who liked to "bet on a sure thing."

One of his favorite stunts with a newcomer to his golf habitat was to grow expansive and say, "I'll tell you what. I'll play you left-handed." The suckers never seemed to ask if left-handed was his natural style.

He once bet he could drive a golf ball 500 yards, and won. He picked a tee overlooking a long lake that was frozen over. No one ever did find the ball after it went out of sight. Another time he bet he could drive a golf ball into a rowboat in the middle of a lake and make it stay in. Naturally, the ball would hit the floor of the boat and bounce out, so he lost. Next day, pretending to be stubborn, he said he would still make the same bet, for double the money, of course. And he did it, three times at the same odds. He had filled the bottom of the boat with sand overnight (although it still showed his confidence and his skill with a golf club).

Titanic had a trick to make long putts. He would take a water hose, leave it on a green that had just been watered (with the end in the hole), then move it the next morning. When the green was mowed, a trough was left that led directly into the hole. Then Titanic would bet someone he could sink three of five putts from 30 feet. He would select that green, then just hit his balls right down the trough.

Lee Trevino grew up in that same atmosphere. While working Hardy's Driving Range at Tenison in the early 1960s, he started playing the 9-hole pitch and putt course with a family-sized 32-ounce Dr. Pepper bottle. After cutting his hand when one broke, he taped the bottle neck and wore a glove. He practiced for a year, throwing the ball into the air and batting it onto the green, then putting between his legs croquet style. Then he went looking for matches. He played three years against all comers, allowing his opponents to use their regular equipment, and he never lost.

THE LEGENDARY ALVIN "TITANIC" THOMAS.

ditch the rules!

FRANKIE LAINE, WHOSE SAVINGS GOT BIGGER WITH LITTLER.

the strokes mounted on the next holes, so did his anger. On the fourth tee it took him four swings to make contact with the ball and he finished with a 21. His nine-hole score was 114.

Some of the more common betting versions of golf are the Nassau, the Greenie, the Press, the Bingle-Bangle-Bungle, the Gammon, the Calcutta, and the current favorite, the Skins Game.

The Nassau is a match based on three bets—so much for the front nine, so much for the back nine, and so much for the overall 18. In a Greenie, the player whose shot ends up closest to the hole on a par-3 collects. The Press is a request for a new bet on the remaining holes, usually by a player who is "down" and hopes to recoup. The Bingle-Bangle-Bungle (sometimes shortened to Bing-Bang-Bong) requires a bookkeeper, since it involves three points or payoffs for each hole—for the ball reaching the green first, the ball nearest the cup after all players are on the green, and the ball into the cup first.

R.C. Dunlap, Jr., of Macon, Georgia, announced the advent of the Gammon in 1979, modeling it after the board game Backgammon. "You bet on each hole," he explained, "and players may challenge opponents to double on a hole by announcing 'gammon', though the challenge does not have to be accepted."

The Calcutta is a form of betting in which the golfers are divided into teams and each team is auctioned off to the highest bidders. The guy who collects the most money is the one owning the tournament winners, which, of course, could be themselves if they had bid for themselves.

One of the biggest Calcuttas was the 1929 U.S. Amateur at Pebble Beach, where the total pool exceeded $200,000. Most people also remember it for the huge upset that took place. Bobby Jones, the reigning U.S. Open champion and the big favorite, was auctioned off at $60,000, but Johnny Goodman eliminated him in the first round.

Probably the all-time leading money winner for Calcuttas was Frankie Laine, the singer, who made a fortune betting on Gene Littler in the Tournament of Champions held in Las Vegas. Laine bid $13,000 for Gene in 1955 and collected $72,900 when he won. Laine bid $16,500 for Littler the next year and won again, collecting $68,120. Then Laine really hit the jackpot. He bid $15,500 in 1957 and Littler won for the third year in a row, with a $100,000 payout. He seemed to be in a zone where nothing could go wrong. On one hole, for example, Littler hit his putt about two feet past the hole, but it U-turned and rolled back downhill—right into the hole.

PROBABLY THE ALL-TIME LEADING MONEY WINNER FOR CALCUTTAS WAS FRANKIE LAINE, THE SINGER, WHO MADE A FORTUNE BETTING ON GENE LITTLER IN THE TOURNAMENT OF CHAMPIONS HELD IN LAS VEGAS.

chapter three

For years, the Masters ran its own Calcutta, as did a lot of the pro tour events. In fact, the Calcutta was once the golf gamblers' pride and joy. The hustlers spoiled it for themselves, though, by angering the USGA, which commenced an anti-Calcutta crusade. Bing Crosby, at the tourney he sponsored annually, was

> "Isn't it amazing, Arnold," rejoiced Player. "Here we've been playing for more than 30 years and it's our greatest day ever!"

among the first to back them up by eliminating it. The event that prompted the ban occurred in 1955 when players lied about their handicaps in a $5,000 Calcutta at the Deepdale Golf Club on Long Island. Two Massachusetts golfers with posted handicaps of 17 and 18 bought themselves and easily won the $16,000 first prize. Then it was learned that they both had 3 handicaps, and the USGA began an ultimately successful campaign to ban all Calcuttas.

Currently, the big money tourney is the Skins Game. That name comes from a gambling term used in weekend matches common to country clubs and municipal courses all over the country. A "skin" is a pre-established unit, maybe $5 or $10. The player who wins a hole, wins a skin from the other players. The 9-hole or 18-hole scores are meaningless. If no player wins a hole—ties are not wins—the money carries over to the winner of the following hole.

The first nationally televised Skins Game took place in Scottsdale, Arizona, in 1983. The prize money was $10,000 for each of the first six holes, $20,000 for the next six holes, and $30,000 for the final six. Sponsor Trans-World International hyped the event by suggesting a scenario whereby the entire $360,000 could be riding on the final hole. It was kept taint-free by making it an invitational for only four top professionals: Jack Nicklaus, 43, Arnold Palmer, 54, Gary Player, 48, and Tom Watson, 33. Palmer and Player recaptured earlier glory by converting two lightning thrusts into a quarter-million dollars. The four had won 41 major pro tournaments and more than 320 tournaments between them, but Palmer remarked, "I'd never won more than $50,000 in any tournament before, and today I come up with $100,000!"

"Isn't it amazing, Arnold," rejoiced Player. "Here we've been playing for more than 30 years and it's our greatest day ever!" Player led the money winners over the two day match with $170,000, making $150,000 of it on the 17th hole alone because of carryovers. And he hadn't won on the American tour since 1978!

Palmer hadn't won on the American tour for over 10 years. The $140,000 he collected was more than he had made on all his Masters and British Open wins combined! Nicklaus won two holes, for $40,000, while Watson, the dominant pro on the tour at that time, got only one, for $10,000.

The infamous toilet seat hole from the Cow Pasture Open.

ditch the rules!

More, You Say?

Actor William Gargan, a Brooklyn boy who made his film debut in 1932, was nominated for Best Supporting Actor in 1940, and made 78 movies before he died in 1979, had lost his voice box to cancer, so he sponsored an annual tournament at La Costa for the benefit of cancer research. The first tee was off a mattress, from which players had to loft over a spread-eagled pair of long johns on a washline, then curve around an outhouse on the fairway. Each hole had similar innovations added to its regular hazards, not the least of which were three "watering" holes—5, 13 and 18—as well as a traveling bar operated by actor William Powell (of the *Thin Man* series) and his wife, which serviced the other holes and all off-the-fairway duffers.

The Hazard Tournament idea was carried a bit further by Betty Abbott, a recreation supervisor in Concord, New Hampshire, for her Housewives Golfing League. Each player teeing off was given a list of the "hazards":

HOLE 1: Blindfolded for the tee shot.

HOLE 2: Drive with left-handed club (unless left-handed).

HOLE 3: Use driver on all shots, including putts.

HELD EVERY FALL, THE COW PASTURE OPEN NEAR WISDOM, MONTANA, ATTRACTS A VARIETY OF FREE-RANGE GOLFERS BRANDISHING SPURS AND NINE IRONS. MOOSE, DEER, ANTELOPE, EAGLES, COYOTES, WOLVES AND MOUNTAIN LIONS HAVE ALSO BEEN KNOWN TO MAKE UNANNOUNCED APPEARANCES.

The Cow Pasture Open
Your Guide Around the Golf Pasture

Golf the Big Hole Valley Wisdom, Montana

Battlefield Send Off
Tradition of the Big Hole Golf Tournament, the blast of the cannon starts the fun.

HOLE 4: Putt with croquet mallet.

HOLE 5: Hole out on temporary green (in rough).

HOLE 6: Tee off from sand trap.

HOLE 7: Putt left-handed (unless left-handed).

HOLE 8: Blow up balloon while driving, with five-stroke penalty if can't.

HOLE 9: Play ball through a barrel and onto the green.

Abbott, with a ready imagination, innovated several other zany variations on golf. Scramble Golf, for example, is a best-ball tourney for teams of four. Each player drives off, the best lie is selected and other members of the team bring their balls to that spot for their next shots. This continues throughout the round, with the lowest team score winning.

Years later this idea went national with the Oldsmobile Scramble, founded by Richard Garn of Coldwater, Michigan. Previously, he had conducted a Michigan Scramble involving players from 17 states. It went so well he bought out his partner in the event and gained the okay of the PGA of America to expand nationally. He gained the Oldsmobile sponsorship Dec. 27, 1983 and held the first "national" in Sept. 1984. Fred Couples won it, but it involved 43,000 golfers competing in more than 1,300 qualifying tourneys in 41 sections of the PGA. In 1996, 120,000 golfers participated. It was the largest pro-am conducted by the PGA.

In Abbott's Blind Partner Tournament, partners are selected only after all players have teed off. The club pro draws names from a hat and players don't know who they are paired with until the end, when combined scores are totaled up.

> JIM ENGLAND OF BULLHEAD CITY, ARIZONA, BET FRIENDS HE COULD BREAK 50 ON NINE HOLES AT THE CHAPARRAL CC PLAYING BLINDFOLDED. AND HE DID IT, WITH A 46.

In her Blind Bogey Tournament, each player selects a handicap he thinks he needs in order to par the round. Then the club pro draws final score numbers from a hat for each contestant, without letting them know what they are. The player whose net score—actual stroke score less the handicap he selected at the start—is nearest the score drawn for him wins.

In an actual "blind" game, Jim England of Bullhead City, Arizona, bet friends he could break 50 on nine holes at the Chaparral CC playing blindfolded and using only 5 and 8 irons and a putter. And he did it, with a 46.

Next day, using his eyes and his whole bag of clubs, he went around the same course in, yup, 46 again.

Another Abbott brainstorm was her Tombstone Tournament. Players were allowed the number of strokes for par, plus their handicaps.

ditch the rules!

FOLLOWING PAGES: PSYCHEDELIC GOLF AT THE BLACK ROCK SELF-INVITATIONAL TOURNAMENT.

Then they were permitted to take that many strokes. A name marker was put where the ball ended up after that many strokes, and the winner was the player to go furthest. The name of the tourney came from the markers Abbott used, small tombstones printed: "Here lies ____, in ____ strokes."

Attempts have been made to streamline and to miniaturize golf, but the consequence has been either to eliminate the long tee shot or to rely on windmills. However, in 1980, Ted Vallas, then a 59-year old California golf course developer, designed Olympic Golf, which is actually neither golf nor an Olympic event. The first, and only, course was set up on the outskirts of Palm Springs, California. Vallas designed it to eliminate the grandiose aspects, and costs, of the sport and its attendant country clubs, while retaining its challenges and satisfactions. "I got the idea while watching the touring pros simulate different shots at the practice tee," he explained. "They aim at caddies they position at various points along the fairway."

He imitated this training technique by squeezing many of the vital elements of a course onto only 10 acres—a grassy rectangle 170 yards wide and 320 yards long. At the "clubhouse" end were 18 AstroTurf driving mats facing nine greens-sized pools of water, each of which is surrounded by bunkers and sports a hole flag. Distances from the tee are marked off in ten-yard increments by lines and side signs. Behind each driving mat is a small putting green and a tiny sand trap. Playing the "course" requires a bucket of balls and creative thinking, turning target practice into Pebble Beach or another of your course choices. To do this, any course's scorecard may be used, simulating its holes by superimposing them on the Olympic Golf layout, in three steps.

A new ball is used for each shot since the player doesn't do any chasing. The first step is the tee shot. Say, for example, a hole is designated as a 360-yard par-4, and the drive is 200 yards. The second ball is put down and the Olympic Golf course card checked to see which "green" should be shot to simulate the needed 160 yards, or which distance marker. If still short of the green, a chip shot must be taken. Third step is putting, which is done on the green most appropriate, by placing the ball where your chip shot landed, as near as eyesight can tell. A round of Olympic Golf takes about 90 minutes.

Doug Keister has run the Self-Invitational Black Rock Desert Classic Golf Tournament every June since 1988. Held at the Playa of the Black Rock Desert ("the largest flat spot on Earth") 120 miles northeast of Reno, Nevada, the

THE LESSER CRIME

A CRIMINAL TRIO KIDNAPPED THE WIFE OF A PROMINENT BUSINESSMAN FROM HIS COUNTRY CLUB. THE BUSINESSMAN RECEIVED THE DEMAND: "BRING $50,000 TO THE 17TH GREEN MONDAY MORNING FOR THE RELEASE OF YOUR WIFE." WHEN HE ARRIVED THERE MONDAY, A MAN IN A SKI MASK CONFRONTED HIM FROM OUT OF A GROVE OF TREES AND DEMANDED, "WHAT TOOK YOU SO LONG?" "MY HANDICAP IS A 27," SNAPPED THE BUSINESSMAN.

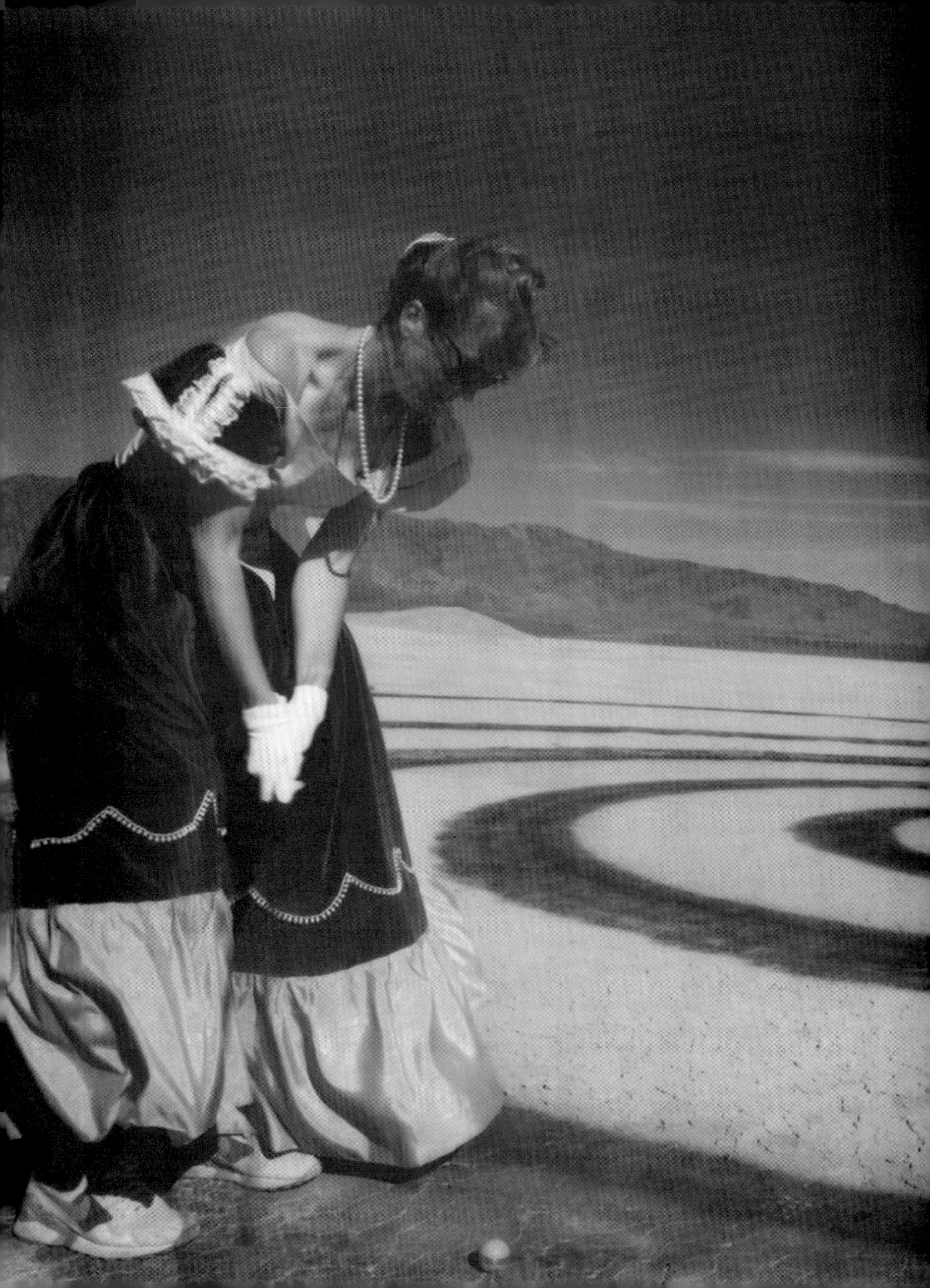

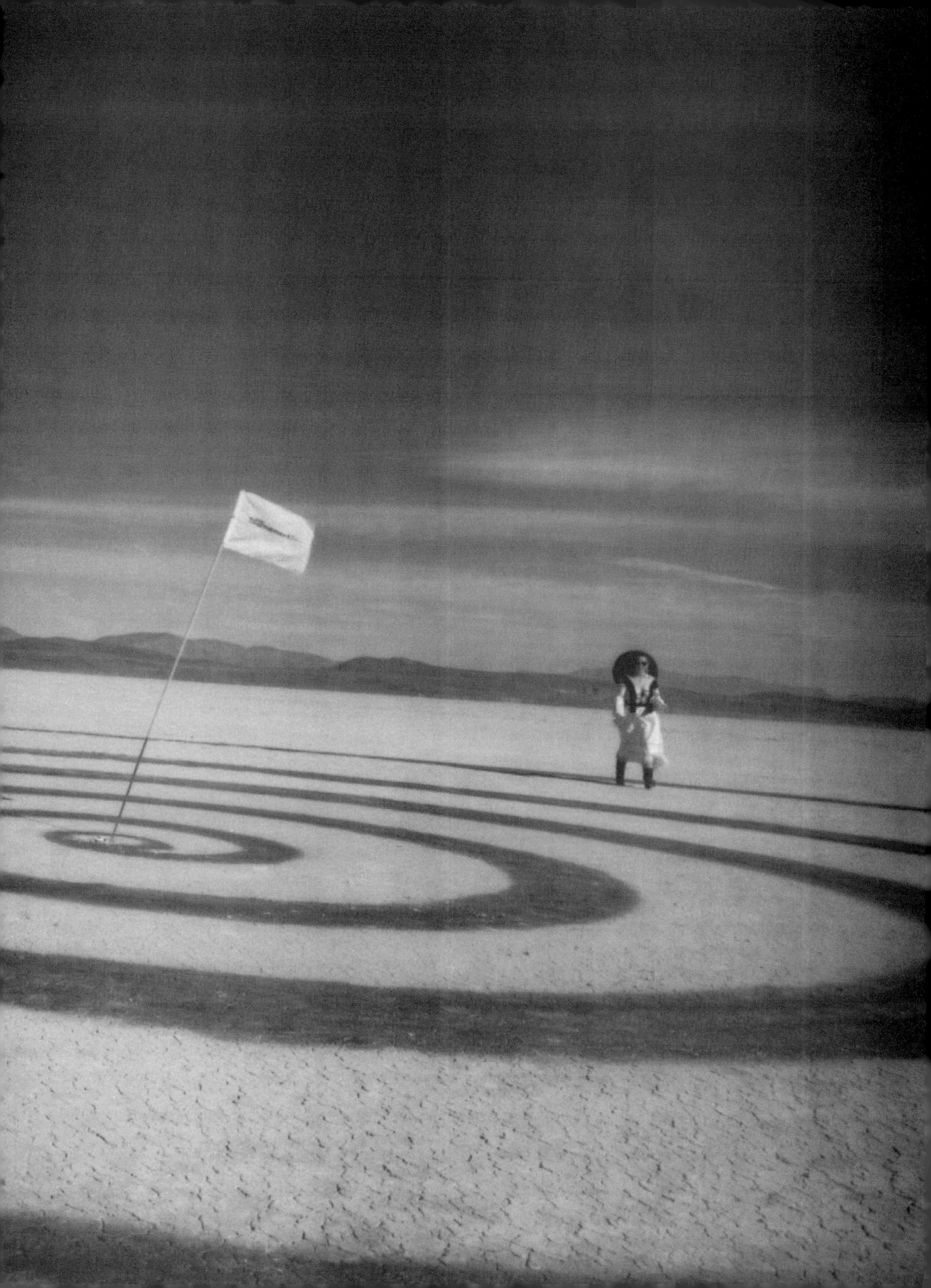

chapter three

THE LIVING ROOM HOLE AT THE BLACK ROCK SELF-INVITATIONAL.

tournament is played on the Lucifer's Anvil Golf Course—a course that volunteers actually *paint* onto the desert floor. "Hell Hole," for example, is a 702 yard hole featuring a fairway decorated with yellow arrows pointing toward the "green," which is painted in bright yellow and red. The Black Rock Desert was a bombing range during World War II, and players in the tournament often find discarded machine-gun shells in the fairways. "They make great tees," Keister says.

If all the foregoing aren't enough variety for the golfing nut, Ligonier, Indiana is the home of an annual Marshmallow Festival, which includes the wildest ever golfing contest, using marshmallows for balls! And, on the foreign scene, there is a game called Colf in the Netherlands, played on ice, where a ball is golfed toward a post; and a game called Golkey in Bangalore, India, that is sort of a combination of golf and hockey, using a field hockey stick and ball on a simulated golf course.

Finally, there is even "square-ball golf,"

> THE BLACK ROCK DESERT WAS A BOMBING RANGE DURING WORLD WAR II, AND PLAYERS IN THE TOURNAMENT OFTEN FIND DISCARDED MACHINE-GUN SHELLS IN THE FAIRWAYS. "THEY MAKE GREAT TEES," KEISTER SAYS.

invented by crew members of the HMS *Albion*, a British commando carrier. They found, not surprisingly, that regular golf balls kept rolling off the flight deck. So someone carved some square wooden "balls," utilized hockey sticks and set up a sporty little course around the hazards of ringbolts, launchers and other ship's nautical impedimenta.

And, for those who grow impatient with their lack of accuracy in any of the above-described games, Ben Davidson, retired Oakland football legend and sometime actor, added a special event to his personally-sponsored golf tourney in 1971—a club-throwing contest!

But it was an amateur event compared to the one held by Harry Stephens, golf pro at the Druid Hills course in Atlanta, Georgia, in the 1930s. He had over 60 contestants, with the winner heaving a putter 61 yards. The altitude winner was the person who tossed a pitching wedge 20 feet over the top of an 80-foot pine tree—a feat that must have benefited from *mucho* practice!

Trick Shot Artists

chapter 4

If you have ever seen professional trick shot artists perform, you have seen what can be done with an array of cast-off clubs, plumbing parts, garden implements and the like. Trick shot artists have intrigued pros and duffers alike for years with their wild and woolly innovations and seeming impossible shots.

Joe Kirkwood is generally recognized as the first professional trick shot artist. Born in Australia in 1897, Kirkwood played a key role in spreading the game of golf around the world. He not only won many of the world's most coveted golfing championships, but also played exhibitions in cities, jungles, and deserts—from one end of the globe to the other. During his life, he played golf with—and gave lessons to—many famous people, including the Queen of England, the Emperor of Japan, Warren Harding, Calvin Coolidge, Dwight Eisenhower, Richard Nixon and John Kennedy.

One early trip to China proved to be full of surprises. While preparing to give an exhibition at a course outside of Shanghai, some of the local warlords began fighting. Joe was understandably

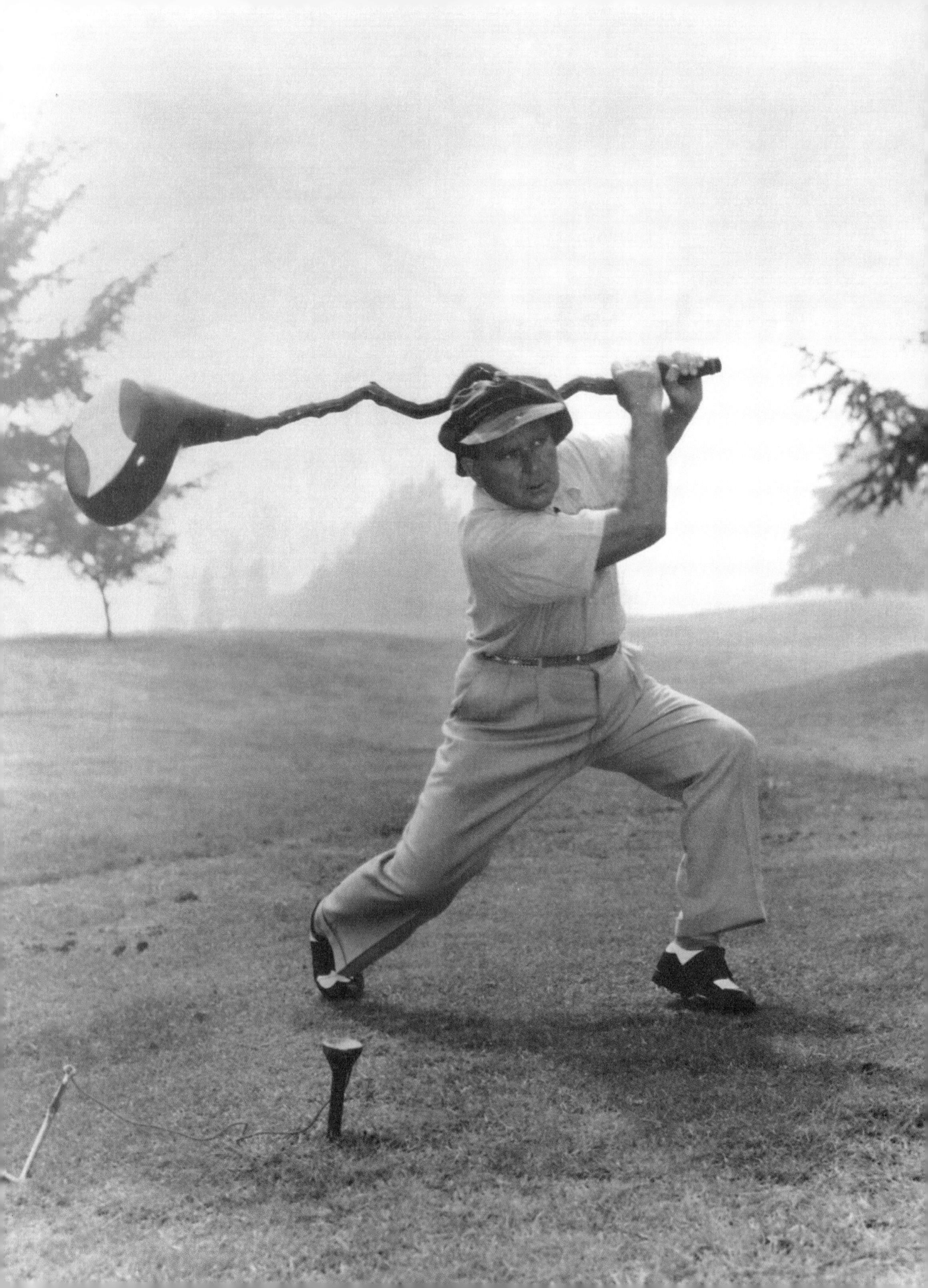

trick shot artists

> JOE KIRKWOOD WAS SO STRONG THAT HE COULD WRAP A CLUB WITH A LEAD SHAFT AROUND HIS NECK.

a bit reluctant to continue with bullets flying around. However, because both sides wanted to see him perform, a temporary truce was called. The soldiers, though, had laid their dead on the surface of the ground and covered them with dirt, so Kirkwood had to contend with a course covered with mounds. At one point, his legendary powerful swing with an iron club even caused a bone to fly out from one of the graves.

Another memorable event took place at Sea Island, Georgia. Kirkwood came across sportscaster Grantland Rice, while Rice was making a movie called *Sportlite*. Rice was seeking to capture a hole in one on film. A pro Rice had hired had been trying to accomplish the feat all day on a 150-yard hole without any success. Kirkwood calmly walked up to the tee and nailed a hole in one with his 6-iron! Certainly the first hole in one ever captured on film. In fact, Kirkwood had 26 holes in one during his career, including one played off the crystal of a watch. He even shot two holes in one during a single round of play.

The USGA Museum has a collection of the trick clubs used by Kirkwood—and others like him—including drivers with double-jointed shafts, a 9-iron with a face the size of a pie tin, and clubs with heads turned inside-out. There is also a picture of Kirkwood hanging by his teeth from a rope that is dangling from an airplane (flying 175 mph through a blizzard) and another of him hitting a ball 250 yards with a rubber-shafted driver . . . from a bad lie! He could hit a low shot, high shot, two balls with one club, curve the ball to the right or left, hit off of somebody's toe, play right-handed shots with left-handed clubs, and vice-versa. He was so strong that he could wrap a club with a lead shaft around his neck. Elected to the Golf Hall of Fame in 1969, Kirkwood died of liver cancer in Vermont in 1970.

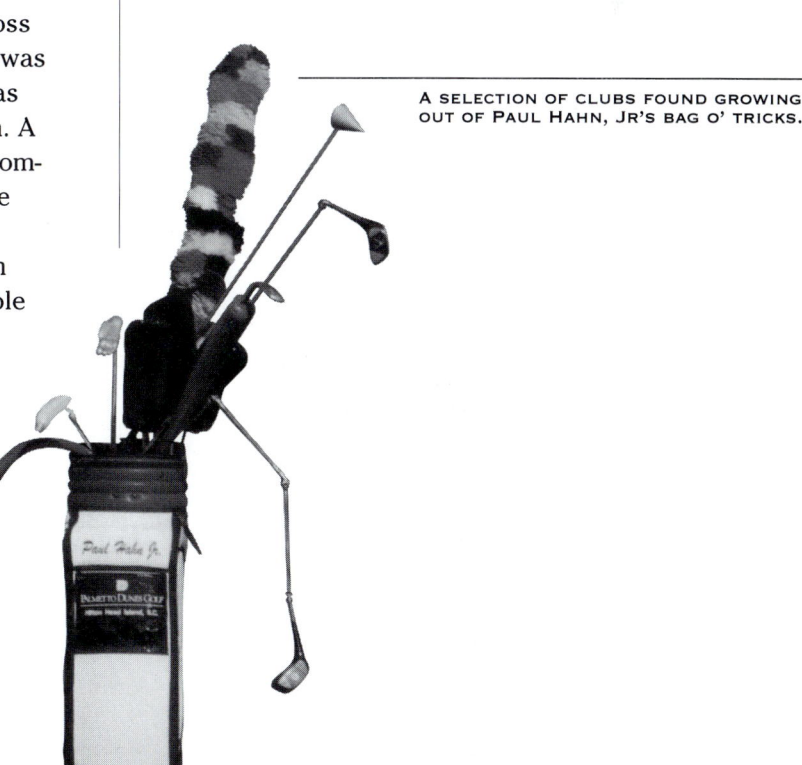

A SELECTION OF CLUBS FOUND GROWING OUT OF PAUL HAHN, JR'S BAG O' TRICKS.

FORE! JOE KIRKWOOD IN FINE FORM. WONDER HOW BIG THE BALL WAS . . .

chapter four

PAUL HAHN, JR., DEMONSTRATING THE HIGH-TEE SHOT. (IT SHOULD BE NOTED THAT MICHAEL JORDAN CAN DO THIS WITHOUT THE STOOL.)

Paul Hahn, Sr., the Lake Worth, Florida pro, was another early trick shot exhibitionist. He was most famed for his trick of driving a ball off a tee held in someone's teeth while they lay supine on the turf. He traveled 1.5 million miles—five times around the earth—over 25 years performing weird shots with a wondrous variety of Rube Goldbergian clubs and contraptions. He died while on tour in March 1976, at the age of 58. His son, Paul Hahn, Jr, has taken over where his dad left off. One of his best-known tricks is hitting a ball over 200 yards using a club with a rubber hose for a shaft. If you'd like to catch him at work, surf the net to www.golftrickshots.com.

John Montague became a legendary figure back in the 1930s when he fascinated Hollywood's movie colony golfers by beating them on the course using only a baseball fungo bat, a shovel and a rake. Sports columnist Grantland Rice saw him shoot an 84 with these bizarre tools and promptly columnized him, claiming he could beat anyone. In 1963, at an advanced age and in retirement, Montague fell from a ladder and was paralyzed from the hips down for five and a half months. Then, one day after being released from the hospital, he was out on the course playing two holes with a friend. He played on crutches and parred both holes.

DENNIS WALTERS AND MENAGERIE.

trick shot artists

Dennis Walters, another of today's top pro trick shot artists, has a similar tale. Walters, who once finished 11th in the U.S. Amateur Championships, was in a golf cart accident in 1974 that left him paralyzed from the waist down. After lengthy hospitalization, therapy and rehab, he longed to get back on the course. His solution? He cut the legs off a swivel bar stool and mounted it on top of a cart. Now, he claims, with a twinkle in his eye, "I beat my handicap every time I play." Included among his repertory of shots are hitting low, medium and high shots at the same time with a "unique" 3-iron (a club with three heads); hitting balls with a crutch (which he also uses while putting one-handed), fishing rods, baseball bats, and radiator hoses; and stacking three balls and then effortlessly hitting each ball, one at a time. His golf show has been called "Golf's Most Inspiring Hour."

MIKE CALBOT WITH YET ANOTHER VARIATION OF THE HIGH-TEE SHOT. KIDS—DON'T TRY THIS AT HOME!

EVEN MORE IMPRESSIVE THAN THIS TRICK SHOT IS JOEY O'S ABILITY TO PUTT IN A STRAIGHT JACKET WHILE SUSPENDED UPSIDE DOWN IN A TANK OF LIQUID NITROGEN.

A number of other trick shotters are now in business along with Hahn, Jr., (not to mention Lee Trevino and Chi Chi Rodriguez, who have been known to clown around when occasion calls for it).

Joey "O," who bills himself as the acrobatic golf comedian, proves the title by stroking golf balls while riding a unicycle, balancing himself on top of a large rubber ball, and making other seemingly impossible drives off of pedestals and other weird tees.

Mike Calbot hits shots with a clubhead attached to a Samurai sword and draws on an assortment of one-legged tricks. In one, he stands on one leg atop a three-legged stool and hits a ball off a baseball tee. In another, he stands on his left foot, holds his right foot up in front of himself, and irons the ball off a tee stuck into the toe of his right shoe.

chapter four

OPPOSITE: DIVOT, "THE WORLD'S GREATEST GOLFING CLOWN."

WEDGY WINCHESTER CAN ROUTINELY CHIP A COIN INTO THE HOLE FROM 20 YARDS AWAY.

Bob Brue, 22 years the pro at Ozaukee Country Club, has won 22 golf tournaments, including back-to-back PGA Match Play Championships. He set the Senior Tour records for the fewest putts over nine and 18 holes (7 and 17 respectively), and scored only the tenth double-eagle in Senior Tour history. He has now turned to specializing in clinics where his trick shot skills teach his lessons. One of his favored tricks is a modification of the old Paul Hahn, Sr., trick of driving off a tee clenched in the teeth of a supine subject. But, because of insurance costs today, he uses a dummy head, even

WEDGY WINCHESTER DEMONSTRATES THAT FOUR CLUBS ARE BETTER THAN ONE.

though he has never so much as scraped its chin in several hundred demonstrations.

Wedgy Winchester, a former winner of the National Long Driving Championship, can

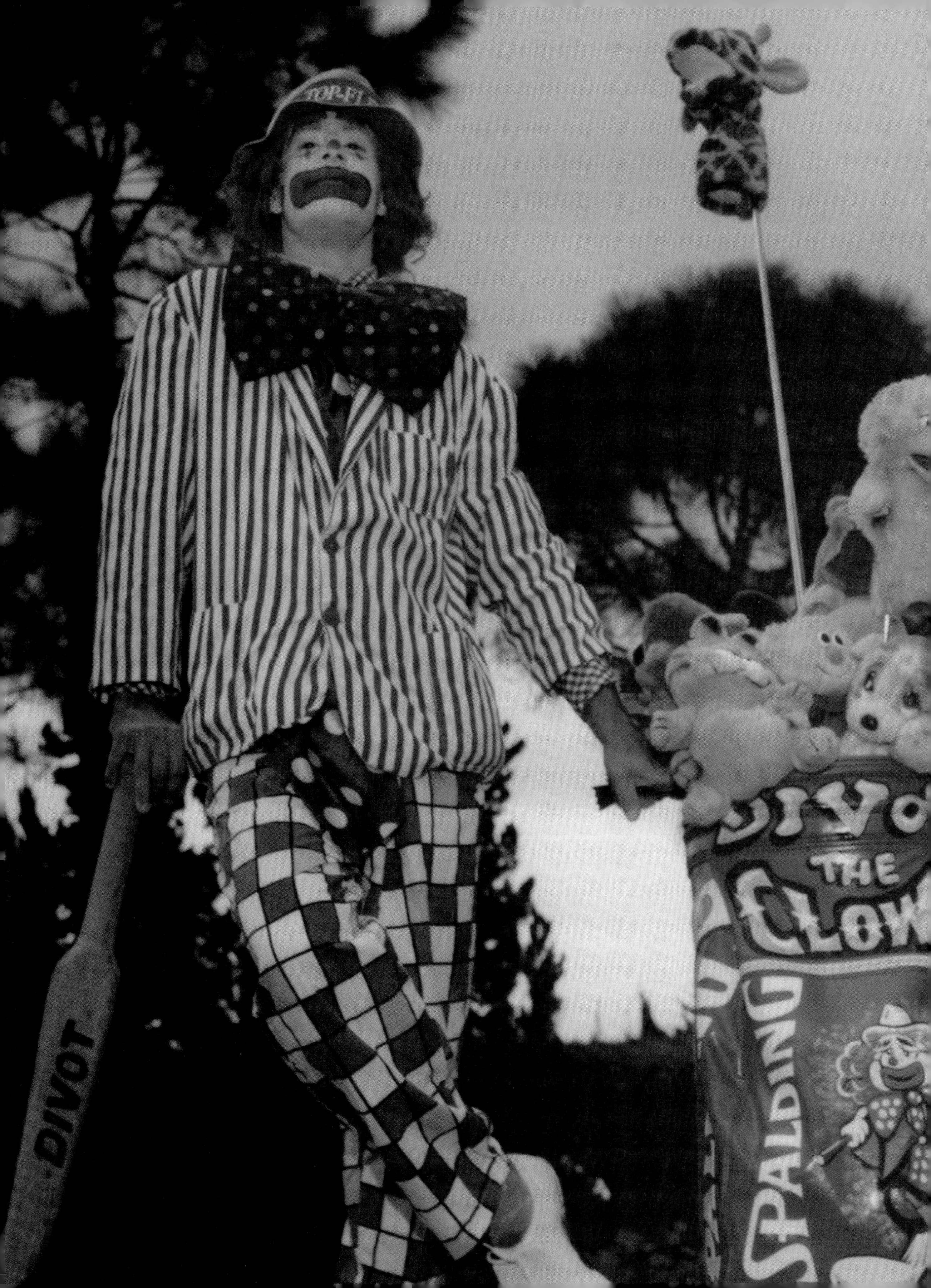
DIVOT
THE
SPALDING

chapter four

routinely chip a coin into the hole from 20 yards away. He's also been known to shoot a 71 left-handed (he's right-handed) and blast shots down the fairway while using a seven-foot club.

Peter Longo, the "King of Clubs," has over 200 trick shot routines that he has relied on to entertain fans for over 20 years. Among Longo's more famous tricks are his ability to drive a ball 275 yards from a 40 inch tee and drive a ball right down the middle of a fairway using everything from a claw hammer to a club with a car steering wheel for a grip. In addition to his trick shot skills, Longo is known for creating Challenge Golf, the world's first video for physically handicapped people. The video features instructions for golfing with one arm, golfing with one leg, golfing from the seated position, golfing for the blind, and golfing with arthritis.

THE FAMOUS "GOLFING GORILLA" REGULARLY DRIVES BALLS OVER 300 YARDS AND IS TOP BANANA ON THE FAIRWAY WITH HIS APPEALING ANTICS. HE DOES PARTICULARLY WELL IN SKINS GAMES . . .

PETER LONGO AND A FEW OF HIS TRICK CLUBS. AT LAST COUNT HE HAD GONE THROUGH 42 CADDIES DURING HIS ILLUSTRIOUS CAREER.

Curious Courses

c h a p t e r 5

Today, we tend to think of golf courses as being standardized at nine and 18 holes—the average 18-hole course using about 150 acres—without ever stopping to wonder why. But the origin dates back to a decision made two centuries ago at the Royal & Ancient Golf Club of St. Andrews in Scotland. Until then, the round at St. Andrews had consisted of 22 holes. In 1764, though, the club passed a resolution that their first four holes should be converted into only two. As this change automatically converted the same four holes into two on the back side, the round was reduced from 22 to 18. St. Andrews gradually established preeminence in the golf world and its 18-hole course was accepted as standard.

This "Old Course" is still a magnet today. The worshipper has not made a proper pilgrimage until he has played this championship course. But it is a course that tries men's souls, being peculiar by modern standards, with its hidden bunkers, unforgiving whins and heather, unexpected bounces and 14 of 18 "double" greens (two holes cut into each of seven huge greens, the largest almost an acre). Still, as exacting as it is, it was first holed with 79 strokes almost 125 years ago, by Allan Robertson, the first great golfer (and later the leading maker of "feathery" balls).

chapter five

In spite of the edict of standardization made at St. Andrews, however, enough rebels exist to see that imagination and whimsy never forsake the game entirely. This chapter will explore some of the more unusual golf courses in existence today.

NO, THIS IS NOT AN IMAGE FROM THE GALILEO SPACECRAFT OF ONE OF JUPITER'S MOONS. INSTEAD, IT'S AN OVERVIEW OF ST. ANDREWS DURING THE OPEN GOLF CHAMPIONSHIP IN 1957. THOSE ARE THE 7TH AND 11TH GREENS ON THE LEFT, AND THE 8TH AND 10TH ON THE RIGHT. REFER TO THE MAP ON PAGE 13 TO GET YOUR BEARINGS.

North vs. South

The Fairbanks Golf and Country Club bills itself as "The World's Northernmost Golf Course." This nine-hole, par-36 course is located just a few miles from North Pole (the town) and less than 200 miles from the Arctic Circle. Needless to say, it is only open during the summer months.

A close second is Canada's nine-hole non-regulation course at Yellowknife, located just a Sunday commute—250 miles—south of the

68

curious courses

Arctic Circle in the huge and largely unexplored Northwest Territories off Great Slave Lake. This location makes it possible for the club members to hold a midsummer tournament where tee-off time is midnight. At this latitude there are 24 hours of daylight on the first day of summer.

Being this far north, one has to expect different golfing conditions. Only one "known" golfer has ever played at Yellowknife. That was Marlene Streit, six-time Canadian

ONE OF THE BOULDER TEES AT THE YELLOWKNIFE COURSE IN CANADA'S GREAT WHITE NORTH.

women's champion. And she never came back for seconds.

The first difference encountered is that the 2,480-yard course is *all* sand-like tundra. It is essentially one giant sand trap. Even the greens are sand, heavily soaked with bunker oil to give them some semblance of consistency. To save wear and tear on clubs, rubber mats are placed at all tees, many on platforms atop boulder outcroppings. Sand wedges have, not unexpectedly, become favored clubs for fairway play.

Borders? What Borders?

Llanymynech Golf Club in Wales was built on the highest point for 10 miles around, with three of its holes bordering a gaping 100-foot deep quarry. Fifteen of its holes are in Wales, two in England and one straddles the border. And this across-the-border sharing isn't unique. Located some 50 miles south of the Arctic Circle, the Green Zone Golf Course in Tornio, Finland and Haplaranda, Sweden is surreal. Straddling the border between the two countries, the game enjoys constant daylight in the summer months—making 24-hour golf possible. But the two countries are in different time zones, so a 15-foot putt from the Finnish to the Swedish side of the sixth green will technically beat the clock, rolling backward in time. Non-Scandinavians are required to carry a "borderline passport" as they hit back and forth across the fairways and boundaries. It's even possible to drive a hole in one lasting over an hour!

Portal, North Dakota is another place that has a nine-hole course that splits a border. Eight of its holes are in Canada. Meanwhile, players on the Yale University Golf Course in Connecticut play through several borders, too. The course crosses the boundaries of four towns—West Haven, Woodbridge, Orange and New Haven.

chapter five

One plus is that there are no water hazards. The average rainfall during the mid-May to mid-September golfing season is eight inches, and the sand absorbs water so rapidly there are only seven or so unplayable days per season. Things change after September 15, however. Then the occasional golf addict and the ground slowly freeze together.

Other hazards include a copious crop of mosquitoes and black flies that swarm over the course from the bordering spruce swamp, and ravens, which have made ball thieving a fine art, sometimes lifting them before they've even stopped rolling. With such distractions, it is small wonder there has never been a verified ace on the course since the members built it in June 1948. Par rounds are almost as rare.

The farthest south golf course, on the other hand, is Puntas Arenas at the southernmost tip of Chile. It has one big water hazard, the Strait of Magellan. And a big, *big* wind! In fact, the greens have had to be set below the level of the fairways, so balls don't blow away. Trees on the course grow up about two feet, then follow the prevailing wind direction.

SMOOTHING OUT ONE OF THE "GREENS" ON THE YELLOWKNIFE COURSE. LAWNMOWERS NEED NOT APPLY.

•

OTHER HAZARDS INCLUDE A COPIOUS CROP OF MOSQUITOES AND BLACK FLIES THAT SWARM OVER THE COURSE FROM THE BORDERING SPRUCE SWAMP, AND RAVENS, WHICH HAVE MADE BALL THIEVING A FINE ART, SOMETIMES LIFTING THEM BEFORE THEY'VE EVEN STOPPED ROLLING.

•

Why Wedges are Best Sellers

Sand courses, which are better than no courses at all to golf addicts, can be found all around the world.

One is located near Dhahran, the American oil town in Saudi Arabia. It has sand roughs, sand fairways (which have, however, been smoothed) and sand greens (which have been oiled). Players use red balls.

The Awali Golf Course in Bahraini is similar, except it has portable grass-hung simulated trees that can be "planted" at various spots to change the course layout periodically. Players tee off from a strip of plastic grass, which they carry with them. Fairways are outlined in oil, so players always know when they have hit the rough. Usually they can tell by the puff of dust that occurs when their ball lands.

The golf club at Walvis Bay, South Africa, a remote fishing port bordered on one side by the South Atlantic Ocean and the other by the Namib Desert, uses part of the desert as its golf course. Regulation equipment includes goggles to combat dust and the

curious courses

> IN A BURST OF OPTIMISM ONE YEAR, A FIVE-GANG MOWER WAS PURCHASED,
> BUT IT DIDN'T TURN A WHEEL FOR THE NEXT SEVEN YEARS.

LIFE IN THE OUTBACK: AUSTRALIAN FOR GOLF, MATE.

sun's glare. The club's landmark and pride is a single grass green, which requires almost constant watering because of the heat and scarcity of rainfall, as well as regular fine combings to remove the grass-destructive mica particles deposited from blowing sand.

At Alice Springs, in the heart of the Australia outback, there is a course that can try even Aussie souls. It is a pastiche of yellow stubble, specimen rock formations and clinging brown dust. Grass has no hope there because it almost never rains in Alice Springs. In a burst of optimism one year, a five-gang mower was purchased, but it didn't turn a wheel for the next seven years. The greens are actually called "browns," and are oiled (the usual solution). Local rules allow two swipes with a bar rake before every putt. And a ball under a rock or in a wagon rut on the fairway can be moved a club length to a preferred lie. A six-inch move is allowed *anywhere* in the rough. "It wouldn't do any

Golf in Demand

The National Golf Foundation has estimated there are 30 million golfers in the U.S., two million of which just took up the game two years ago (40% of which were young, college-educated, professional women). So, to keep up with foreseen demand for playing areas, we need to build 400 public courses a year—more than one a day! Golf also is the fastest growing sport in Asia, where there are more than 4300 courses (1997), with hundreds of new ones planned.

good to allow more, because all the rough is alike anyhow," stated one who knew.

Lakepoint Country Club, outside Fort St. John, BC, Canada started out in 1957 as a sand course. But, showing things do get better sometimes, nine grass greens were installed in 1969, and another nine in 1975, which gave the course a new distinction as the "farthest north course with grass greens." The course is within a game preserve, though, so ducks and deer cross the fairways, muskrats build homes in water hazards, and a fox will occasionally dart out and mangle a ball (and you can't do a thing about it).

An all-sand course was also constructed on the U.S. Navy's Harold E. Holt Communications Station on the northwest cape of Australia, four miles outside Exmouth, by off-duty sailors. Other than smoothing the terrain a bit, the only construction necessary was the sinking of the hole cups. Almost no maintenance is needed, either, except occasionally finding and digging out the cups after a sandstorm. The storms, along with ant hills that grow to seven feet in height and can spring up overnight anywhere on the course, assure changing contours and challenges. But one Australian local was heard to comment, "Who but Yanks would work so hard to have fun?"

Extreme golf. Watch for it at the next X-games . . .

curious courses

THE SINKHOLE AT THE NEFYN & DISTRICT GOLF CLUB IN WALES IS ALL THAT REMAINS OF THE FIRST, SADLY MISCALCULATED TEST OF THE POPULAR "EXPLODING GOLFBALL" FOUND ON PAGE 158.

In the 1920s, residents of Ascension Island in the South Atlantic—112 employees of the British Eastern Telegraphic Company—built the Georgetown Golf Course, a nine-hole, 2,019-yard, all-sand course currently listed in the *Guinness Book of World Records* as "the worst golf course in the world." Five fairways criss-cross at a central point, so "instead of caps, we wear helmets," stated club president R.C. Huxley. Wayward shots end up in impenetrable thorns, cacti-ridden lava flow or people's back gardens.

How Much Do You Love This Game?

There are courses with hazards worse than mere sand, however. At Rose Bay in New South Wales, for instance, a media report stated that S.J. Baily MacArthur once stepped into a bunker and began to sink. He yelled for help but wasn't rescued until he was in up to his armpits. However, a note from Jim Grant of the Australian Golf Club, Ltd., states club records do not show MacArthur, a member "from 1905," ever suffering such a mishap. Instead, he states, it was Dr. N. Rowlands who sank up to his armpits in a "low lying section" of the course, where it took the help of several other golfers, alerted by his cries for help, to extricate him. In another part of the world, the 12th hole at Nefyn & District Golf Club in Morfa Nefyn, Wales, also features a sink hole (which must be handy for getting rid of offending clubs.)

The site of the Camp Bonifas one-hole, 170-yard, bunkered golf course has been called "the most dangerous golf course in the world." Along one side are minefields, because just 200 yards away is the Demilitarized Zone between North and South Korea. "Hook one off the tee and you're in the minefield," smiled one knowledgeable player.

The same type of hazards plague players at the Stanley Golf Club in the Falkland Is-

chapter five

Location, Location, Location!

A location doesn't have to be icebound or desert land to furnish players with problems. A legion of other distractions can do it as well. Like landing strips.

It has been estimated that 6,000 California golfers alone fly their own planes. And more and more golf pros are finding it convenient, and profitable, to fly between tournaments while on tour. So, many resort courses are adding what they call "the 20th hole"—an airstrip—to their layout. Bud Holscher was one of those flying pros, and he created a membership organization called The National 20th Hole Committee. Bob Hope was his co-chairman. He started promoting 2500-by-75-foot airstrips adjacent or near courses that would allow members playing privileges and preferred starting times, as well as package plans at the resort courses.

Not quite as modernized, the golf course at Capetown, South Africa adjoins a railway station. Players there have gotten used to the noise of train comings and goings, but once, during an important match, while one player's ball hung on the lip of the cup, a train thundered by and the ball dropped because of it. That caused a rules hassle.

Players on a course in Colorado would *love* to have landing strips or train stations adjacent their course. It is located at the Colorado State Penitentiary.

lands, ever since the British short-war of recovery was fought there in 1982.

Animals are common as "moving hazards" on courses. Ocean Shores course near Aberdeen, Washington had to call in a police helicopter to chase a large black bear off its fourth fairway and back into the forest. The incident evoked considerable nervous levity, including the posting of a sign near the first tee revising summer rules: "If a ball is picked up by a bear, player may replace it and take

> "IF A BALL IS PICKED UP BY A BEAR, PLAYER MAY REPLACE IT AND TAKE ONE PENALTY STROKE. IF PLAYER GETS BALL BACK FROM BEAR, TAKE AUTOMATIC PAR FOR HOLE."

one penalty stroke. If player gets ball back from bear, take automatic par for hole."

A course in Nairobi, Kenya has an even more frightening rule: "Ball lying less than 10 yards from a lion need not be played." And the Mwanza Club on Lake Victoria, when it was British East Africa, once ruled: "If a ball comes to rest in proximity to a hippopotamus or crocodile, another may be dropped at a safe distance, no nearer the hole, without penalty."

curious courses

Run! Run for your life! Stork on the course! Stork on the course!!

At 200 feet below sea level, the golf course at Death Valley's Furnace Creek oasis is the world's lowest grass course. Play is free during the sizzling hot summers, but players must watch out for the coyotes that like to lounge on the cool greens.

Golfers on a course in New South Wales are harassed by crows that swoop down, pick up golf balls and fly off with them. The Chembur golf course in Bombay, India has the same problem, but with kites, a local bird. These birds evidently think the balls are eggs, which they dearly love as a meal. But the humans, for once, have out-thought the wildlife.

> "Ball lying less than 10 yards from a lion need not be played."

They started hiring *agaie wallahs*, or forecaddies, whose job it is to range ahead of golfers, get to balls before the birds can, and cover them with red cloths until the golfers are ready for their next shots.

A somewhat similar story comes out of Texas A&M University. Joe Prieve of Wellborn, Texas is groundskeeper of the student course and he collects old, worn-out balls to take back to his farm and lay out in fake chicken nests. Snakes come onto the farm in search of chicken eggs, which they love. They gulp them whole and crush them internally. But they can't tell the difference between golf balls and chicken eggs. And, if they swallow a golf ball, they die of indigestion. "One ball will usually get one," Prieve said, "but we did open a six-foot snake to find four golf balls in him."

In Australia, kangaroos of various varieties can turn up anywhere. So the Yeppoon Golf Club in Queensland has included in its rules: "A ball hitting a kangaroo—play it as is." (The possibility of a ball landing in or being taken into a kangaroo pouch isn't considered.)

High Tee

The visitor paid his greens fee and went out to the first tee. Taking a stolid stance, he made a rather wild swipe at his ball and missed completely. "By Jove," he exclaimed to his playing mates, "It's a good thing I found out early that this course is at least two inches lower than the one I've been playing on."

chapter five

INTREPID GOLFERS ARE CONDITIONED TO PLAY THROUGH WHATEVER MOTHER NATURE HAS UP HER SLEEVE. HERE, JOE KIRKWOOD AND GALLERY ROUGH IT IN AUSTRALIA.

A rule at the Elephant Hills Country Club in Zimbabwe states that "players may take a free drop with any ball that lands in a hippopotamus print." (Providing the hippo isn't still standing in it, we presume.) This course, which was carved out of the African bush by pro Gary Player, is 7,734 yards and includes "the biggest water hazard in the world," Victoria Falls, which lies alongside the course, not to mention some 500 free-roaming wild animals. Signs on the Zambezi River bank, which flanks the course, warn golfers to watch

curious courses

out for crocodiles. Rules state: "A ball striking or deflected by a wild animal may be replayed from as near as possible to the spot from which the original ball was played without penalty," and "The hippo fence on the north side of the 14th fairway marks out-of-bounds." The falls, with a drop of 355 feet, is not actually a part of the course, but they have proved an irresistible hazard for golfers to try their drives on. As Simon Hobday, a golf pro who failed to overdrive it in six tries, said, "It has to be a par-1. If you don't get it on the drive, forget it. Who's going to go after the ball?"

The Hua Hin course in Thailand, cut through thick jungle, has rough which is usually several feet deep. Bengal tigers have been seen on the premises and large boa constrictors were not uncommon when it was opened in the mid-1970s. Players could hire "beaters" to go ahead, making a lot of noise to scare off the jungle denizens.

The pressure in championship golf is nothing compared to what a player had to deal with at the Chapman Golf Club in Harare, Zimbabwe. A five-foot long crocodile named Cuthbert lived in the water off the sixth hole. "We tried to catch him but without success," admitted club pro Roger Baylis, "It's a joke when they talk of a 'sudden death playoff' here!"

Sites themselves sometimes dictate course hazards. A course in New Zealand has three holes—6th, 9th and 13th—that gobble up golf balls and digest them in 240-degree mud craters. A golfer is not encouraged to try to retrieve his errant ball,

ONE OF THE MORE UNUSUAL TEES AT A COURSE IN INDIA, BIRTHPLACE OF THE PGA (PACHYDERM GOLFERS ASSOCIATION).

chapter five

lest his foursome boils down to an instant threesome.

During a civil war that ended in 1980, the Hillside Golf Club in Zimbabwe allowed a player a free drop if his ball landed in a crater caused by mortar fire. On another course, in Centenary, players were permitted to repeat a shot if their swing was interrupted by gunfire or explosions and, at the same time, they were admonished to check for land mines before putting.

"Note: Beware of crocodiles on 4, 5, 6, 8, 9, 13, 14, 15, 17, 18."

At the Konkola Golf Club in the small mining town of Chililabombwe, Zambia, one golfer was nipped by a cobra while another was attacked by a crocodile, which was, however, dispatched by his playing partner with a nine-iron. Crocs are a problem there as signs along the lakefront attest: "Note: Beware of crocodiles on 4, 5, 6, 8, 9, 13, 14, 15, 17, 18."

A course in India posted this sign: "Balls may be moved to avoid cutcha roads, cattle tracks, runnels adjoining same, patches of dung and dangerous snakes." Religious taboos play a large part in rules formulated here, as illustrated by a club in Hyderabad that conceded: "Balls eaten by sacred cows or monkeys may be replaced without penalty."

Finally, professional golfer Howard Twitty, back in 1975, was playing in the Malaysian Open, using a caddy that spoke no English. Halfway around the course, after Twitty had just taken a club from his bag, the caddie began to scream and jump up and down. Then he very gingerly turned the golf bag upside down and out plopped a King Cobra.

GOLFERS TEE OFF A TERMITE MOUND AT AN AFRICAN GOLF COURSE.

A STROLL THROUGH THE VALLEY OF THE TERMITES, PAST THE INTIMIDATING INSECT BUNKERS.

curious courses

Recent Hazards

The newer courses are experimenting with an old hazard in an entirely new way. Oristo, a seaside family resort on Edisto Island, South Carolina has an 18-hole par-72 course that includes a green that is an island in the middle of a lake.

A floating golf green was incorporated into the course at Lake Coeur d'Alene, Idaho in 1991, though not without problems. No one anticipated that the lake water could recede an average of six feet each winter. So, to keep the 15-million-pound barge holding the island afloat, the owner had to dredge a 430-foot long

P.C. GOLFERS

HAVE YOU READ ABOUT THE POLITICALLY CORRECT COUNTRY CLUB? ITS MEMBERS AREN'T LISTED AS HAVING "HANDICAPS." THEY ARE REFERRED TO AS "STROKE CHALLENGED."

Space Saving Ideas

It has been said that golf courses and cemeteries are the two largest wastes of real estate. In an effort to deal with a dwindling supply of land, several courses have been built on top of garbage dumps. A $41 million 18-hole public course was built on top of 18 million tons of garbage in Japan. Since rotting refuse produces potentially explosive methane gas, 74 vent pipes stick up allowing the gas to escape. Smoking on the course, naturally, is banned, since a spark could blow up a fairway. The smell isn't exactly rose-like either. Still, the course is always booked solid, at $110 to $140 for greens fees.

In Duarte, California, a nine-hole course was built on a 33-acre recycled landfill. They solved their gas problem even more ecologically, by fueling a generator supplying power to Southern California Edison. Other courses built on landfills include the Merrick Road Park Golf Course in Hempstead, New York and the Detwiller Municipal Course in Toledo, Ohio.

Denver-based Metrogolf Company has a plan to save even more space. They have proposed building a golfing facility on top of the midtown Manhattan Port Authority bus terminal. Plans include a three-story 220-yard driving range, a putting green, a clubhouse, food shops and a corporate meeting space.

79

chapter five

FLOATING GOLF GREEN AT LAKE COEUR D'ALENE, IDAHO.

trench for it. Surprisingly, nine holes in one have been made here in seven years. And this, evidently, gave the owner the idea of holding a big $1,000,000 hole in one competition.

Going the floating green courses one better is the Oustoen Country Club at Oslo Fjord, Norway. The entire island there *is* the course. Its fairways are carved through virgin woodlands allowing deer to roam freely about.

It is a sad commentary, though, on a game already fraught with hazards of all varieties, that people have to go looking for ways to add more, like these floating island greens. Maybe course designers should start thinking about the first course on the moon. That should give them plenty to do. They will need synthetic grass—lots of it—since the gravity there is one-sixth of the earth's, thus making 1,000-yard drives commonplace.

> MAYBE COURSE DESIGNERS SHOULD START THINKING ABOUT THE FIRST COURSE ON THE MOON. GREENS WILL HAVE TO BE ABOUT THREE BLOCKS WIDE, WHILE CUPS WOULD HAVE TO BE VERY SHALLOW, SINCE THE LOW GRAVITY WOULD MAKE PUTTS TAKE FOREVER TO DROP.

Greens will have to be about three blocks wide, while cups would have to be very shallow, since the low gravity would make putts take forever to drop. It appears, in fact, that we will have to get ready for a whole new ball game!

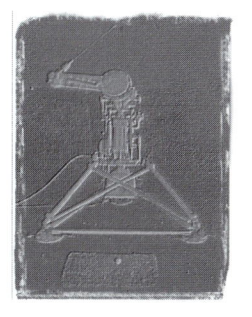

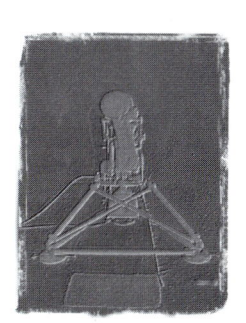

Automated Golf

chapter 6

The idea of a perfect mechanized golfer for frailer human counterparts to study reaches back to 1927, when John Mesple of San Francisco invented the first golfing robot. Since live players moved too fast for the eye to catch the nuances of their swing, Mesple planned a skeleton of bolts, gears and pulleys that could be manually cranked in slow- or stop-motion so that the ideal swing (as Mesple saw it) could be studied in detail. Mesple had definite ideas of how the swing should look. He wrote in his Patent No. 1,703,403: "In the up swing the body is pivoted on the right hip and the shoulders turn substantially to a right angle from the position of address. The left arm remains substantially straight, the right arm is flexed and there is an upward movement of both the wrists and arms . . . The downswing is substantially the reverse of the upswing.

"After the club engages with the ball, the weight of the body is completely shifted to the left hip, the right arm is substantially straight, the left arm is flexed, the shoulders turn substantially to a right angle toward the left and the club goes up in a horizontal position over the left shoulder, parallel with the line of play."

chapter six

J. L. MESPLE

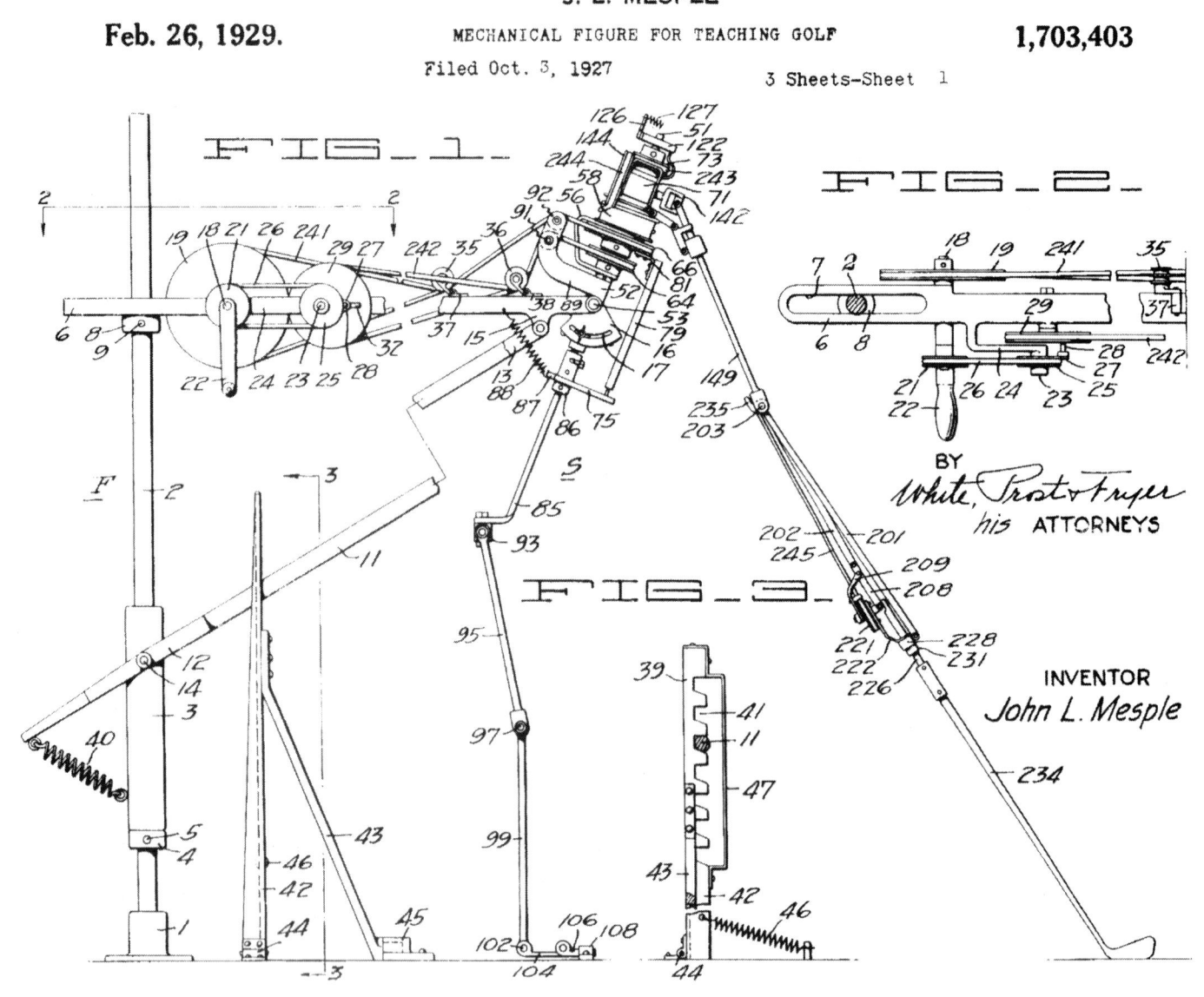

Feb. 26, 1929. MECHANICAL FIGURE FOR TEACHING GOLF **1,703,403**

Filed Oct. 3, 1927   3 Sheets—Sheet 1

J. L. MESPLE'S 1929 PATENT DRAWING FOR HIS GOLFING ROBOT, WHICH BEARS A STRIKING RESEMBLANCE TO A GOLFER LEAVING THE CLUBHOUSE AFTER ONE TOO MANY.

Mesple's mechanical man presumably enacted such a swing. It took him about 6,000 words to "substantially" describe the operation, including: "The rotation of the crank 22 in a clockwise direction drives the belt 241 and the belt in turn is arranged to drive the pulley 66 also in a clockwise direction (as the pulley 66 is viewed from above) . . . ."

It wasn't until some 40 years later that a newer version was invented that made this idea actually practical. In January 1967, the second robot was announced to the world, this time from Palm Beach Gardens, Florida where True Temper Corporation was headquartered. This project started with a series of action films being taken of outstanding golfers to analyze swing similarities and differences and graph the classic pattern swing. Then a computer program developed the geometry of this swing so the design of the machine could simulate it for any club from driver to wedge. Slight variations in the settings of the club faces made it hook or slice on command.

True Temper—all business—had no nickname for its working "monster." It was simply

automated golf

True Temper's golf club testing device in action, circa 1967. It has since been disassembled and re-engineered as Tiger Woods.

chapter six

called the Golf Club Testing Device, or GCTD if you were on more familiar terms with it. Developed in cooperation with Batelle Memorial Institute of Columbus, Ohio, it cost more than a quarter million dollars and took over two years to develop.

Around the same time, out in California, William J. "Bill" Glasson, golfer-engineer-inventor, started toying with his first mechanized mannequin. He had graduated from the Massachusetts Institute of Technology and was working on the Falcon missile at the time. As has been usual in golfing inventions, Glasson was looking for ways to cut strokes from his own game.

"The monster was a crude thing then," Glasson reminisced, "mounted on a wooden tripod. And I had to crank it manually to get it to work. At first it would only hit the ball about 125 yards. But, after several modifications, it started belting the ball 200 yards and I got excited about its possibilities."

Glasson's Frankenstein-like monster machine was put into operation at Golfcraft, Inc. of Escondido, California for testing new designs and materials in clubs and balls. A simple screw adjustment could set it to pitch 25 yards or blast 400 yards on the fly, and its accuracy was amazing. When pitched the shorter distance, ten balls would land within a one-foot diameter circle; when driven 400 yards, ten would land within a 15-foot circle.

Some of the company's employees, who also dabbled in divots in their leisure time, started studying the grooved swing of Mr. Automatic, as the robot golfer came to be called, and all claimed to have knocked strokes off their games. The robot could hit every shot in the Palmer-method (Arnold Palmer, that is) manual: fade or draw, hook or slice, high or low trajectory, and all with perfect wrist action, pronation and follow-through. And, unlike us, he could do each when he was supposed to.

Neither the Golfcraft nor True Temper robots caused panic among golfing profes-

•
THE ROBOT COULD HIT EVERY SHOT IN THE PALMER-METHOD (ARNOLD PALMER, THAT IS) MANUAL: FADE OR DRAW, HOOK OR SLICE, HIGH OR LOW TRAJECTORY, AND ALL WITH PERFECT WRIST ACTION, PRONATION AND FOLLOW-THROUGH. AND, UNLIKE US, HE COULD DO EACH WHEN HE WAS SUPPOSED TO.
•

sionals. In fact, the pros liked the innovation because these robots were strictly specialists. They were to be used by their owners—golf equipment manufacturers Golfcraft and True Temper respectively—to test designs and materials of new golf clubs and balls. Even then, however, these farsighted company officials could see possible adaptations for teaching golf and tailoring clubs to individual customers.

Today, of course, most golf equipment companies have their own testing machines, as does the U.S. Golf Association. The USGA's "Iron Byron" tests all new equipment submitted for use in official tournament play. The USGA has worn out three versions of the True Temper model since 1974.

Computers and Cameras

The technological advances of cameras and computers has made it much easier to study human anatomy in motion—including the all-important golf swing. The advent of the

---

"MR. AUTOMATIC" GETS READY TO SWING AT GOLFCRAFT'S HEADQUARTERS IN ESCONDIDO, CA. NOTE THAT THE ROBOT'S "HAT," LOOKS CURIOUSLY LIKE A HUBCAP FROM A '66 IMPALA.

chapter six

THE STROBOSCOPE: ARE YOU EXPERIENCED?

sequence camera, like Polaroid's Graph-Check Sequence Camera which shot with eight shutters at 1/1000ths of a second, aided the teaching pros immeasurably. "Most people don't believe they have certain faults, even when you tell them," explained Jack Ellis the resident pro at Los Coyotes Country Club in Buena Park, California back in 1964. "But they (have to) believe instant feedback pictures."

Oddly enough, though, this camera pointed out that, far from a picture swing, Arnold Palmer "lunged at the ball scandalously," Jackie Cupit had a noticeable loop in his backswing, and Doug Sanders was jerky and too short with his swing.

Dramatic action images are relatively recent in the annals of photography, largely because the technical development of cameras was slow. It wasn't until the 1870s that itinerant photographer Edward Muybridge developed a spring-loaded shutter fast enough to stop motion on a glass-plate negative. He had been hired by a railroad tycoon who wanted to prove that all four hooves of a trotting horse leave the ground at once, even if only for an instant. Muybridge proved that they do. Until that breakthrough, such evidence could not be produced with camera shutters controlled by hand.

Muybridge went on to photograph a series of landmark motion studies of horses and humans, but action photography advanced little from there for decades. Lenses were short, cameras were cumbersome, and inspiration was lacking. Even as late as the 1950s, most sports photographers used cameras they called Big Berthas, shooting plays far from the action. The genre didn't begin to blossom until the late 1940s, when Mark Kauffman started moving about sporting events with telephoto lenses mounted on a 35mm camera, focusing on the human drama rather than the execution of play.

Today any golfer may blueprint his swing using, for example, Golfsmith's 4X Action Cam or Golf Day's Action Tracker. Basically

POLITICAL PAR

FORMER PRESIDENT DWIGHT D. EISENHOWER, AN AVID GOLFER, WAS PUTTING ON HIS SPIKES FOR A ROUND ONE DAY WHEN HE WAS ASKED BY HIS SON, JOHN, "DAD, HAVE YOU NOTICED ANYTHING DIFFERENT SINCE YOU LEFT THE WHITE HOUSE?" "YES," SMILED IKE. "A LOT MORE GOLFERS ARE BEATING ME."

automated golf

a 35mm camera, the former clicks four frames per half-second, from the top of the backswing to follow-through. These four pictures appear on one printout. The shutter sets automatically when the film is advanced. No batteries (gasp!) needed.

The portable video camera, when it came along, did Muybridge's job better than he could have conceived. The golfers could set the camera to automatically record themselves. It could even be mounted right on the golf cart so as to be continually at the ready.

The next step—computer analysis—has actually been on the scene much longer than most people realize. On July 27, 1941 two Lewiston, Idaho inventors, J.R. Jenks and W.F. Gilbert, unveiled a golf machine that measured the distance and direction a golf ball would take if driven on the open course—though it was done in a little cubbyhole of a research building located under the flight path at the Lewiston airport.

Their work was furthered by a consulting mathematician and former IBM computer analyst from Chicago named E.J. Betinis. He invented his Betinis Swing Recorder because his father pestered him to come up with a "Tinkertoy" that would take his picture at ball contact. The result, after four years of complicated ballistics studies, consisted of a black box less than two feet high with a Polaroid camera and a series of electric eyes. When the club shaft passed through an electric eye beam, it triggered the camera and a picture resulted. With the aid of a computer, Betinis worked around aerodynamic drag and gravitational pull to develop a series of equations that could measure impact and trajectory and convert them into distance.

Bud Blankenship, owner of Golf Technology, Inc., introduced his first portable golf computer models in 1977. One model was specifically for putting. It told the puttee his club face angle at impact, the path of the clubhead, and the impact point of the ball on the club face. It also precisely measured 10 to 20-foot putts. Digital readouts could be programmed to display "number of perfect putts" and "total putts," allowing the

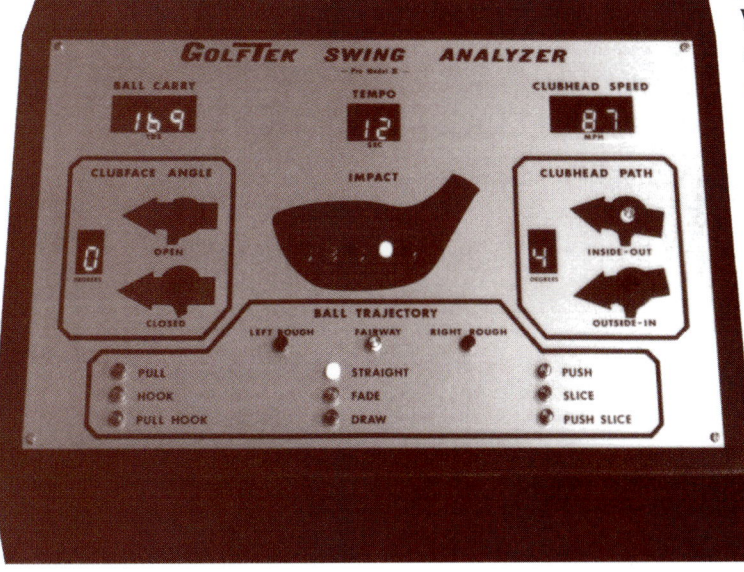

IN LIEU OF THE MORE TRADITIONAL COUCH, THE SWING ANALYZER OFFERS GOLFERS THERAPY WITHOUT CHARGING BY THE HOUR.

A CONSULTING MATHEMATICIAN AND FORMER IBM COMPUTER ANALYST FROM CHICAGO NAMED E.J. BETINIS INVENTED HIS BETINIS SWING RECORDER BECAUSE HIS FATHER PESTERED HIM TO COME UP WITH A "TINKERTOY" THAT WOULD TAKE HIS PICTURE AT BALL CONTACT.

chapter six

COMPUTER Miya SHOT ANALYZER PAT.P

Works with any wood or iron clubs, indoors or out, with or without ball

Model No.SM-306-1

9 Features of Shot Analyzer

1. Shows **HEAD SPEED** by meter per second.
2. Shows distance of **CARRY**.
3. Shows direction of **PATH** made by the club head before impact.
4. Shows **AREA** of club head hitting the ball at impact.
5. Shows club head **ANGLE** as Open, Square or Closed.
6. Shows club head **ANGLE** in degree. For calculating Deviation.
7. An "E" instead of the **CARRY** reading appears for over 25 degree open or closed head angle at impact. Possibly **OB**.
8. **No** need to attach Magnet strip to any of your clubs.
9. It's completely **PORTABLE**. Powered by 4 "AA" batteries or 6 volt D.C. adapter.

ANOTHER BRANCH OF GOLF ANALYSIS.

individual to compare day-to-day improvement. The machine could even set up a percentage point statistic to work with, if desired.

The second model was for other clubs. It registered tempo or timing of the swing for maximum clubhead speed, angle of club face at impact, impact point of ball on club face, how many yards the ball would have carried, ball trajectory, and something about the correct club weight, length and flexibility for an individual's physical build and ability. The device utilized 40 light beams and cells, coupled with the specially designed computer.

In spite of the revolutionary concept, it took Golf Tek (after a name change) from 1977 to 1980, and an intricate merger with Automated Golf Technology, Inc., to get national sales attention. One of the early sales problems was that the unit was intimidating to golf pros. They thought it would put them out of business, until they were educated to all of its potential uses: teaching, club fitting and year-round indoor practice. Soon, the company had trouble keeping up with orders.

John Cromarty of Old Saybrook, Connecticut, was another amateur inventor who wanted,

automated golf

at age 53, to get rid of his slice. His Sportech, a 4 1/2-foot high computer—encased in heavy-duty fiberglass and equipped with some 30 functions, a video display and a printer—was the result of his tinkering experiments. When a golfer swung on its special platform, sensors along a two-foot mat at the bottom of the machine followed the clubhead through the hitting area. At the same time, scales, located under each foot, measured weight distribution throughout the swing. As each swing was completed, the computer instantly displayed a graph and, if desired, a printout that included the path of the clubhead away from and through the ball in relation to the target line, the position of the clubhead during the backswing and at impact, the angle of the club face at impact, and the weight distribution at address, at the top of the swing, and at impact.

The cost of this 1984 machine was about $20,000, but about 30 were in use at golf teaching facilities across the country by mid-summer of that year. Peter Kostis, the teaching pro at St. Andrews Country Club in Boca Raton, Florida, used it at the Golf Digest Instructional School very successfully. So Sportech had the unqualified blessing of golf commissioner Deane Beman.

More Golf by Illusion

Back in 1968, the Brunswick Company, via Virginia inventor Robert Hopp, came out with an

HOME ON THE RANGE: BRUNSWICK'S ELECTRONIC GOLF RANGE (OPTIONAL WADING POOL FOR SIMULATED WATER HAZARD NOT SHOWN).

chapter six

early computerized 18-hole golf course designed for home use and which allowed employment of all clubs. Requiring an 18 x 14-foot space when assembled for play, it had scale layouts of water hazards, sand traps and other obstacles, and a transistorized computer that measured the distance of a shot, allowed for bounce and roll, and registered any hooks or slices, telling the golfer where a ball had stopped on the course. William W. Bertka got the brainstorm of using the Brunswick Electronic Golf Range on a weekly television sports show as a teaching aid and the sales of the unit took off.

Still more extensive—and expensive (originally $5500)—was the Golf-O-Tron, which allowed the golfer to play 18 holes in his living room, lending eye-catching reality to the usual drudgery of practice swinging. This 14-year project, was the handiwork of Austrian-born engineer M.R. Speiser of S&M Products Company of New York. It worked digested by the works of the Golf-O-Tron, a computing machine about the size of a very large TV set. How far the ball was hit was shown by numbers on a screen facing the golfer, while moving lights passing over a representation of a fairway indicated whether he hooked, sliced or pumped the ball right down the groove. The distance of each stroke was successively subtracted from the total yardage assigned each hole as it was played, allowing the golfer to choose his clubs—woods, irons or putter—realistically.

One of the first successful commercial installations of the Golf-O-Tron was at Sam Anziano's East 54th Street Golf Club (encompassing the whole fourth floor of a nondescript brick building) in 1976. For $10 per hour players could swing out over any of four computerized championship course simulations, including famed Pebble Beach.

The next logical step was units like the Snowy White, Inc. coin-operated Golf It

A SCENE FROM AN AS-YET-TO-BE-RELEASED STANLEY KUBRICK FILM.

like this: When you blasted a ball, it hit a nylon net 18 feet away. The speed with which the net kicked back, together with the angle the ball took, triggered four electric eye beams. The electronic impulses thus registered were electronic driving ranges and the Golfomat centers, to help take the pressure off courses and driving ranges that hadn't been able to handle the sudden influx of working men, youths, and women into the world of golf.

automated golf

PUTT FROM 5 FEET

It's always a sunny afternoon inside a Golfomat!

chapter six

GOLF-TEK IS A GREAT STRESS-RELIEVER AT THE OFFICE. HERE WE SEE A THREESOME TAKING IN A FEW ROUNDS DURING A LULL AT A LARGE METROPOLITAN NUCLEAR POWER PLANT.

Using the Golfomat, players hit a regulation free-flying ball into 100-square feet of nylon motion picture screen. A computer calculated velocity and direction, then advanced a film strip—from any one of several world famous golf courses—to the spot on the fairway, rough or hazard where the ball would have landed and/or rolled to on the actual course. Yards driven and yards to go appeared after each shot, so players used every club in their bags of tricks. They putted out on an undulating green from any of 37 positions. The units could also be set to practice just driving. An individual, without all the walking between holes necessary on an actual course, could shoot 18 holes in about 40 minutes,

> AN INDIVIDUAL, WITHOUT ALL THE WALKING BETWEEN HOLES NECESSARY ON AN ACTUAL COURSE, COULD SHOOT 18 HOLES IN ABOUT 40 MINUTES, WITH A DUO FINISHING IN ABOUT AN HOUR AND A HALF, AND A FOURSOME TAKING ABOUT TWO AND A HALF HOURS.

automated golf

with a duo finishing in about an hour and a half, and a foursome taking about two and a half hours.

Every hole was color photographed at 10-yard intervals to within five feet of the cups and to 80 yards beyond them, for playback of overshoots. Any ball missing the screen was a whiff stroke. And holes in one were scored when the ball landed within five feet of the flag.

clubs and balls and stand on a grass-like mat. When the golfer hits the ball into the nine-foot by twelve-foot screen, the ball falls to the floor. The ball's image, however, is projected onto the screen, and follows the same path that it would have taken on a real course. The ball's speed, direction, spin and elevation are all taken into account. Once the ball stops on the fairway, the view changes to reflect the golfer's new position, and an on-screen

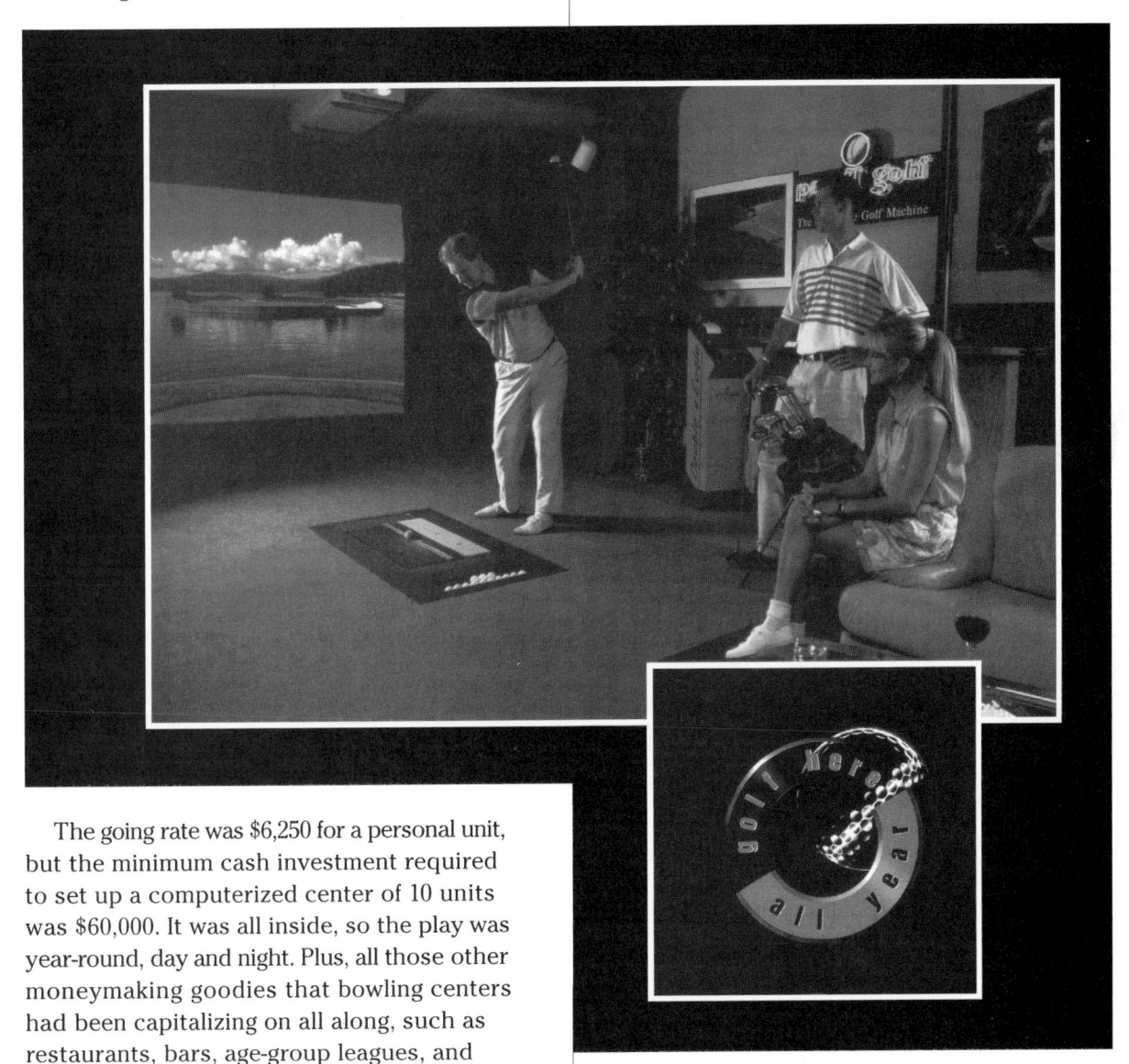

The going rate was $6,250 for a personal unit, but the minimum cash investment required to set up a computerized center of 10 units was $60,000. It was all inside, so the play was year-round, day and night. Plus, all those other moneymaking goodies that bowling centers had been capitalizing on all along, such as restaurants, bars, age-group leagues, and attached pool parlors could be incorporated. It was an ideal solution to the lack of space for actual courses within major urban areas.

The latest state-of-the-art golf simulator is the Par T Golf Double Eagle 2000, manufactured by Optronics LTD. The Double Eagle 2000 uses a LCD video projector and digital technology. Golfers use their own favorite

ONE DAY, ULTRAVIOLET LIGHTS WILL ALLOW YOU TO TAN AS YOU PLAY!

readout offers such statistics as the distance hit and the number of yards to the pin.

When it comes time to putt, the golfer has two choices: for putts that are less than 20 feet, the golfer putts on an actual artificial turf green with a real cup. For longer putts, the golfer uses the screen technology. An average round takes approximately 45 minutes to complete, and a foursome should finish in less than three hours. While the flight time of the ball is calculated in real time, the elimination of walks to balls or between holes—not to mention the disappearance of such tasks as replacing divots and raking sand traps—is where the time savings is accomplished. Extra bonus: the screen doubles as a movie screen for satellite reception, VCRs, video games and the like!

The Future of Golf?

The next step, of course, is already in development—virtual reality golf gaming!

It is difficult to believe that at one time in U.S. history the patent bureau closed down because its administrators figured "everything had been invented that could be." The disunited state of golfdom, with the advent of the computerized and filmed indoor courses, seemed to have arrived at this same conjecture. Yet one has only to imagine the potential of virtual reality technology and the innovations in automating education to know better. We have subliminal teaching through audio-visual aids, and self-made movies for slow-motion and stop-action analysis. Now we are looking at another concept, which may prove to be the real cure-all we've been searching for in both golf and education in general. It's been called the "Learning Box."

As envisioned for country club pro use, or even for the college golf teacher's use, this "learning box" would be a 20-foot-square soundproofed, one-person "studio." The student could be completely isolated from all outside influence and distraction, except those selected. And these selections would electronically bombard him with sounds, vibrations, words, sights and maybe even smells from a controlled battery of recorders, players, projectors, computers, et al. The machine could provide an intense package of golf lore, history, rules, sensations, and scientific knowledge within a very short time period. The student would, in effect, osmose all this.

Bad habits, confused skills, wrong impressions and mental blocks could probably be programmed out just as easily.

Picture, if you can, the year 2020 or so. A golf widow has badgered her husband into teaching her the game. They arrive at the club, hubby parks the Mrs. inside the golf pro "booth," inserts his credit card in a meter, and in a half-hour—which he wiles happily away in the bar—his wife emerges with a good working knowledge of the game. He may even have spent the waiting time in an adjacent booth taking a refresher course on sand trap escape or psychological enhancement for driving over water himself.

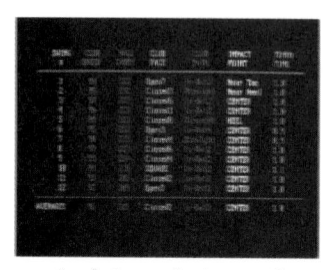

Analysis pgm/swing results 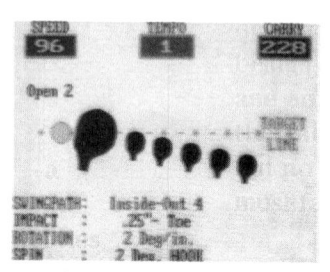   *Teaching pgm/clubhead action* 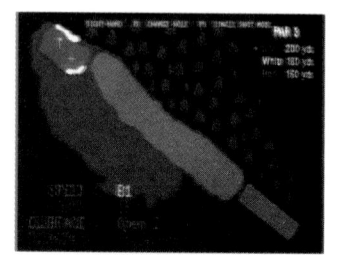   *Practice pgm/3 & 4-par holes*

COMPUTERIZED GOLF WILL DRIVE THE BALL INTO THE 21ST CENTURY. NEXT STOP: VIRTUAL GOLF, PROMISING TO BE THE BIGGEST MIND GAME YET.

Groovy Gadgets to Improve Your Game

chapter 7

This chapter is not meant to be a catalog, but a compendium of the unusual, shown through the development of the game and its equipment over the years since its inception. Because rules and equipment have changed often and are, in fact, in a nearly continual state of flux, specific items shown here, as well as the companies selling the items, are not necessarily current . . . Trying to trace some individuals or companies that produced golf equipment and gadgetry has been impossible in many instances. Many have since moved with forwarding addresses no longer available, sold out to other firms, changed company or product names, or simply gone out of business. In those instances we have still included their products. I do not advocate nor decry the use of any item, nor do I judge on whether items included herein fit the rules of the game. I have merely reported.

• • •

The well-adjusted person is the one who plays golf as though it were just a game. The reason soon becomes obvious— there are so many different things that can go wrong, singly or in bunches, that a person could quickly go berserk if he took the game too much to heart. This is why so many "how-to" books and videos on golf have been written and filmed. Each golfer's game between tee and green requires personal knowledge of three things—his physical limitations, his skills limitations with each club, and his mental conditioning. And each limitation depends upon the other: game skills without both power and finesse won't foster a champion, neither will strength without the knowledge of how to use the equipment. And without a positive mental outlook, what good are the other elements?

Luckily, we have golf gadget inventors for help. The following pages contain some of the more useful—and unusual— gadgets that have been developed over the years. Who knows, maybe you'll find that perfect product that will take strokes off of your game!

chapter seven

Muscling In

groovy gadgets

(Opposite and left) For the really physically pffft, Tommy Bolt, terrible-tempered titan of the links in another generation, recommended the Muscle Matic belts—pellet-filled leatherette belts for wear around the waist, ankles and wrists while on the job, around the house and on the golf links.

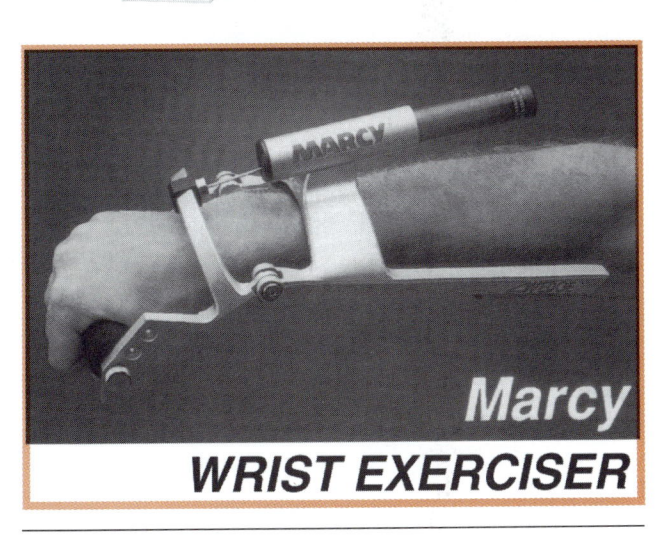

Marcy WRIST EXERCISER

The Marcy Wedge Wrist Exerciser, with adjustable hydraulic tension, can create resistance up to the equivalent of a 15-pound dumbbell.

Animal, vegetable or mineral? You make the call! Actually, Bill Cox, a former Los Angeles area golf pro and current president of SportsHealth, took Silly Putty a step further and came up with Power Putty, marketing it as a hand-strengthening aid.

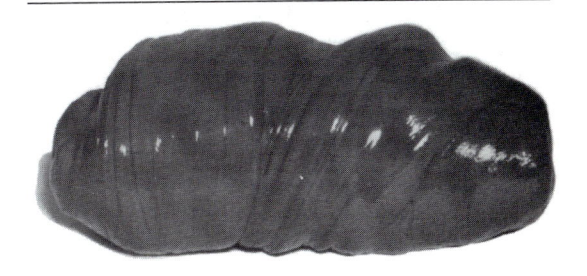

97

chapter seven

Net Returns

R.A. JOHNSON, THE ORIGINATOR AND MARKETER OF THE NY-LO-SCO PRACTICE NET, SAID THAT AT THE AGE OF 60 HE DROPPED HIS HANDICAP FROM 13 TO 5 IN ONE YEAR USING A NET SETUP ON HIS FLOODLIT PATIO. THEN HE PUT ONE IN HIS OFFICE WITH A MIRROR BEHIND IT FOR FORM STUDY AND CONTINUED TO LOWER HIS SCORE.

groovy gadgets

MAKES PRACTICE FUN INDOORS AND OUTDOORS, REGARDLESS OF WEATHER

If you want to reduce your handicap, you can take strokes off your game as you enjoy good exercise. It's fun to practice regularly when you have a NY-LO-SCO Net in your yard or play room with a "T-T-F" Saver to tee off turf or floor. This is the all-year, all-weather way to stay in that groove of happiness.

DCC Professional Bobby Morris Hits Toward Net and Glass

Young Woman Drives into Net in Glass-Cornered Country Club

LEADING PROS RECOMMEND NY-LO-SCO

Teaching and other Professionals across the country recognize the value of regular practice as well as lessons, and they welcome the aid this Net gives their efforts to help lower scores.

Use "T-T-F" SAVER Indoors and Outdoors
(Turf-Tee-Floor)

Save your lawn or floor and enjoy a better base for hitting balls into your Net. A blend of tough, green natural and synthetic fibers like grass, will withstand wood and iron shots by the thousands. Use wood tees, if you wish. Rust-resistant, Aluminum base.

$12.95 POSTPAID

Back Yard Chipper Net

THE NY-LO-SCO SPAWNED NUMEROUS IMITATORS, INCLUDING ONE FEATURED IN THE FAMOUS TEXAS NEIMAN-MARCUS DEPARTMENT STORE CHRISTMAS CATALOG. DESIGNED FOR THE GOLFER WHO HAD EVERYTHING (INCLUDING LOTS OF MONEY) IT FEATURED A FRAME MADE OUT OF GOLD.

START CHIPPING SHOTS INTO THIS NET ON A CONSISTENT BASIS AND YOU'LL BE READY FOR THE TOUR!

chapter seven

NEW

ENTIRE UNIT CAN BE SET UP FOR USE OR FOLDED AGAINST WALL IN LESS THAN 2 MINUTES BY 1 PERSON...

Pak-A-Way GOLF DRIVING RANGE

BERLIN CHAPMAN OF BERLIN, WISCONSIN, PROMOTED PAK-A-WAY GOLF DRIVING RANGE, WHICH WAS DIFFERENT IN THAT IT COULD BE ARRANGED IN A MODIFIED-U CAGE WITH TEES FOR TWO SWINGERS AT THE SAME TIME.

THE HOT SHOT NET IS A FREESTANDING LIGHTWEIGHT NET THAT'S GREAT FOR WORKING OUT THE KINKS IN YOUR GAME.

HEADS-UP ADVICE

THE GOLFER WAS HAVING A TERRIBLE DAY. FINALLY ARRIVING AT THE 18TH TEE, WHICH FACED A LARGE WATER HAZARD, HE GAZED AT IT DOUBTFULLY, TURNED TO HIS CADDY AND SAID, "TAKE MY CLUBS, THEY'RE YOURS. I'M JUST GOING TO WALK INTO THAT WATER AND DROWN MYSELF." THE CADDY, JUST AS DISGUSTEDLY, REPLIED, "YOU WON'T DROWN. YOU CAN'T KEEP YOUR HEAD DOWN LONG ENOUGH."

100

groovy gadgets

Puttering Around

Hammacher Schlemmer currently carries this adjustable electronic putting green. It has 72 different surface positions that change slope and angle automatically to precisely simulate the differences in golf course greens. It features four 18-hole courses (two amateur and two pro levels) and allows play for as many as four persons. Sensors on the green compute all scores, total strokes per game, average putts per hole and lowest score. Each player's score is displayed on a digital scoreboard and a computerized voice announces each player's turn, the hole number and the number of penalty strokes while a simulated crowd applauds. Golf Magazine called this putting green "the closest thing to reality you'll find."

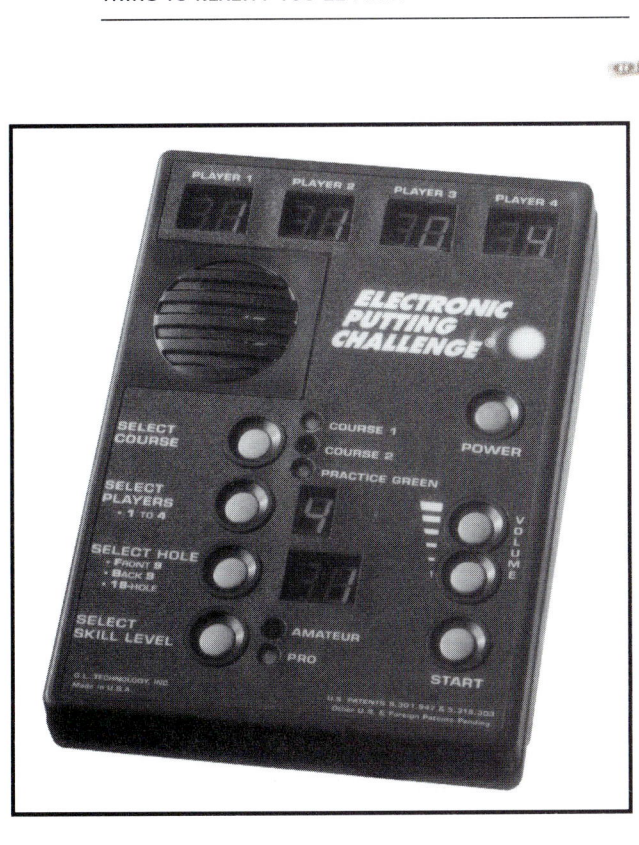

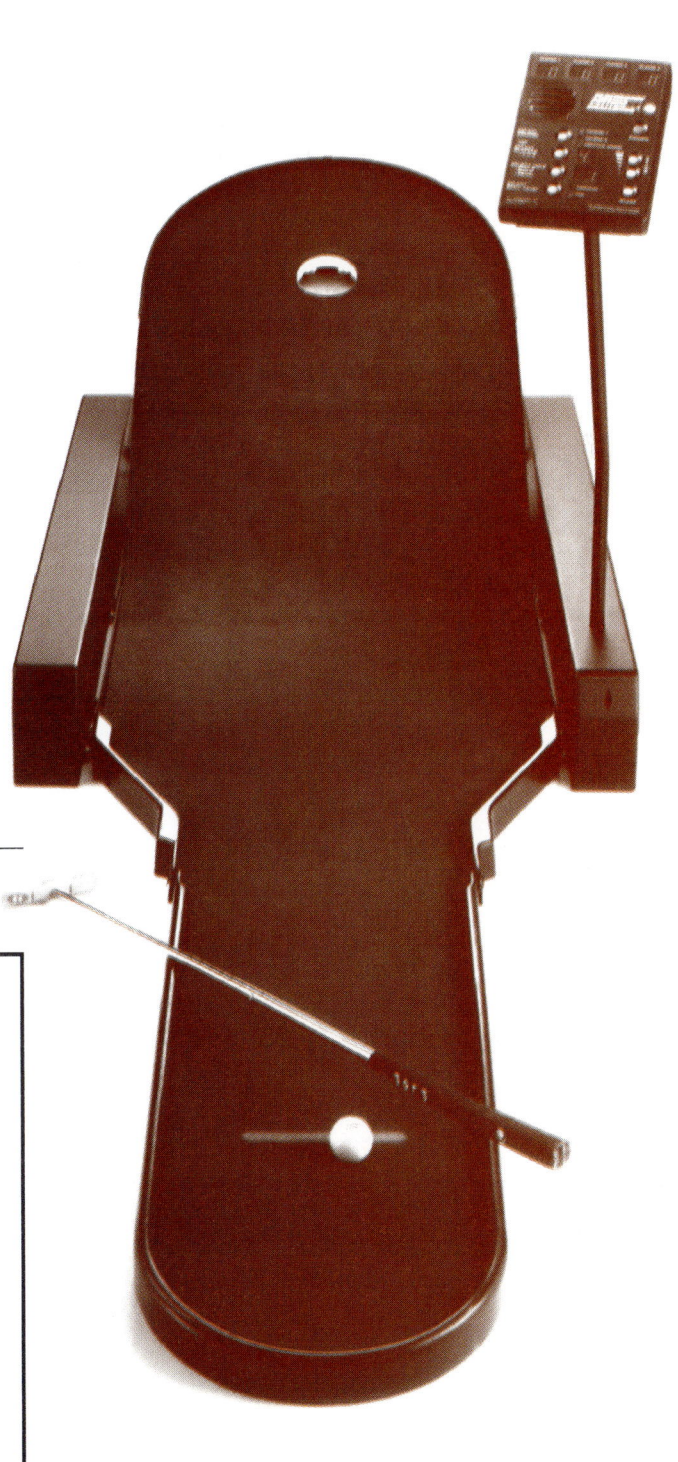

chapter seven

Does It Pass the Test?

Tests of new products have shown that modern technology is capable of changing the game and outmoding present courses. That's why the USGA has a watchdog arm called the Implements and Ball Committee. It's also why, back in the early 1970s, a mechanical engineer named Frank Thomas was hired away from Shakespeare Company to fill the then-new position of USGA Technical Director. His job, basically, was to keep the game on a *status quo*.

That job has been made easier over the years by the establishment of a complete Research & Test Center, where all new equipment is tested and passed on for its effect on the game. For many years this role had been carried out at the Polytechnic Institute of New York. But in 1984, the new center—complete with a main test laboratory and an outdoor test range—opened in Far Hills, New Jersey. The main lab actually has three test labs in it. One is for testing equipment under impact conditions, another holds a wind tunnel for conducting aerodynamic tests, and the third weighs and sizes equipment and tests balls for initial velocity performance.

PUTT-CASTER
Golf Practice Fixture for Clubs
PATENT PENDING

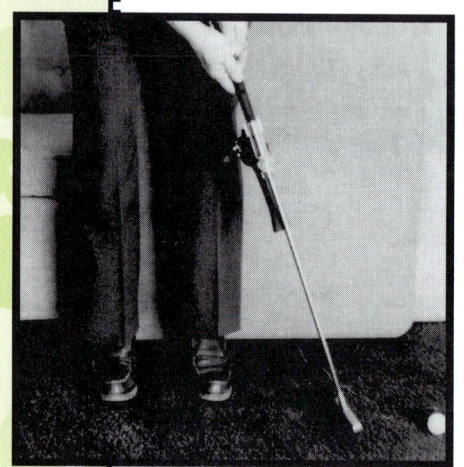

THE PUTT-CASTER ATTACHES TO YOUR PUTTER OR CHIPPER AND WORKS LIKE A FISHING REEL. PRESSING YOUR FINGER DOWN ON THE LINE RELEASES THE BUTTON, ALLOWING A TETHERED BALL TO TRAVEL FREELY. ONCE STOPPED ON THE GROUND, THE BALL CAN BE SIMPLY REELED BACK IN—ALL WITHOUT CHASING, SEARCHING AND STOOPING FOR THE BALL! EXTRA TETHERED BALLS WITH A SWIVEL CAN BE PURCHASED FROM THE MANUFACTURER.

groovy gadgets

The Putt Teacher uses a putter attached to a belt on rollers. If the golfer's swing is not straight through the ball, the belt will twist.

103

chapter seven

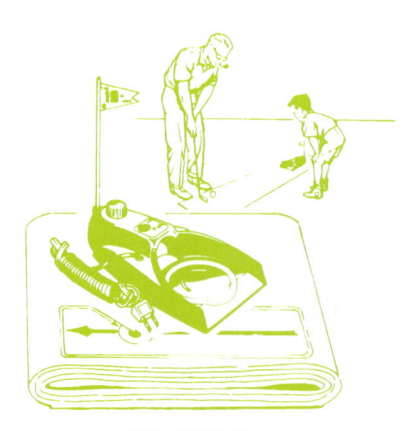

PAR-COMBO
The Par Putting Cup in one package with putting green and guide boxed in corrugated container suitable for individual unit shipments.

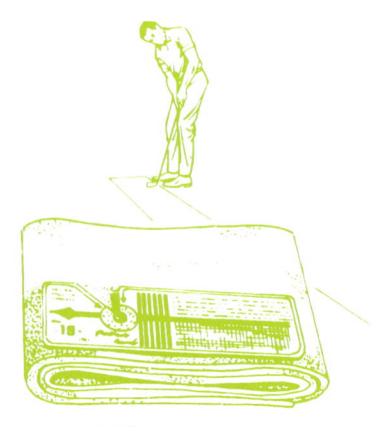

PUTTING GREEN
A realistic, durable putting surface made from green foam rubber, 9 feet long and 12 inches wide. Complete with 19th Hole instructional putting guide.

BIRDIE-COMBO
The Birdie Putting Cup in one package with putting green and guide boxed in display type corrugated carton.

PAR ELECTRIC PUTTING CUP
The "original" electric putting cup — helping thousands of golfers year after year! Automatic and adjustable ball return. Exact golf cup size.

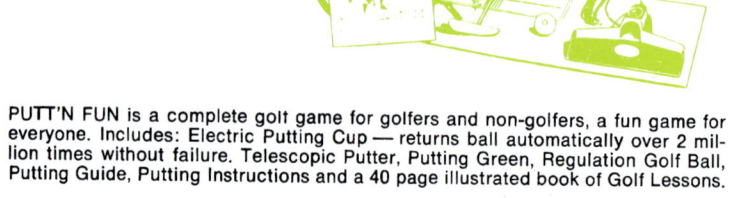

PUTT'N FUN GOLF GAME

PUTT'N FUN is a complete golf game for golfers and non-golfers, a fun game for everyone. Includes: Electric Putting Cup — returns ball automatically over 2 million times without failure. Telescopic Putter, Putting Green, Regulation Golf Ball, Putting Guide, Putting Instructions and a 40 page illustrated book of Golf Lessons.

EAGLE-COMBO
The Eagle Putting Cup in one package with putting green and guide boxed in display type corrugated carton.

PUTT'N BOX™ HOME GOLF GAME
A new concept for indoor golf. Box converts into realistic putting cup. Complete with 9 foot putting green and putting instructions. Fun for all and serious practice for golfers.

EAGLE ELECTRIC PUTTING CUP
Features automatic, adjustable ball return plus the ringing, spinning no-peek bell — you hear the perfect putt. Extra width also returns near misses.

104

groovy gadgets

Sometimes the simplest ideas are the most effective. The Birdiemaster starts you off with a regulation size cup and gradually shrinks the cup with its concentric rings. By the time you can sink a putt into the smallest ring, your putting game will be comparable to the pros!

The Birdiemaster
Makes putting look much easier!

The Miya Putting Checker uses a computer to check and control your putting stroke. Computer data helps you identify the correct sweet spot position and fix those putting yips.

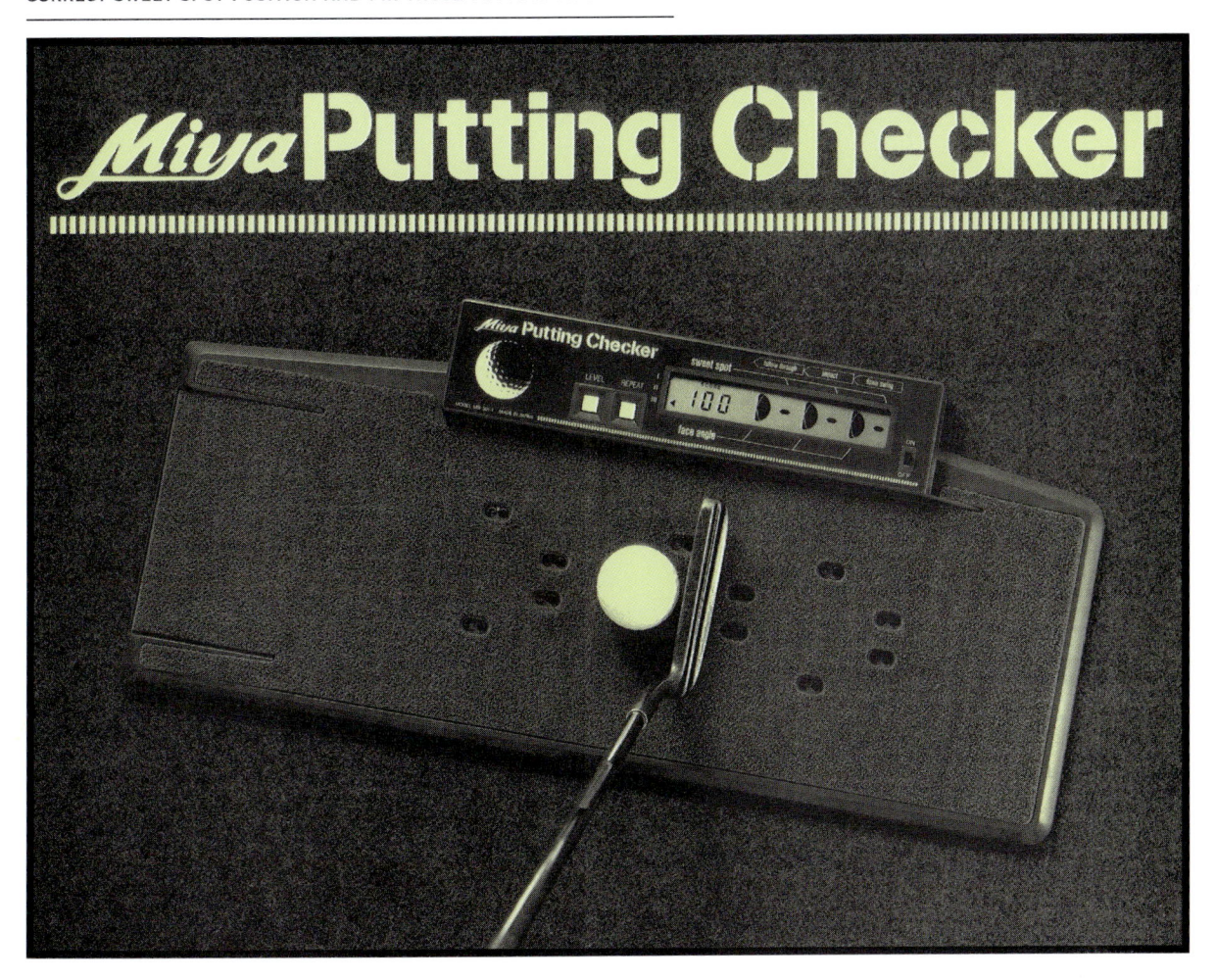

Miya Putting Checker

105

chapter seven

スライス、フックラインの練習もできる!!
ミヤパッティングトレーナー

特徴

■ミヤパッティングトレーナーは、付属のスペアカップと底部の脚の調節で、パッティングの最も大切な、「距離感」「方向性」はもちろんスライス、フックライン等、グリーンを想定したいろいろな練習ができます。

■サイドには、ボールの帰ってくるミゾがあり、又、カップの上には傾斜の目やすをつける水平器がついています。

■本器は、持ち運び、収納に便利なように、センターより2つに折りたたむことができます。

★パッティングの軌道を科学的に立証した画期的な家庭用練習機コンピュータ、「ミヤ・パッティングチェッカー」とドッキングしてのご使用は、なお一層効果的です。

スペアカップの種類と用途

※パッティングトレーナーに付属している2種類のスペアカップを利用すると、次のような練習ができます。

▶小さなカップ(正確さ)
規定のカップよりも一回り小さくしてありますのでより正確さをつかむことができます。(スペア付)

▶ダ円カップ(距離感)
特にパットでは距離感が大切です。ダ円カップを図のように置くことにより、より正確な距離感をつかむことができます。(スペア付)

▶ダ円カップ(方向性)
パットでは方向性が大切です。ダ円カップを図のように置き練習することにより、より正確な方向性をつかむことができます。

▶ダ円カップ(スライスライン用)
ダ円カップを図の様に置き、トレーナー下部の脚の調節で本体に傾斜をつけることによりスライスラインの練習をすることができます。

ミヤパッティングトレーナー仕様

種類 寸法	巾(W)mm	長さ(L)mm
I 型	230	1,866
II 型	300	1,866

YET ANOTHER PUTTING TRAINER BROUGHT TO YOU BY THE FOLKS AT MIYA. MY KNOWLEDGE OF JAPANESE IS LIMITED, BUT THIS DEVICE ESSENTIALLY ALLOWS YOU TO PRACTICE PUTTS OF A VARIETY OF DISTANCES AND BREAKS WITH ITS USE OF SEVERAL DIFFERENTLY SHAPED CUPS.

Secrets of the Professional and Not-So-Professional

Golf instruction has progressed greatly since the days when a devotee expected to perfect his game by reading a book by a pro who thought he had all the answers, or by taking lessons from a crusty old Scot in knickerbockers. The magazines play up the innovations, inventions and current fads, while the books search for promotable gimmicks to make them sell. And the golf pros, we've learned, have just about as much trouble with their games as we do. So where do we look for our answers?

There is no easy answer. The trouble is that what works for one player often means nothing to another. And the little variations that different players work out to cure their personal yips and hitches are secrets of little worth to others.

One pro, for instance, developed a touch of arthritis in his left elbow and it hurt when he bent it. So he broke a general rule by keeping it relatively straight. Plastic surgery left him with a touchy right foot as well, so he learned to get off it fast, transferring his weight from right to left quickly. After an appendectomy, permanent stitches were left in his right side, which left it tender. To protect it, he kept his right elbow in close. And, while in his early golfing days he had gone hatless, he later started wearing a Sam Snead-type hat because of a thinning pate. "The hat gives me confidence!" he grinned.

Nick Faldo, after winning the British Open in 1987, revealed his then-current technical quirk: "Set the angle by letting the right hand govern the take-away." Other golfers, were they to try this, would probably hit a passel of coathanger hooks.

Bob Falkenburg, the 1948 Wimbledon tennis champ-turned-golfer, once admitted he periodically had a head-lift problem. So he kept a piece of tape on the head of his driver imprinted "KYFHDYFI," standing for "Keep Your Foolish Head Down You Fatuous Idiot," or whatever other choice words one might choose to substitute for "foolish" and "fatuous."

Dave Stockton, who had had putting problems on tour, won the 1976 PGA Championship by "doubling the size of the hole in my mind. I aim at the right lip and hood the blade of the putter. I can't miss." And that week he couldn't!

When Ed Butterworth, assistant professor of communications at Brigham Young University, decided to give up golf, he was shooting around 100. About 12 years later his children discovered his old clubs in the attic and cajoled him into instructing them in the basics. Of course, the golf bug bit him again and, in the month that followed, he found himself, to his astonishment, shooting in the low 80s. The improvement was a puzzle until he finally worked out a theory. He had become near-sighted so, now, peering over the bottoms of his bifocals helped him keep his head down.

Tim Gallway, author of *The Inner Game of Tennis*, after taking up golf, discovered that humming to himself during his swing improved his shot making. "The sound amplifies the feedback you are receiving from the over-tightening of muscles," he explained. "By listening to changes in the sound, you can soon gain more control over subtle muscular tightness than you might have thought possible."

For years Ben Hogan refused to divulge his secrets, until he had announced his retirement and *Life Magazine* (1955) came out with not one, but two mysterious maneuvers he used. "I moved my left hand one-eighth to one-fourth of an inch to the left so that the thumb was almost directly on top of the shaft," he stated. "The second adjustment, which is the real meat of the secret, was nothing more than a twist or a cocking of the left wrist. I cupped the wrist gradually backward and inward on the backswing so the wrist formed a slight V at the top of the swing. The angle was not more than four or six degrees, almost invisible to the human eye. This simple maneuver, in addition to the pronation, had the effect of opening the face of the club to the widest practical extreme at the top of the swing." He added that this secret made his swing hook-proof, resulting in that "lovely, long fading ball which is a highly effective weapon on any golf course."

But another pro said Ben had told him that "he only put that stuff in *Life* to stop people from asking."

chapter seven

In The Swing

19th HOLE BRAND Swing Trainer & EXERCISE CLUB

Read instructions thoroughly before using Swing-Trainer

CLICK

Teaches
RHYTHM • TIMING • TEMPO

The greatest of all indoor and outdoor golf-swing trainers — No golf ball required!

A PRACTICE CLUB with instrumentalized head that transmits the "CLICK" and "FEEL" of hitting a real golf ball to the hands indicating EARLY, CORRECT or LATE HAND ACTION.

INSTRUMENTALIZED HEAD

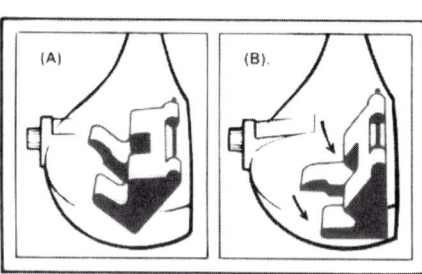

(A) (B)

THE HEAD OF THE SWING TRAINER FEATURES AN ADJUSTABLE SPRING-LOADED RELEASE MECHANISM. AT THE START OF THE SWING, THE SWING-WEIGHT IS IN POSITION "A" (SEE ABOVE). THE SETTING ON THE POWER-SCALE (SEE BELOW) DETERMINES THE CENTRIFUGAL FORCE REQUIRED TO OPERATE THE RELEASE MECHANISM. WHEN THE CLUBHEAD DEVELOPS THE PRE-DETERMINED CENTRIFUGAL FORCE, THE SWING-WEIGHT MOVES TO POSITION "B," EMITTING A LOUD "CLICK." AT THE INSTANT THIS OCCURS, THE WEIGHT CHANGE TRANSMITS TO YOUR HANDS, THUS SIMULATING THE "FEEL" OF HITTING A REAL GOLF BALL.

THE POWER SCALE

POWER SETTING
0 1 2 3 4

The setting on the Power-Scale represents the centrifugal force required to operate the weight-change in the head. An approximate guide follows:

0 — 50   Pitch shot with wedge
50 — 100   Short and mid-iron shots
100 — 150   Full shot average woman
150 — 250   Full shot strong woman or average man
250 — 325   Full shot for strong hitter
325 — 400   Full shot for most powerful hitter

WHAM-O Golfers DRIVING RANGE

NO BALL TO CHASE! **USED BY PROS TO WARM UP!**

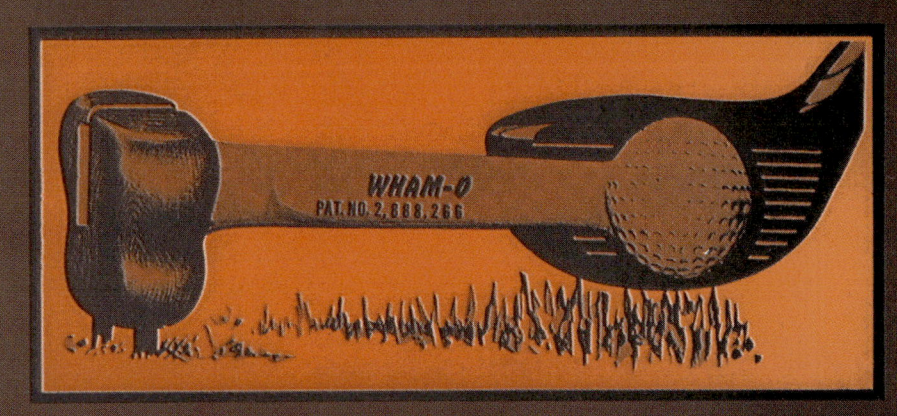

GROOVE YOUR SWING AT HOME! DEVELOP FORM CORRECT HOOK AND SLICE!

Simply push into ground and hit. Returns to position after club swing. Incorrect swings are indicated by action of Wham-O. Practice just 5 minutes a day with our instructions and play 100% better on Sunday! Folds to 8" for golf bag. Use to warm up at starting tee. Tough pliable plastic, ash hardwood stock, 5" steel spikes. Withstands violent abuse.

Help your golf friends improve their game — Whamo-O is a practical and popular gift.

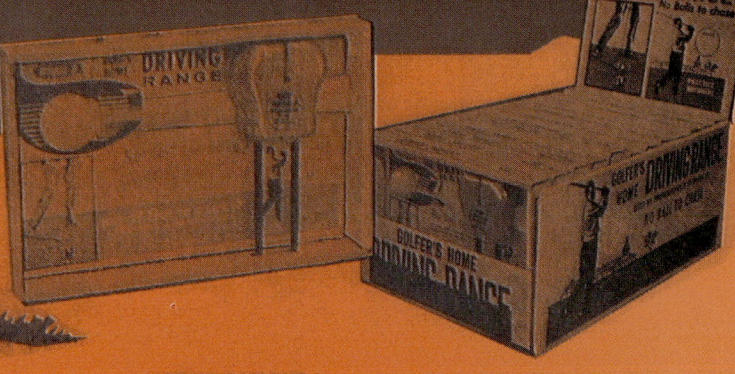

STOCK NO. 116

SPECIFICATIONS
Packed: 12 Per Display Carton
Weight: 8 lbs.

©1965 U.S. Pat. No. 2,888,266   WHAM-O MFG. CO., 835 E. El Monte St., San Gabriel, Calif. 91776

chapter seven

The Golf Coach—a promotional item given away by Bowser, Inc. in the early 1970s—was an extremely affordable alternative to hiring the real thing.

How to Play Lousy Golf

A minister and a professor, being evenly matched on the golf course, had developed a keen rivalry over the years. But one Spring the professor's game suddenly improved so much he started winning regularly. The preacher's efforts to improve his own game were unsuccessful—until he came up with the following plan. Going to a bookstore, he picked up three how-to-play-golf books and sent them as a birthday present to the professor. It wasn't long before the two men were again evenly matched.

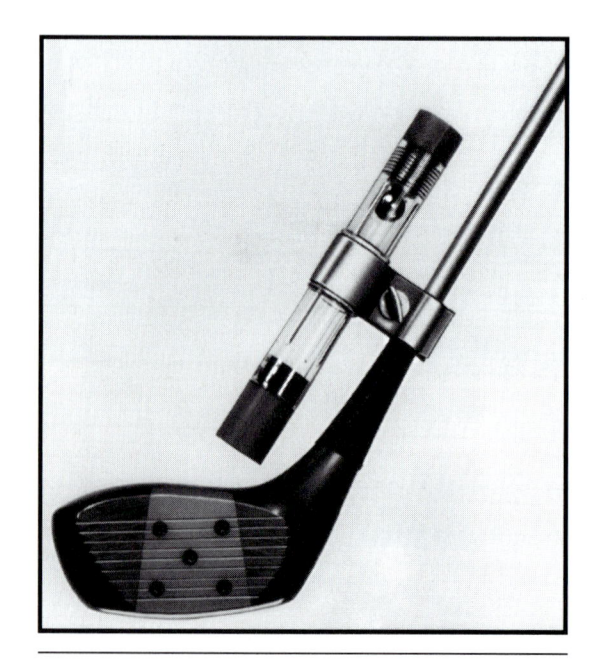

Time-Rite's floating magnetic ball bearing clicks to the other end of the cylinder upon the correct release of power on the downswing.

110

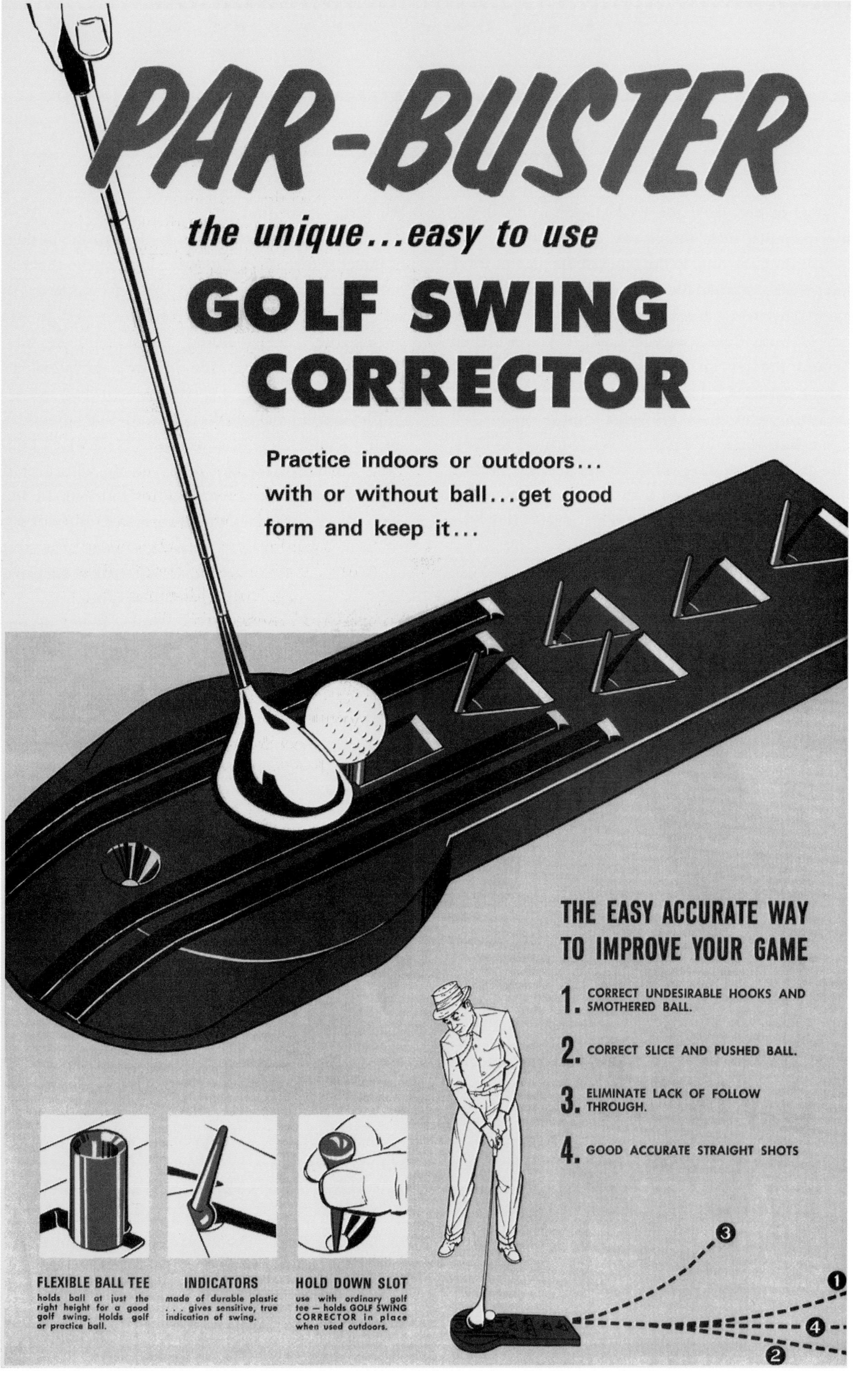

PAR-BUSTER

the unique...easy to use
GOLF SWING CORRECTOR

Practice indoors or outdoors... with or without ball...get good form and keep it...

THE EASY ACCURATE WAY TO IMPROVE YOUR GAME

1. CORRECT UNDESIRABLE HOOKS AND SMOTHERED BALL.
2. CORRECT SLICE AND PUSHED BALL.
3. ELIMINATE LACK OF FOLLOW THROUGH.
4. GOOD ACCURATE STRAIGHT SHOTS

FLEXIBLE BALL TEE
holds ball at just the right height for a good golf swing. Holds golf or practice ball.

INDICATORS
made of durable plastic ... gives sensitive, true indication of swing.

HOLD DOWN SLOT
use with ordinary golf tee — holds GOLF SWING CORRECTOR in place when used outdoors.

chapter seven

More Tricks . . .

True or not, there *are* tricks to the trade. In big tournaments, little things can make a difference, even if they are only in the mind of the player. Dave Paul closely studied the leading pros for a 1963 article in *This Week Magazine* and uncovered a number of individual idiosyncrasies. If you watched Arnold Palmer on TV, perhaps you noticed his "glove gimmick," for example. When he's driving or hitting iron shots, he wears a glove on his left hand. But, when he's putting, his left hand is bare. The glove is dangling out of his hip pocket. "Hitting the ball hard, you need a sure grip and the glove provides that," he explained once. "But putting is a matter of feel, and I found I never had the proper feel between my fingers and the club when I kept my glove on."

Once, during hot, humid weather, Dow Finsterwald, the 1958 PGA champion, took his glove off between shots. "Otherwise," he explained "it gets so wet from perspiration that it's slippery when I grip the club." (New types of gloves have since largely solved this problem.)

Gene Sarazen had a little trick he would use before playing in brisk weather: He would bathe his hands in the hottest water he could stand, to get his finger muscles loose and hands supple.

Palmer, like many other pros, hits a certain spot on the ball when driving. "I like to hit it on the manufacturer's name," he said. "It gives me a target,"

Sam Snead had another reason for positioning the ball for clubface contact. "That's where the cover is thinnest." And George Bayer, the game's longest driver for many years, expanded on that: "Hitting it on the name, you get the most compression in the ball and, therefore, the greatest distance."

Some "secrets" are obvious and perfectly sensible, but difficult to duplicate. Fuzzy Zoeller, the 1984 U.S. Open champ, addresses the ball in the middle of the club face, then slides the club out so that the ball is lined up at the heel. "This tells me to try to pull the heel of the clubhead down first in my downswing," he explained. "Most amateurs take the club back okay, but they throw it down instead of swinging it."

Playing in cold weather, as sometimes happens on the winter tour, pros prefer to hit a warm ball. "You get more distance than you do with a cold ball," opined Tony Lema, 1963 runner-up in the Masters. To keep them warm, a caddy will put a few in his pocket. Some pros even change their ball at each tee in cold weather.

On the green, Tommy Bolt set his ball so that the manufacturer's name pointed lengthwise at the proper putting line. If it's a straight putt, all the better," he said. "But on a putt where you know it's going to break to the right or to the left, I found it helps to have the name aiming at the line you want the ball to take."

Veteran pro Tom Watson has said that, when he is on the green, he envisions a tack sticking out of the away side of his golf ball, and taps the tack in with his putter. Pros Jim Nelford and Mac O'Grady both swing righty and putt lefty. So did Blaine McAllister when he won three tournaments between 1989 and 1991.

Non-golfers can't comprehend why a pro, faced with what appears to be a tap-in putt, marks the ball, cleans it and replaces it. "If a ball bites into a green, it invariably picks up a little dirt," according to Jack Nicklaus. "Even a speck of dirt can throw your putt off-line. To give yourself every chance, your ball must be clean."

... of the Trade

Also, after nearly every shot, the pro's caddie will carefully clean the club with a towel. This is especially important for the wedges. "On a wedge shot," explained Julius Boros, two-time U.S. Open champion, "you want backspin. The grooves help you get backspin, but if they are clogged with dirt, the face is too smooth." Otherwise, Boros admitted he ignored the various gimmicks other pros use. "I have enough trouble just trying to hit the ball," he chuckled.

Harvie Ward, two-time winner of the U.S. Amateur title, placed his tee so it leaned slightly forward. "That way," he said, "there is less friction when the ball goes off the tee."

Billy Casper, Jr., was careful not to wash his hands for a couple of hours before playing. "It can puff up your fingers and you can lose all your putting feel," he said. A similar belief was held by Ben Hogan when he was winning a record-sharing four U.S. Opens. He seldom shook hands with an opponent before starting play. "If somebody really squeezes your fingers," he grinned, "you won't feel right holding a club all day."

To prepare himself physically for the Senior Tour, George Archer played his last few years on the younger circuit wearing three-pound weights on his ankles—an idea he picked up from Tommy Bolt. Lugging these weights around paid off since playing the Senior Tour between October 1989 and November 1994 he won more than four million dollars.

Every golfer, no matter whom he strives to emulate, or how much he reads how others do it, or how much he studies the ideal swing performances, will swing a club differently. Thus each will have to find his own optimum "groove." Everyone is just built differently, concentrates disparately, follows directions variously, and intakes learning at different rates and by different methods. These are the reasons no one really can tell which method, gimmick or gadget will be successful for a golfer while learning the game, or for correcting his learning after he has started to play. The magic cure-all may be simple or complex. It may come from a book, a video or a pro, even a next-door neighbor. It may even come by accident, from personal experimentation.

Some secrets sound a little far-fetched: John Schlee, the tour's "official" astrologer, wouldn't play unless the stars were just right. Some may simply be due to natural phenomena: The secret of Sam Snead's magnificent swing was probably that he has uncommon flexibility in his joints; even at age 76 he could kick the top of an eight-foot high doorjamb!

One suggestion, from Fred Akel's book *A Different Approach to the Game of Golf*, stated that reader-golfers should find their "dominant side" by studying the direction of the hair whorl on the crowns of their heads. However, Akel didn't say what to do if one's whorl has departed.

Another comment, from Allan Starr's book, *The Easy Way to Lower Your Golf Score*, recommended the golfer use "psycho-control," by programming his mind with positive pictures of golf balls sailing serenely over water hazards, for example, and safely onto greens. Psycho-control, however, presumed one already knew how to use a club and a ball to realize these serene scenes.

Phil Cooper's Golf Improvement Plan, circa 1975, included instructions for making a device to visually show the path of a clubhead, by using two three-by-five-inch index cards and a can of Campbell's soup. Use your own imagination on this one. It wasn't explained any further.

chapter seven

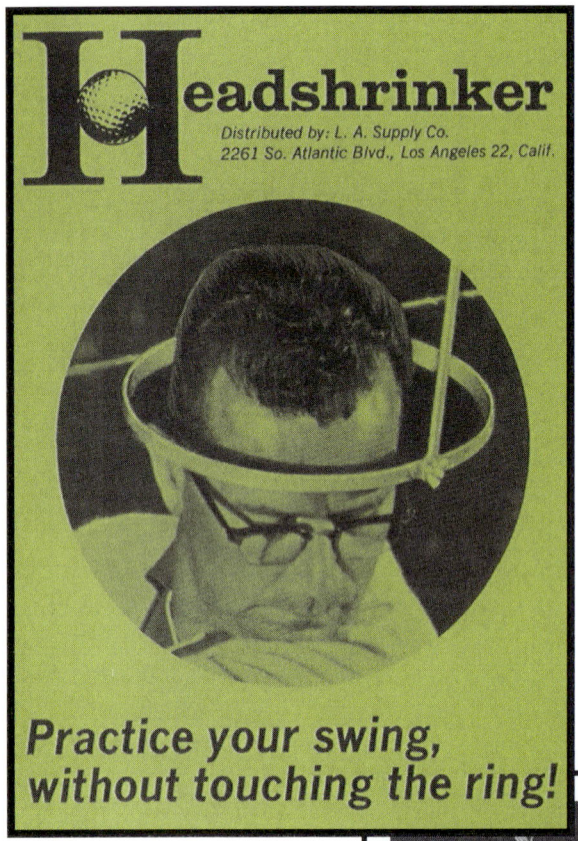

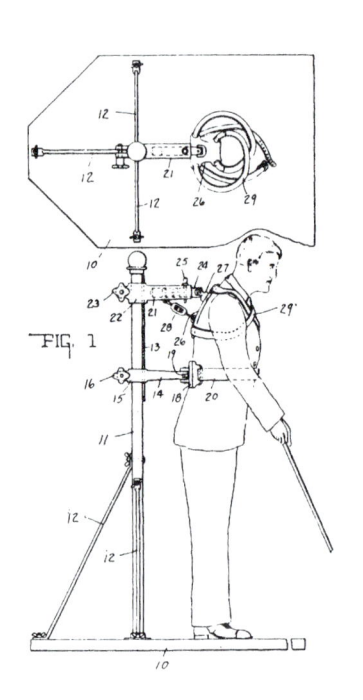

Headshrinker

Distributed by: L. A. Supply Co.
2261 So. Atlantic Blvd., Los Angeles 22, Calif.

Practice your swing, without touching the ring!

groovy gadgets

A number of Rube Goldbergian devices have been invented for the special problem of a bobbing bean. They include the Headshrinker (opposite), Head Stabilizer (this page), Stroke Saver, Head Trainer, and Head Freezer. All of these items were superseded by a 1925 body brace, however, showing there is little that is new under the golfing sun. The patent drawing on the opposite page shows a body brace attached to an anchored post behind the golfer. It was supposed to be strapped on "to teach proper form by preventing elevation of the torso during the swing." The Headshrinker ($9.95 originally, circa 1968) originated with a Cal Tech engineer named George Kendall. It differed in that it fitted a metal halo around the head to hold it in correct position throughout the swing. On this page, golf legend Gene Littler is shown demonstrating the Head Stabilizer, also circa 1968.

chapter seven

groovy gadgets

14 Tips From Arnold Palmer

1
You are out to enjoy yourself, so give the ball a healthy whack and have fun.

2
Ninety percent of golf is mental.

3
Think about your game as you drive out to play, but think constructively.

4
Before you tee off, warm up.

5
Keep your head still during the swing.

6
Don't break your wrists during the first 12 inches of the backswing.

7
Take the club back only as far as you can maintain complete control of it.

8
Use enough club on iron shots. Most golfers don't.

9
Do not try to correct fundamentals during play.

10
Concentrate especially hard during the first three holes.

11
Always play aggressively—attack the course or it will attack you.

12
Try to hit those "impossible" shots. Most amateurs give up too quickly.

13
If you begin to get tired, swing at the ball easier, not harder.

14
Give the game your best and it will, in turn, give you the most pleasure.

Power Swing—It Puts The Power In Your Game

THE POWER SWING IS A SIMPLE YET EFFECTIVE DEVICE THAT DEVELOPS THE STRENGTH AND MUSCLE MEMORY REQUIRED TO PERFECT A SMOOTH, POWERFUL SWING. 30 TO 40 POWER SWINGS PER DAY WILL STRENGTHEN YOUR WRISTS, ARMS AND SHOULDERS, ADDING POWER AND CONSISTENCY TO YOUR SWING.

(OPPOSITE) THE PERFECTO-ARC UNIT USES ARNOLD PALMER'S FOOTPRINTS AND DIAGRAMMED SHOT AIDES TO TEACH THE BEGINNER OR GIVE A REFRESHER COURSE TO THE MORE ADVANCED PLAYER.

chapter seven

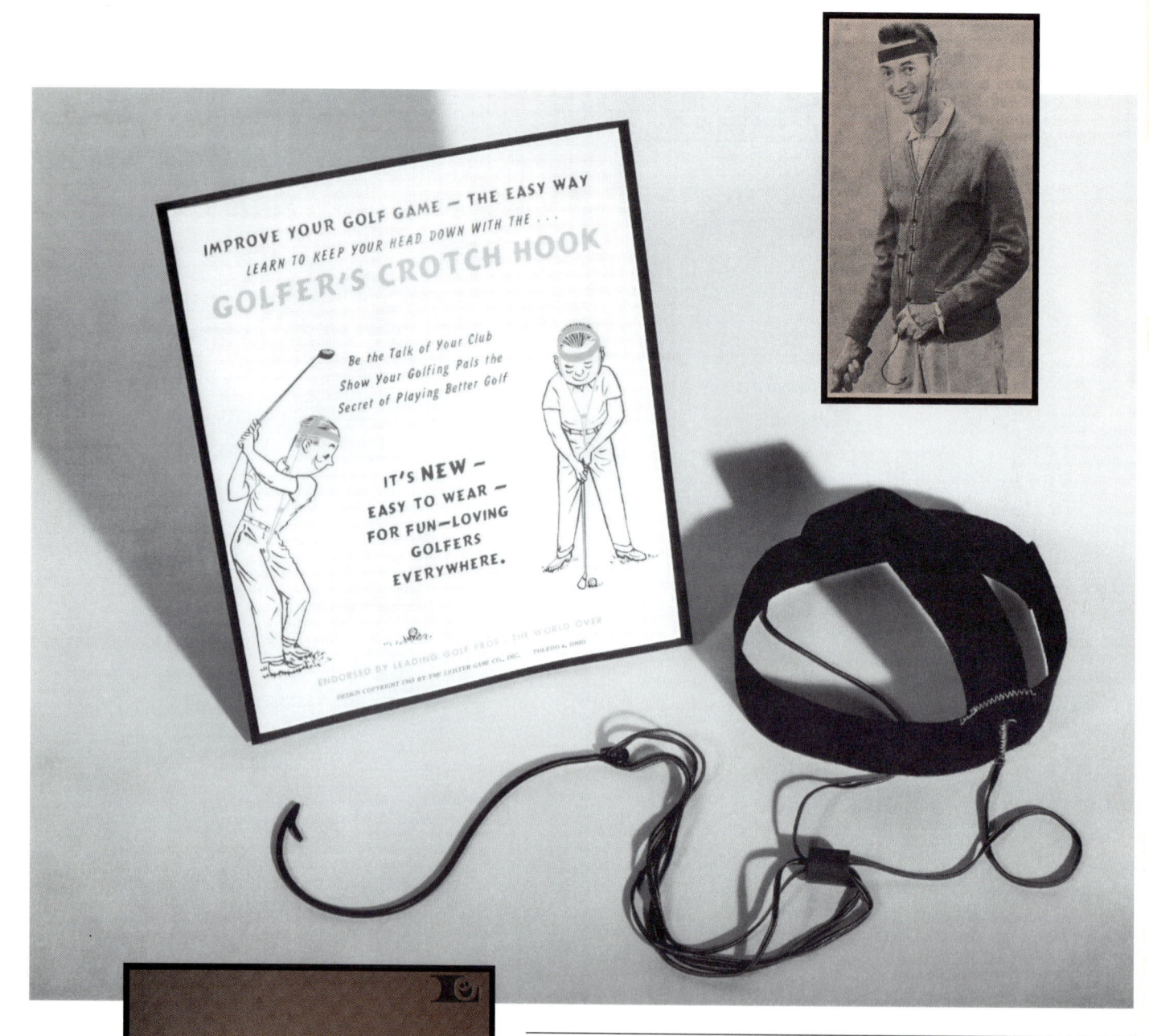

The Crotch Hook is the most diabolical of all the strap and brace devices designed to keep the head down during the swing. It consists of a headband with an elastic cord attached to a giant seven-inch fishhook which, of course, is fitted into the crotch of one's trousers. Lift your head up too high during your swing and, well, you get the idea. Pavlov would've been proud.

(Opposite) The Holt Swing Glasses are shaped like glasses but don't use optical glass. The glasses force the golfer to keep his eyes on the ball throughout the swing, since opaque plastic ridges surround the eyeholes. The wearer is, in effect, looking through two eye tunnels. All side vision is cut off, reminding one of horse blinders. If the head is moved, the ball disappears from view. All outside distractions, including head and club movements, are also thus eliminated, making this a valuable aid on the putting green as well.

HOLT
GOLF SWING GLASSES

THE REVOLUTIONARY GOLF TEACHING AID...

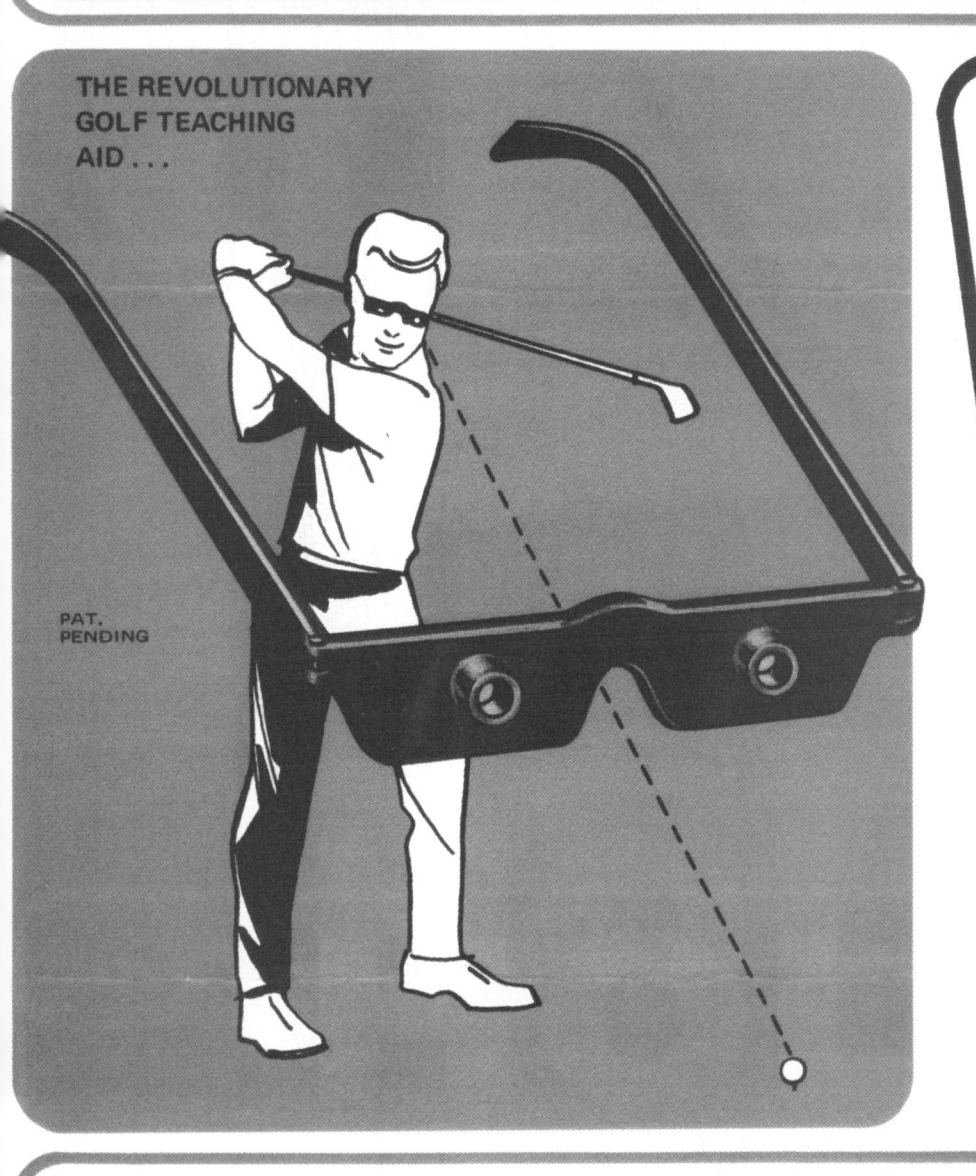

PAT. PENDING

TEACHES YOU TO:

- STOP SWAYING
- STOP LOOKING-UP
- HOLD HEAD STILL
- GET A FULL SHOULDER TURN
- KEEP YOUR EYE ON THE BALL

ONLY $4.95

TEACHES YOU TO CUT DOWN

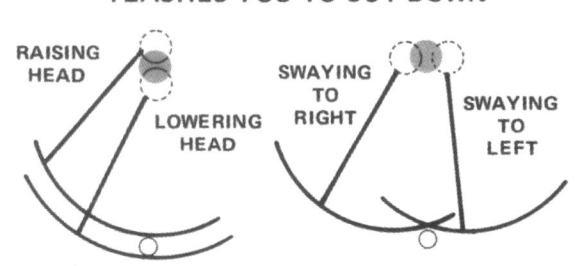

RAISING HEAD / LOWERING HEAD

SWAYING TO RIGHT / SWAYING TO LEFT

ON THOSE "EXTRA STROKE" MISTAKES

"KEEP YOUR EYE ON THE BALL"...

...is the first rule of golf and without question the most difficult one to conquer!

Holt Golf Swing Glasses train you to keep your eye on the ball during the entire swing. If you lift, nod, sway or turn your head...the ball disappears from view!

Ideal for both men and women, Holt Golf Swing Glasses fit over prescription glasses where required.

Develop a "grooved swing" with a full shoulder turn and you will take strokes off your game...

PLAY BETTER GOLF...ENJOY GOLF MORE!

MANUFACTURED BY E. L. HOLT COMPANY, 6714 GIRARD AVENUE SO., MPLS., MINN. 55423

FORM NO. 1071

chapter seven

Ever since a patent was granted in 1934 for a swing-grooving circle of steel that "imprisoned a pupil inside its coils," the idea has periodically resurfaced. The Duf-Mar, Inc. Swing Guide (this page) claimed to groove a consistent inside-out swing, eliminate slices and fades, and restore lost touch and timing.

Groove your swing Play better golf

With SWING GUIDE

AMAZING RESULTS!

This revolutionary golf aid helps beginners and the duffer get results they never thought possible. Your swing and stance are developed to the maximum for consistently better results. Just rest your club lightly on the swing ring and describe your arc, which soon grooves your swing. If your stance or arm position is faulty, "Swing Guide" will immediately let you know **and** show you how to correct it. Each practice swing trains your muscles to make those consistently perfect swings that positions the ball where you want it on the fairway and green.

SWING GUIDE BUILDS UP MUSCLE MEMORY...

Practice puts you in the groove without guesswork

CONSISTENTLY PLACE YOUR BALL WHERE YOU WANT IT

groovy gadgets

The Golf Swing Groover was developed by golf school operator Frank Zega of Bridgeport, Connecticut. With his unit, a swinger steps onto a platform set inside adjustable tubular steel "tracks." These tracks then follow the arc of the swing. It is guaranteed to help the duffer develop the perfect golf swing. Today this same basic unit is still marketed, but under the name the Perfect Swing Trainer by Golf Day.

"THE RING WITH THE BUILT IN SWING"

Get Your Golf Swing in the Groove!
With The New Scientific Golf Swing Groover

Height Adjustment Pin

Club guided by track (Not attached)

This track guides your club to swing inside out preventing you from cutting across the ball.

NOW BEING USED AT
FRANK ZEGA'S GOLF SCHOOL
THE PLACE TO PRACTICE THROUGH THE WINTER
— 2 INDOOR PRACTICE NETS —

chapter seven

It Could Make A Difference

Ed Snead, the Ryder Cup member, wrote: "When you consider that the golf ball, which is of either solid or wound construction and has a Balata or Surlyn cover and must not exceed 1.62 ounces nor be less than 1.68 inches in diameter, is struck with a club, the shaft of which may be made of aluminum, titanium, graphite, hickory or moon rock, and is tipped 3/4 of an inch and is 3/8 of an inch longer than standard, especially when most manufacturers on the deflection board drop it 4.3612 inches with a one-pound weight placed two inches from the end, and when the grip on that shaft, which is either rubber, cord or leather, is 1/64 of an inch over standard or perhaps 1/32 under standard, and such a shot is struck off of fairways mowed at 29/54 onto a green that is cut to 5/32 on Thursday or Friday and then 7/64 on Saturday or Sunday, it is then of course very easy to see how a groove in an iron club that is a thousandth of an inch off can be one hell of an advantage."

TEE-OFF® Golf PRACTICE AID

FOR HOME PRACTICE THE YEAR AROUND

Clint D. Moffatt of Long Beach, California couldn't seem to lower his right shoulder properly on his downswing. So he bent a piece of welding rod 90 degrees, pushed one end into the turf, tied a plastic practice ball to the other end with a nylon cord from his lawnmower and, presto, the basic idea for his Tee-Off Practice Unit was born. The unit allows the ball to swing freely around the bent metal rod. It shows both hooking and slicing errors. Upon hooking, the ball orbits inside-out. Slicing forces the ball to orbit outside-in.

It Don't Mean A Thing, If It Ain't Got That Swing

c h a p t e r 8

As late as the 1840s golfers used long, thin clubs with whippy ash shafts. But when feather-filled balls were replaced by the rubber-like gutta-percha balls, clubs all had to be re-designed because this new type of ball was too hard for the slender clubs.

Actually, many different woods have been tried in golf shafts of the past. The first recorded happened to be hazelwood. Then came ash. Then holly, hornbeam, dogwood, and finally beech and hickory. One story is that the hickory came from Russia, as ballast in ships. A more likely story, though, is that it came from American axe handles and pit props.

Anyway, when hickory replaced ash in quantity, the game lived through it, as well as through the later advent of the lively rubber ball, and steel shafts that replaced hickory in 1924, courtesy of Brunswick. Also in 1924, the Union Hardware Company of Torrington, Connecticut, introduced a seamless shaft of high carbon steel capable of being heat-treated and tempered. In 1926, True Temper Corporation developed the stepped-down steel shaft. Brunswick began production of high alloy golf shafts from roll-formed steel in 1938. Steel shafts were replaced by aluminum ones in 1967, primarily on the strength of Arnold Palmer's successes with it. A.G. Spalding introduced stainless steel shafts in 1969, and Brunswick came out with its Chrome Vanadium alloy steel shaft in 1976. By the mid-70s, the shopping golfer could select clubs made with shafts of carbon steel, lightweight steel, glass, glass and steel and aluminum, and stainless steel.

chapter eight

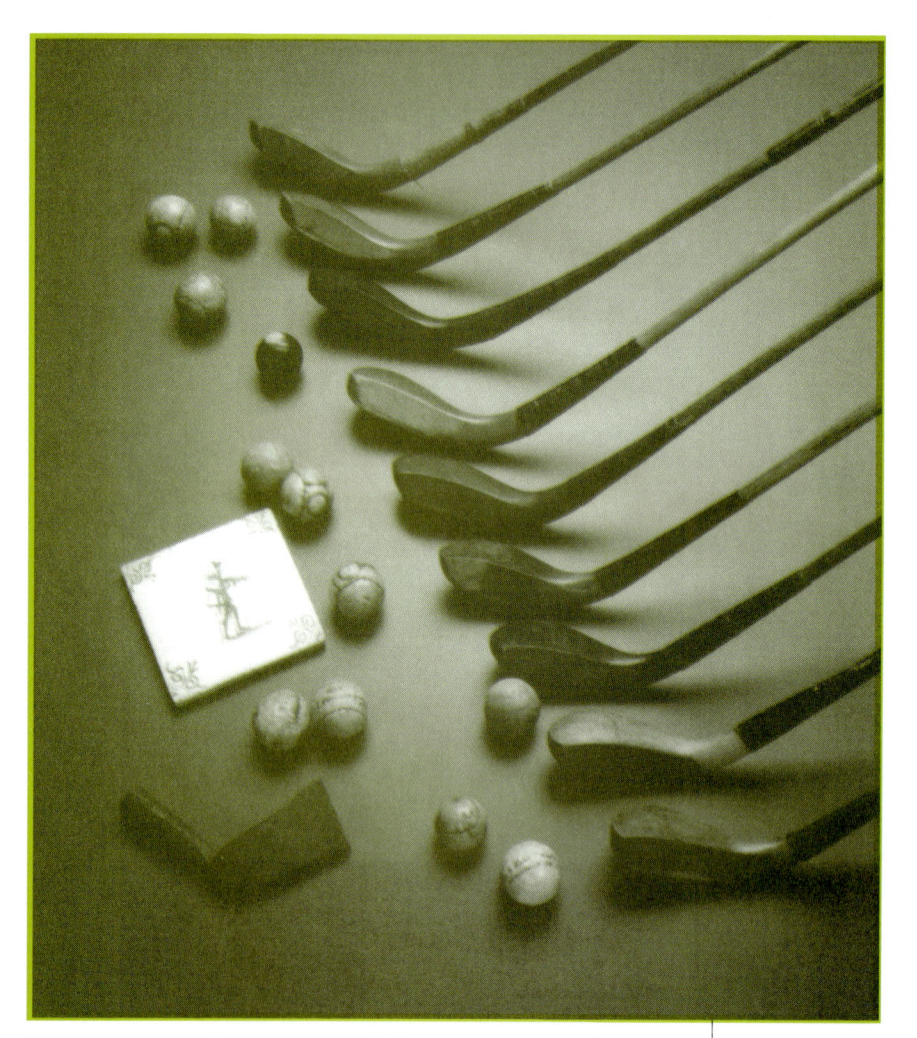

A DISPLAY OF ANTIQUE CLUBS AND FEATHER BALLS. THE CLUB HEAD AT LOWER LEFT DATES FROM CIRCA 1700, WHILE THE TILE DEPICTING A GOLFER DATES FROM 17TH-CENTURY HOLLAND.

Fiberglass shafts were found to be whippier than steel, as might be expected, but their extreme flexibility tended to exaggerate flaws in a golfer's swing. Developed by the Columbia Products Division of Shakespeare Company, which had a hand in development of the fiberglass fishing rods, the fiberglass shaft was a hollow tube incorporating over 500,000 fibers in one-tenth the diameter of a human hair! In tests conducted by the Equipment Division of Comptometer Corporation, it was shown the head stayed in contact with the ball slightly longer than with steel-shafted clubs. This was said to give greater length to drives, as well as to modify hooks and slices, which was, of course, of interest to duffers everywhere.

Aluminum was more rigid, offering more control than fiberglass. And it was lighter than steel, allowing manufacturers to put more weight into the clubhead and, thus, allow a faster swing with the same effort as before . . . along with increased distance, the supreme test. Another advantage of this speeded-up swing was that the clubhead tended to "rotate" less, thereby reducing the chances of hooking or slicing the ball. Wilson, Spalding and MacGregor were first to lick this problem of tempering aluminum so it wouldn't bend.

Graphite: The Duffer's Dream

It was Jim Flood, a former stockbroker, who heard about a graphite fiber substance and reasoned that it could be molded into golf club shafts. He rounded up a small group of investors, including Glen Campbell and Andy Williams, both singers and avid golfers, and became president and founder of Aldila, Inc. That was in 1972-73, and it's been a classic success story ever since, even though Aldila may not have been the first to study this innovation. Vice President B.J. Lavins, of the Sports Products Group of Shakespeare Company, reported that they had started working on graphite shafts five

it don't mean a thing...

Headcover Plethora

The original idea for club covers, at least according to a *Sports Illustrated* story, came from a traveling salesman named Frank Mitchell. In the 1930s, Mitchell was a manufacturer's rep, selling Kroydon golf clubs, Slazenger tennis racquets and a variety of other lines throughout upstate New York. Golfers were just getting away from drivers, brassies, spoons and cleeks in favor of the new numbered irons and woods. At the time, wooden-headed clubs were finished with several coats of shellac to make them shine. But the shellac chipped easily and clubs knocking together quickly acquired a gray band around the tops of their heads. This was bad for a salesman who had to present his product in pristine condition to dozens of potential customers every day.

Manufacturers used to package them in flimsy white socks, which kept dust off but not much else. However, it gave Mitchell an idea. Next time he was in Gloversville, New York (named because it claimed to be the glove capital of the U.S.), he had a mitten maker prepare two dozen children's mittens without thumbs. When they were delivered, he slipped them over his show display clubheads, tossed them into the back of his Pierce Arrow and headed out on his route again. They protected his display clubs so well he thought about using them on his own clubs on the course. The first Sunday morning he showed up at the Auburn, New York Country Club with his mittened clubs, a half-dozen members asked where they could get them. Word of mouth spread fast and Mitchell's Mittens were sold up through World War II. Then every manufacturer in the country jumped on the bandwagon, selling variations on Mitchell's original idea. Unfortunately, he hadn't thought to take out a patent on them.

The new trend is to cover *all* the club, heads and even the now-expensive shafts that technology has wrought. They are too expensive to be allowed to jostle each other any more. Of course manufacturers have noticed this trend and jumped into the breach willingly, offering about any kind of club cover imaginable.

years before Aldila, and that their shafts were displayed at the PGA show in West Palm Beach in January 1972.

Okay, so we'll split the credit for this duffers' dream. After all, we're only interested in its performance!

The graphite shaft, when it entered the picture, was lighter (by 12 to 13 ounces) and stronger than steel, and seemed easier to swing than any other type of club. It also seemed to be a "forgiving" club, tolerating mis-hit shots to a greater degree than others. The saved weight in the shaft, put into the clubhead, allowed older golfers, women and other less muscular types to approximate the swing efficiency of brutes, after adjusting swing tempo for the added weight.

The flex "recovery," or snap-back-to-original-position, has been found to be quicker than in other shafts, and vibration was found to be reduced—especially noticeable on autumn days when cold hands react adversely to the sting of such vibrato.

As for distance, in the 1973 Masters, Jack Nicklaus borrowed a graphite shaft driver from George Archer and proceeded to drive six balls out of the practice area, over some lofty pines and across a neighboring street— an estimated 350 yards each. That news perked up ears everywhere, in spite of the expense of the new black shafts. Where a pro-type wood with a steel shaft sold for $35, a graphite wood was $167.50. A set of woods (4) and 10 irons cost $2,020.

This was because manufacturers were dealing with a space-age material not yet in quantity production. Union Carbide, which had been processing graphite for a decade for the aerospace industry (used in reinforcing plastic heat shields) was charging $350 to $500 per pound. As demand went up, supply was increased . . . greatly. In 1970, only 5,000 to 6,000 pounds were produced; in 1973, 20,000 pounds were made. 17 manufacturers of graphite shafts had jumped into competition.

Several leading pros, most notably Lee Trevino, Bob Charles and Billy Casper, originally went on record as not thinking too highly of the graphite shafts. The USGA, conversely, thought perhaps too highly of

•
IN THE 1973 MASTERS, JACK NICKLAUS BORROWED A GRAPHITE SHAFT DRIVER FROM GEORGE ARCHER AND PROCEEDED TO DRIVE SIX BALLS OUT OF THE PRACTICE AREA, OVER SOME LOFTY PINES AND ACROSS A NEIGHBORING STREET—AN ESTIMATED 350 YARDS EACH.
•

NICKLAUS NOW MANUFACTURES HIS OWN GRAPHITE SHAFT DRIVERS.

them. They thought them "too effective for some players," and considered banning them "in the interest of stabilizing distance." The thought was that they, combined with recent ball development, would render all existing golf courses obsolete overnight. Not since the discovery of the lead pencil, in fact, had graphite received so much attention!

Ping!

Another revolution in club making was caused by Karsten Solheim, regarded in the late 1970s as the most ingenious club designer by the world of touring pros. This college dropout-turned-engineer/inventor worked for Ryan Aeronautical and Convair, then went to General Electric, where he had much to do with the development of the portable television set. Later he created the early "rabbit ears" antenna, an idea he gave away for free. But then he set up Karsten Manufacturing Corporation and invented the famous Ping Putter, the name of which came from the sound it made upon striking a ball.

In turn, that led to a new design for other clubs that were basically weighted on their perimeters instead of their heels, bottoms or middles. The real revolution was in how he manufactured them, though. He made them from molds instead of forging them, in a process called "investment casting," which insured uniformity and eliminated the grinding process needed to hone a forged club. His new clubs combined the look and feel associated with traditional forged clubs, but added the forgiving quality of perimeter-weighted clubs. And his method changed the whole business. New companies, imitating it, were able to spring up overnight because the clubs were suddenly so easy to make.

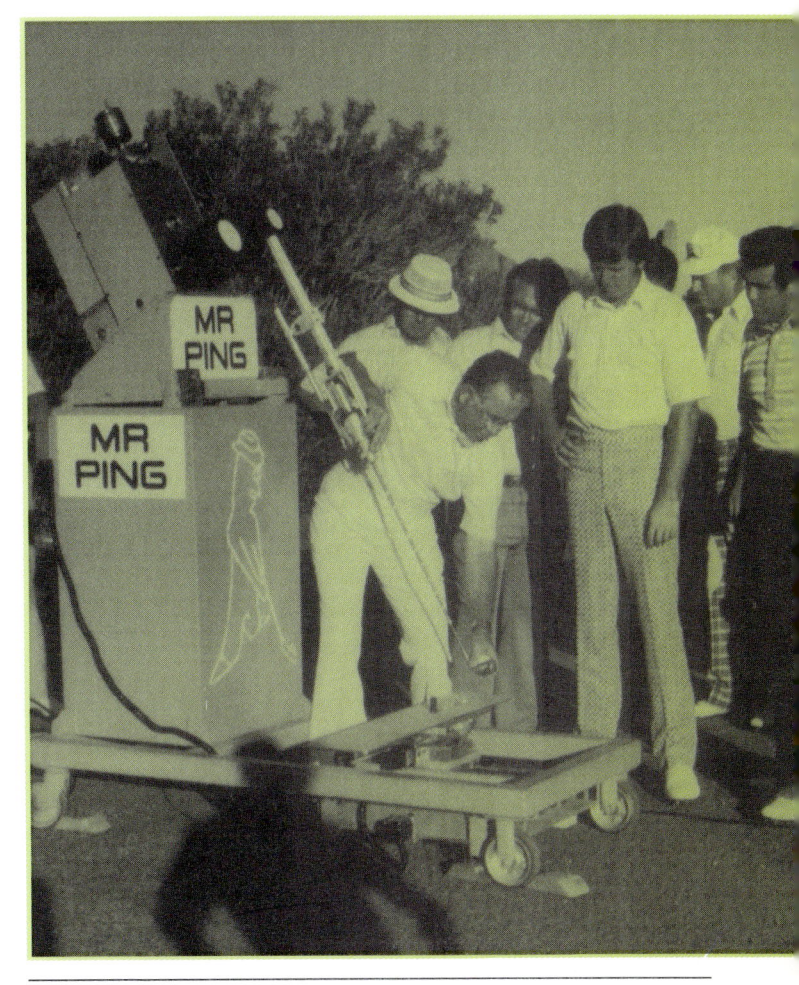

KARSTEN SOLHEIM DEMONSTRATES THE UNIQUE PROPERTIES OF HIS CLUBS WITH HIS ORIGINAL "PING MAN" TESTING ROBOT.

Square-grooved Ping I-2 clubs, developed in 1985 by Karsten, and advocated by a number of touring professionals for increased spin and control of the ball—especially out of roughs and in wet weather—were at first outlawed by the USGA. Naturally! Then inventor Solheim sued the USGA for $100 million and suddenly the USGA pretended that those in use were legal. In exchange, Karsten's agreed to stop making them. A "grandfather's clause," in effect, had been agreed upon whereby the two million sets already sold could be used in PGA tournaments.

chapter eight

The Jumbo Revolution

The most recent tailor-made club to make a splash—maybe the biggest splash ever for a driver—is the Jumbo, more officially known as The J's Professional Weapon (Bridgestone Sports). This metal driver was ballyhooed because superstars Jack Nicklaus (a notorious club experimenter), Greg Norman, Ray Floyd, and Jumbo Ozaki (one of the first international stars to come out of Japan) all enjoyed success with it. Ozaki even played a leading role in designing it for a Japanese firm. The head features a shorter-than-normal hosel and a square face that is hand-ground to ensure a flat surface. Its graphite shaft is specially made to resist twisting. Combined with the club's deep face, the shaft's mid-flex point results in a lower-than-average ball trajectory. J's are also available in most pro shops in 3 and 5-woods, if you don't go into shock when you look at the $400 price tags the Ryobi-Toski Corporation has tacked onto them.

Nicklaus learned about the driver when he played an exhibition match with Ozaki in Tokyo. Jumbo is one of three Ozaki brothers playing with the Jumbo driver—Jumbo (Masashi), Joe (Naomichi), and Jet (Tateo)—for whom the J's are named. Nicklaus asked for one and Jumbo sent him three. When Nicklaus started using them in competition, he unleashed tee shots of 300-plus yards and devastated the field in his senior debut at the Tradition at Desert Mountain.

The Jumbo, as could be expected, started a bigger-is-better trend. Especially after *Golf Digest*, in December 1991, found the oversizers performing better on mis-hits than standard sizes. Other drivers came out bigger and more hi-tech. They were equated with the large-headed Prince tennis racquets that revolutionized tennis manufacturing the previous decade. Manufacturers came up with macho names to fit the Bunyanesque blasters: The Tommy Gun, The Bazooka, The Launcher, The B-52 Bomber, The Power Pod, The Airhammer, Enerjet, Out-a-Site, Demon, King Kong, and even the Peace Missile, which included pieces from a dismantled Soviet SS-23

A PAIR OF JUMBOS.

it don't mean a thing...

MANUFACTURERS CAME UP WITH MACHO NAMES TO FIT THE BUNYANESQUE BLASTERS: THE TOMMY GUN, THE BAZOOKA, THE LAUNCHER, THE B-52 BOMBER, THE POWER POD, THE AIRHAMMER, ENERJET, OUT-A-SITE, DEMON, KING KONG, AND EVEN THE PEACE MISSILE, WHICH INCLUDED PIECES FROM A DISMANTLED SOVIET SS-23 BALLISTIC MISSILE.

ballistic missile. Prince, the company that pioneered the oversized racquet in tennis, and still using its theme "The Sweet Spot Company," introduced the Prince Thunderstick.

President Bill Clinton was seen with one of this new breed in his golf bag—the Big Bertha. It was this Big Bertha, from Callaway Golf, that really commercialized the trend when it was introduced on January 25, 1991. The first jumbo with a metal head, it catapulted a tiny nine-year old company in Carlsbad, California into the rarefied air of the world's top-10 club markets. Sales, at $230 per club, soared 150% to $54.7 million in one year. Its success with the driver spilled over and by 1997 the company had all the rest of the clubs to go with it: Big Bertha War Bird metalwoods, a set of four wedges and a set of "Gold" Irons (actually made of aluminum bronze), all sporting the famed Big Bertha name.

Then came the Wilson Killer Whale, 44.5 inches long, 12.75 ounces in weight, 40% larger than Big Bertha, with titanium shaft and head, for $600. And Golfsmith came out with its "beyond jumbo," the Jetstream, and its Big Gun. New for 1997 was the 350cc Long Jon advertised by Golfsmith as "one of the largest driver heads in golf history."

Big Blasters

Some physicists have stated that, on level ground, with normal grass and no wind factor, the human limit for socking a golf ball is about 340 yards. But be honest. Haven't you ever thought about hitting a drive 1,500 yards?

The Sarazen Sand Wedge

In 1931, Gene Sarazen (given name Saracini) developed the sand wedge, primarily to compensate for his generally poor trap play. He was taking flying lessons when he noted that when he pulled the stick back the tail went down and the plane took off. He thought that, if he did that to a niblick, it would have the same action in the sand, though he also considered the possibility that the flange would hit the sand and bounce. He wired Wilson Company to send him a dozen niblicks, then bought up all the solder in town, along with a collection of rasps and files. He spent two months in secret at a little nine-hole course remodeling and trying out his brainstorm beauties.

Tinkering completed, he went to the British Open, never letting his new club be seen—even taking to putting it under his coat to take to his room. He was in three traps in the first nine and came out about a foot and a half from the hole each time. Leading by nine strokes at one point, he won that Open by five.

chapter eight

DIAGRAM OF THE 'EXPLODING CARTRIDGE' CLUB CIRCA 1910. THE CARTRIDGE WAS DESIGNED TO EXPLODE WHEN THE BALL WAS HIT HEAD-ON—IN THEORY PROPELLING IT (THE BALL, NOT THE CLUB), FARTHER. WELL, IT LOOKED GOOD ON PAPER . . .

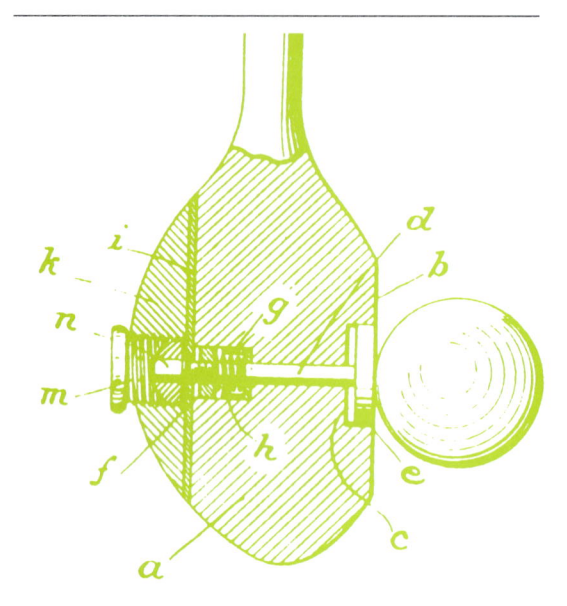

Every golfer has. The first one to seriously ponder it was the 1910 inventor of the clubhead with a "cartridge" implanted that exploded when the ball was hit head-on. But his idea reached only as far as the patent application.

One man who has actually not only accomplished this feat, but surpassed it, is Niles Lied. He drove a golf ball across a frozen lake in Antarctica in 1962. The ball was claimed to have traveled 2,640 yards, or more than a mile and a half.

Another man had the chance, in wildly different surroundings, but blew it. Alan Shepard, when he was getting ready to go to the moon in Apollo 14 in 1971, learned that the moon has one-sixth the gravity of earth, so a ball there would go six times as far and stay airborne six times as long. So he took a 6-iron head and two golf balls—personally paid for—in his space suit pocket. He planned to use a collapsible aluminum handle that they normally used for scooping moon dust samples, replacing the scoop with the golf clubhead.

Once on the moon, he practiced several swings inside his cumbersome and highly restrictive space suit, and found that he couldn't even get both hands on the club. So, using a one-handed, off-balance half-swing, he did succeed in getting good contact and drove the first ball over 200 yards, with the ball staying airborne nearly 30 seconds. He

PAR FOR THE MOON: A PORTION OF THE EXHIBIT OF ALAN B. SHEPARD'S FAMOUS LUNAR GOLFING EXCURSION. THE SPECIALLY CRAFTED ALUMINUM/TEFLON 6-IRON IS SHOWN IN THE CENTER DISPLAY CASE.

it don't mean a thing...

swung harder at the second ball, but shanked it into a crater . . . for a hole in one—even if the hole was several miles in diameter.

The balls are still there, but the club is in the USGA building in Far Hills, New Jersey.

With Shepard's chance at golfing immortality aborted, we can look at more mundane, yet exemplary, blasting. For instance, Nate Sherman of Moses Lake, Washington is credited with a 440-yard drive using—are you ready for this?—a 2-iron.

It was during an insurance men's convention in Seattle in October 1953 and Sherman was playing at the Sand Point Golf & Country Club nearby with Bill Grant of Spokane and John Herbick of Seattle. On the par-5 568-yard eighth hole, Herbick sliced to the side of the fairway. Grant dubbed his shot about 100 yards up the fairway. Sherman, who had had wood trouble all day, used his 2-iron and uncorked a 300-yard drive in the fairway, the ball setting up nicely atop a little knoll. Away, Grant took his second shot. His ball, on the fly, smacked Sherman's ball and sent it another 140 yards, still lying one stroke. Grant's ball stopped dead where it hit Sherman's.

Sherman chipped to five feet from the pin with his 8-iron, looking at an eagle-3. But he rimmed the cup and had to settle for a birdie-4.

Carl Cooper, as a 31-year old struggling pro from Houston, cut an even freakier drive—787 yards, measured by his caddy—in the second round of the 1992 Texas Open. Cooper used "one of those big drivers" on the third tee, hitting 300 yards on the fly, landing on a paved downhill cart path, which the ball followed past the fifth green, beyond the sixth tee, and eventually stopped behind the 12th green, two inches from being out of bounds. To get back to his hole, he had to hit a 4-iron over trees, another that overshot the third green, a chip to 20 feet from the hole and two putts for a double bogey. And he missed the cut for the final two rounds by two strokes.

Craig Wood, in the 1933 British Open, hit probably the longest ball ever in a major

> **SOME PHYSICISTS HAVE STATED THAT, ON LEVEL GROUND, WITH NORMAL GRASS AND NO WIND FACTOR, THE HUMAN LIMIT FOR SOCKING A GOLF BALL IS ABOUT 340 YARDS.**

tournament—430 yards, or 450 yards, depending upon which report one wishes to believe. But he was aided by a stiff tailwind and parched ground. Also helped by a strong wind, F. Lemarchand has been credited with driving a 483-yard hole in Devon, England.

For consistency, Jimmy Thomson, nicknamed Golf's Siege Gun in an earlier era, averaged 347 yards for 10 drives, to win the North American Driving Championship. His longest was 386 yards. But he was once credited with a 480-yard drive. The problem was it was never actually measured, and it was on a downhill lie as well.

Later, George Bayer, a 6 foot, 5 inch, 240-pound ex-football star at the University of

MY WOOD IS SMALLER THAN YOURS

"FOR MOST AMATEURS, THE BEST WOOD IN THE BAG IS A PENCIL."

—CHI CHI RODRIGUEZ

131

chapter eight

The Golf Club Memory Test

Just to mark the passing of one era of golf clubs into another, here is a quiz to test your knowledge of clubs. See how many of the clubs of yesteryear you can equate with their modern counterparts. Match the names in the first column with the correct names in the mixed-up second column.

1.	*1 Iron*	A.	*Playing Club*
2.	*2 Iron*	B.	*Mashie Iron*
3.	*3 Iron*	C.	*Sand Iron*
4.	*4 Iron*	D.	*Driving Iron*
5.	*5 Iron*	E.	*Mid-Iron*
6.	*6 Iron*	F.	*Mid-Mashie*
7.	*7 Iron*	G.	*Lofter/Pitching Niblick*
8.	*8 Iron*	H.	*Baffing Spoon/Niblick*
9.	*9 Iron*	I.	*Baffy/Mashie Niblick*
10.	*10 Iron*	J.	*Driving Cleek*
11.	*1 Wood*	K.	*Green Putter/Putting Cleek*
12.	*2 Wood*	L.	*Short Spoon*
13.	*3 Wood*	M.	*Long Spoon/Brassie*
14.	*4 Wood*	N.	*Mashie*
15.	*Wedge*	O.	*Spade Mashie*

A couple of side notes of interest: The baffing spoon was so named from the noise it made when the club struck the ground and ball together. The spoons were so named because their club faces were slightly concave, not made that way, but from use. The brassie was named from the brass sole plate screwed into the bottom. Others we can only guess at. Even rare out-of-print books researched failed to explain their name origins.

To put the collectors' value on these old clubs, it might be interesting to note that one of these 300-year old clubs was found at the back of a garden shed in Edinburgh, Scotland in July 1992 and fetched $184,800 at auction . . . almost as much as the British Open winner that year received ($190,000).

In a copy of *Hoyle* published in 1796, the following appears: "Game of Goff or Golf. This game is the favorite amusement in Scotland in the summer. It is played with clubs and balls. Of the clubs there are six sorts used by proficients, viz; the *common club* when the ball lies on the ground; the *scraper* and *half scraper* when in long grass; the *spoon* when in a hollow; the *heavy iron* when it lies deep among the stones or mud; and the *light iron club* when on the surface of changle or sandy ground. All these clubs are tapered at the part that strikes the ball, they are also faced with horn and loaded with leads."

(Matchup answers: 1-d, 2-e, 3-f, 4-b, 5-n, 6-o, 7-i, 8-g, 9-h, 10-k, 11-a, 12-m, 13-j, 14-l, 15-c.)

it don't mean a thing...

THE CLUB NO GOLFER SHOULD BE WITHOUT. WHAT'S YOUR PLEASURE?

Washington had a measured drive of 430 yards at Tucson, and one of 420 yards at Las Vegas. He has also smacked the ball 348 yards on the fly. Bayer won every driving contest he ever entered, and he socked balls so hard he wore them out in about three holes of play.

According to Bayer's own memory, his most memorable shot was made at the Lakes Club in Sydney, Australia during an exhibition match in 1956. On a hole that measured 589 yards, he hit a drive that stopped about 50 yards from the green. "But I had some wind with me, the fairway was baked hard by the sun, and it was a little downhill," he admitted.

Mike Dunaway never competed with Bayer, being from a later era. But he was a consistent 300 to 350-yard driver and made the cover of *Golf Magazine* (August 1985) with the challenge: "Outhit me and win $10,000." He claimed no one ever had.

The women's golf drive record was set by pro Laura Davies, who whacked a ball 376 yards down a runway at Philadelphia National Airport in September 1995.

The child champ? Probably Billie Fries, Jr. who whacked a 90-yard drive at the age of 19 *months*. That was in Oakland, California in 1925.

How Many Clubs are in Your Bag?

"The real golfer should use no more than seven clubs!"

I have no idea who first stated that and what his conviction was based upon. It may have started back in 1916 when Chick Evans won the U.S. Open with only seven clubs in his bag, but could date even further back than that. Dr. Samuel Johnson once commented, "Golf is a game in which you claim the privileges of age and retain the playthings of childhood." Just how many of these

chapter eight

TODAY'S WELL-PREPARED DUFFER CARRIES A VARIETY OF SOPHISTICATED CLUBS FOR SPECIALIZED USE IN ANY SITUATION ON (AND SOMETIMES OFF) THE COURSE.

playthings a golfer should carry, or could carry, has always been a delicate point.

"Do not carry more clubs than absolutely necessary," counseled one-time expert Joshua Taylor. "Unless you feel full confidence in a weapon, you had better leave it in your locker." And for a long time, golfers heeded his advice.

Before him, in Scotland, it was thought that any man who needed more than three balls and six clubs was a spendthrift (and probably the sort who couldn't be trusted out of sight in the rough). But at the other extreme, ultimately, was California-based pro Lawson Little, who won the 1934-35 Amateur U.S. and British Championships and the 1940 Open and regularly carried as many as 30 clubs.

Today, of course, the USGA has decreed a

it don't mean a thing...

> MANUFACTURERS KNOW MOST OF US WILL BUY ANYTHING THAT EVEN HINTS IT WILL KNOCK A STROKE OR THREE OFF OF OUR GAMES.

bag limit of 14 clubs, though there has naturally been extensive lobbying by club manufacturers and pros to raise that limit to 16 to allow for more specialized clubs. One expert teacher has stated, "For all the good the standard complement of 14 clubs does him, the average golfer could leave at least five of them home—the driver, the brassie, and the 2, 3, and 4 irons. With their long shafts and lack of loft, these five clubs require extraordinary timing, a timing too exact for the golfer who can devote no more than one or two rounds a week to the game. In their places he would be wise to substitute a one-and-a-half wood, a 5-wood and a 7-wood.

"A one-and-a-half wood is the normal, deeper faced driver with more loft added. The face on a brassie is too shallow for use off a wooden tee, and its lack of loft makes it all but useless for long shots through the fairway, where your spoon could, and should, be used exclusively. The 5-wood can be used instead of a 2-iron, the 7-wood for both the 3- and 4-irons. By sliding through the turf rather than digging into it, the flat sole of a wood offers a margin for error that the blade of an iron does not."

Although purists decry such proliferation of equipage as an attempt to "buy shots in the pro shop" instead of earning them on the course, most players want all the help they can get anywhere they can get it. Even if many new clubs have little more to recommend them than built-in bragging rights! Many new ones are prestige clubs, or conversation pieces, more than "use" clubs. But manufacturers know most of us will buy anything that even hints it will knock a stroke or three off of our games. Thus, every time someone comes out with a new club, or new spinoff from an old club, there is a rush to buy it. Then, to maintain this possibly fallacious seven-club status quo, as well as the 14-club bag limit, we have to rid ourselves of one of our old clubs.

Before the 14-club restriction, pros carried clubs for every conceivable situation, including left-handed clubs for lies where right-handed swinging was impossible. Leo Diegel, for example, carried four drivers—and had more at the ready. Included among his emergency drivers was one with a built-in hook, one with a built-in slice, and a pair tailored for wind conditions—one high-lofted to take advantage of wind at the back and one nearly flat-faced to keep the ball low with the wind in the face.

All-in-One Club

One idea that has been tried—and vetoed by the USGA—was The Adjustable Club. Most average players still think seven irons are sufficient, listing the 2, 3, 5, 7, 9 irons and the putter, with a sand wedge as the seventh. Professionals are about the only ones to master the minute intricacies of the between-numbered ones. But, American ingenuity being the restless thing that it is, tinkering

STROKES

OVERHEARD IN THE CLUBHOUSE: GOLF IS A GAME OF STROKES. I JUST SAW A GUY HAVE ONE TRYING TO GET OUT OF A SAND TRAP!

135

chapter eight

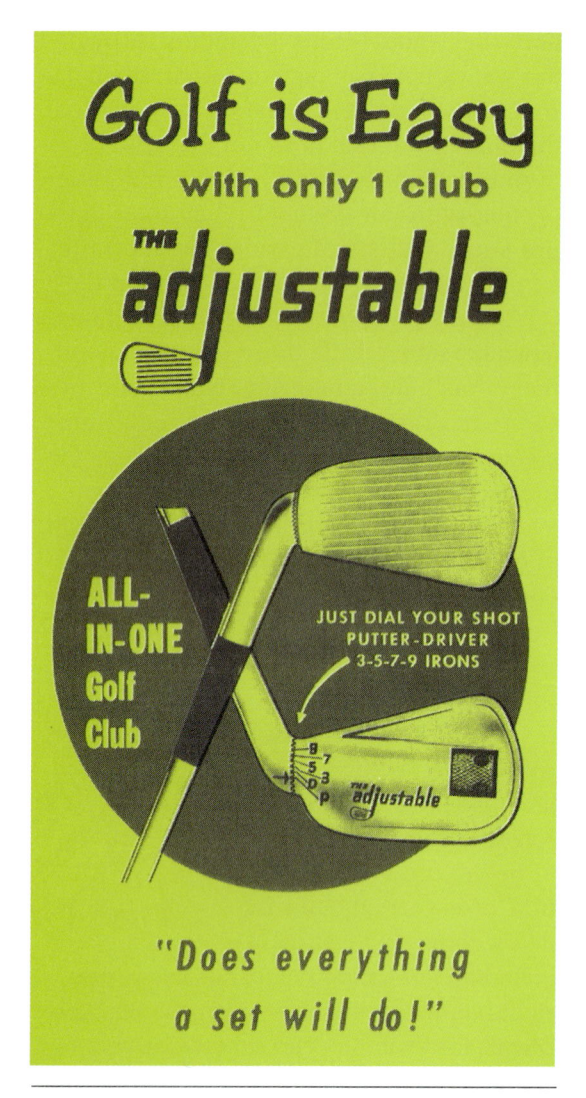

Golf is Easy with only 1 club

THE adjustable

ALL-IN-ONE Golf Club

JUST DIAL YOUR SHOT
PUTTER-DRIVER
3-5-7-9 IRONS

"Does everything a set will do!"

BROCHURE COVER FOR THE ADJUSTABLE, A CADDY'S DREAM COME TRUE!

has continued ad infinitum—to the point where, a few years back, some players were experimenting with a single club that purported to do the job of all seven irons. It was called The Adjustable and featured a clubhead that could be variously positioned, by rotating the head to inscribed settings, so the clubface represented any one of these other irons. Everything was simplified to the max. For $29.95, inventor Joe Novak, one-time president of the PGA, had eliminated the golf bag and the expense of a full set of clubs. With only one club, he maintained, different weights and lengths were eliminated. This would lead, he added, to a standardized grooving of the swing.

It was outlawed, along with any other clubs with any parts not permanently affixed. But, in spite of this ruling, this unique iron is still selling. For some years The World of Golf shop in New York sold it, under the name Super Stick, for $50. It remained popular because (1) it was great for travelers, when taking a full set of clubs was impractical, (2) it was useful for office workers who wanted to get in a little noon hour practice on the driving range or a Golf-O-Mat center, (3) it was a small investment for a family, if several members took up the game at the same time, and (4) it was easy to carry for children learning the game, before it was known if they were going to be serious about it.

Today the adjustable club is still called by the same name, just shortened into one word, Superstick, by Competitive Edge Golf (also handled by Golfsmith) for $94. But, of course, now it can be promoted as "17 clubs in one." It still features a telescoping shaft for easy transport and use by different size players, but is available only for right handers.

Even this wasn't exactly a new idea. In 1927, Howard L. Coles of Tarrytown, New York patented another club that was an engineering wonder. The idea was to be able to play golf "on a reduced scale" with it, even in one's living room. A "small, hollow celluloid ball was used so as not to injure household furnishings." It could also be used left-handed, as well as with a variety of clubheads. In addition, it had a curious advantage over newer counterparts—you didn't even have to swing it! Located about a third of the way down the shaft was a hinge and a circular dial. This self-swinging club was merely "dialed" to regulate the power desired for the stroke. The golfer held the upper part, and the lower part executed the swing on its own. A spring was employed, with putts using less of the spring and drives using more of it. The club was never actually manufactured, though.

Putt 'er There, Pardner!

chapter 9

Early in the game there were three putters—driving putter, approach putter and just plain putter. The first was for driving the ball low into the wind. The second was for lofted approach shots where there were no hazards. The third was, of course, for putting.

As the 19th century neared its end, Willie Park, Jr. reportedly came up with the first "wry-necked" putter. Stories on its true origins vary. One was that it had merely warped into its odd shape. Another was that it was run over by a cart. But it evidently worked for him, and gave other golfers something new to think about.

Much later Ben Hogan, whose yips on the green were monumental and eventually contributed to his decision to retire, always claimed that golf and putting were two different games. And it is true that putting separates the men from the poise!

That's why the history of putter

chapter nine

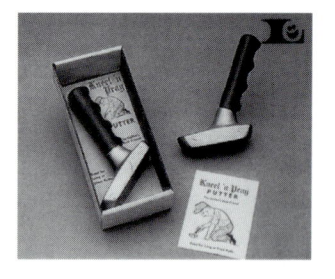

THE KNEEL-AND-PRAY PUTTER—DESIGNED WITH THAT "OTHER" SUNDAY ACTIVITY IN MIND.

puttering has ranged from the ridiculous (the hand-high Kneel-and-Pray Putter from the Leister Game Co.) to the sublime (the Plip Instructional Putter, which forms a U-shape around the ball to help guide it to the cup); and from the beautiful (Golfsmith's Soft Stroke Billet Milled, with a rippled top) to the ugly (Pilcher Company's Pug-Ugly Putter, which

> THE NEVER-ENDING SEARCH FOR A GOOF-PROOF PUTTER, OR PUTTING STYLE, HAS RESULTED IN OVER 2,500 MODELS BEING REGISTERED WITH THE U.S. PATENT OFFICE.

hasn't kept it from selling in nine countries); and from the prosaic (Snake Eyes' Brookline and #88 putters) to the rather wild (The Thing from Natural Golf Corp., which has a large square grip, a shape like a mini-dirigible, a smaller head than a traditional putter but a face higher than the center of a ball, with a zero loft. It was nicknamed by someone among the press who watched Paul Azinger use it while winning a PGA Tour championship).

The never-ending search for a goof-proof putter, or putting style, has resulted in over 2,500 models being registered with the U.S. Patent Office. And that isn't all of the story. Dave Pelz, the "putter professor," who is president of Preceptor Golf, Ltd. of Laurel, Maryland, has stated that once a customer finds the putter head he likes, he, Pelz, can offer any of 135 variations of shaft length and flex, grip size and shape, and angles of lie between shaft and the sole of the blade.

In his heyday, Arnold Palmer used to be sent 300 putters by mail each year by inventors hoping for his blessing. At one time he admitted owning 1,500, "maybe more."

"It's probably closer to 2,000," a friend confided. "If the rules allowed it, Arnold would change putters every hole."

PUTT-PERFECT

A 1989 PGA TOUR STUDY REVEALED THAT TOURING PROS MAKE ONLY 54.8% OF THEIR SIX-FOOT PUTTS, ONE OF THREE (OR 33.5%) ATTEMPTED FROM 10 FEET, ONE OF SIX (OR 16.8%) FROM 15 FEET, AND ONE OF 10 (OR 10.2%) FROM 25 FEET. AND THESE RESULTS WERE TAKEN ON FLAT GREENS! SHOWING HOW PRESSURE WORKS ON PROS THE SAME AS ON US HOI POLOI, WHEN THEY WERE PUTTING THESE SAME DISTANCES, THEY WERE SUCCESSFUL MORE CONSISTENTLY PUTTING FOR PARS THAN PUTTING FOR BIRDIES. ONE POINT THAT SHOWED UP ON THE CHART, BUT WASN'T MENTIONED IN THE REPORT, WAS THAT PROS ALMOST NEVER TAKE MORE THAN TWO PUTTS PER HOLE. THAT'S OFTEN WHERE THE AVERAGE GOLFER WILL FALTER.

putt 'er there, pardner!

PUG-UGLY™ Putter
"It lines itself up!"

- Black anodized solid aluminum head **aligns itself** squarely with the ball on the intended line.

- Complete putting stroke is visible without movement of the head or eyes.

- Provides a complete, smooth, balanced, **on-line** stroke.

- Polished brass faceplate has 1 degree loft for instant roll.

- *Hand crafted* for great touch and feel!

Take strokes off your score!

$60
48" Long John - $75.00
RH or LH available.
(Shipping/handling - $10.00)
(CA residents add 8% sales tax)
Allow 2 weeks for delivery.

"It lines itself up!"

THE PILCHER CO.
♦ 14827 Bluegrass Dr., Box 1456 ♦ Helendale, CA 92342 ♦ (619) 245-8996 ♦

PROVING THAT BEAUTY IS REALLY IN THE LIE OF THE BEHOLDER, THE PUG-UGLY PUTTER PROMISES GORGEOUS RESULTS ON THE GREEN.

chapter nine

So many putters were poured onto the market that, in 1968, the USGA held a purge, rendering scores of these obsolete, including many designs submitted before they even reached fruition. There were putters with little prisms and mirrors on them, with pistol grips,

Croquet, Anyone?

There's been a croquet influence in the putting game, too. When Dean Refram's doctor told him his eyes didn't focus along the same line, he began putting croquet style. He found he could sight his putts better

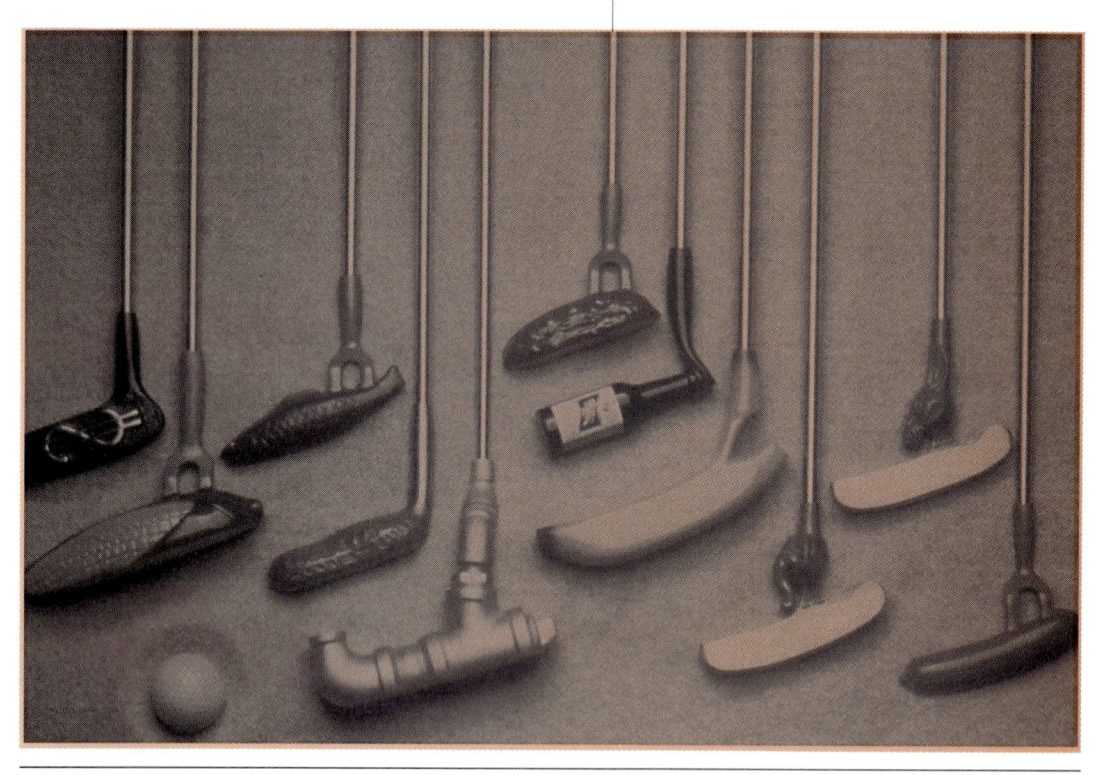

MY PUTTER'S SILLIER THAN YOURS.

with bombsights, and one with two tiny wheels on the blade, fore and aft, so it could be rolled into the ball at the same height every swing. In spite of this ban, there remained a virtual putt-pourri to choose from, including the Plumb-Putt that Baltimore plumber Bud Schuler made from pipe fittings, with a valve handle to "dial the distance" and a relief cock on the side of the valve to "let off some of the putting pressure." He had gotten so frustrated with commercial putters that he had made his own. He had so much fun with it that he started offering copies for $59.95. Today a similar model is sold by Leister Game Company, along with several other laughable putter heads.

while standing astride the ball. And when Slammin' Sammy Snead started admitting to "middle-age shakes" around the greens—after winning more than 100 tournaments since his first in 1937—he also adopted the croquet-stoop style. He started playing so well again he almost won the 1972 Masters. Playing against youngsters, some of whose fathers weren't even born when he joined the pro tour, he also finished in a two-way tie for fourth in the Glenn Campbell Los Angeles Open, the first event in the 1973 tour.

Proving once more there is nothing new in golf, research shows even this idea was not new. Walter J. Travis won the U.S. Amateur championship in 1900, 1901 and 1903, then went on to shock the British by winning their Amateur Championships in 1904 at

putt 'er there, pardner!

Sandwich . . . all with an unconventional Schenectady center-shafted putter. He just didn't use it croquet style.

Soon a plethora of putters shaped for this style of putting hit the market. Marketers called them "pendulum putters," though, not croquet mallets. That would have been demeaning. One produced in Providence, Rhode Island was even shaped like a stubby, squared-off mallet, though, with a sawed-off shaft. Another, John Lambert's Marble Magician ($12 originally), featured a bent-back handle that allowed the putter to "lead the shot with his hands and maintain a truer directional swing."

When the USGA purged all croquet-style greensplay and "unusual" putters, Sam Snead merely switched his crouching, between-the-legs croquet stance—left hand grasping the top of the club and the right hand pushing the club into the ball from a position just above the neck—to a sidesaddle stance. The 1968 ban clause outlawed putting from "a stance astride, or with either foot touching" the line of the putt. Snead moved both feet to the left of the line of the putt to conform. But the outlaw ruling was bitterly cussed and discussed at the time, especially by Snead and Refram, as well as by Dr. William Vallotton, a Charleston, South Carolina ophthalmologist. "Golfers would do well to change their style of putting to take advantage of the fact they have two eyes," was the way the good doctor put it. "All of our daily activities requiring good binocular vision are carried out with the eyes forward, yet we try a difficult task, such as putting, in a most un-physiological way. Most people are right-eyed, so they are looking at the hole out of

SAM SNEAD DEMONSTRATES HIS UNUSUAL "CROQUET-STANCE" STYLE OF PUTTING, LATER OUTLAWED BY THE USGA.

chapter nine

Putting Lore

Stories are rife concerning the pros versus their putters. Ivan Glanz, an earlier-era pro who almost never had an easy win, once became so enraged about his bad play in a match that he bashed himself on the forehead with his club and finished the round with blood pouring down his face. Plagued by a balky putter, he used to get so infuriated watching his putts go offline that he regularly flung himself into sand traps and water hazards.

Ky Laffoon, an earlier-day player as well, used to punish his putter when it misbehaved by dragging it behind his car. Other players sometimes needed such an outlet too. For example, golfing immortal Harry Vardon missed a two-inch putt in the 1900 U.S. Open!

And consider the woes of Chick Evans in a 1922 tournament. He made a fine shot to a par-3 hole, the ball stopping 15 feet from the pin. His first putt sailed four feet behind the cup. He missed the four-footer coming back. He disgustedly putted with one hand, then, realizing that wasn't going in either, he took another swipe as it was still moving. It still didn't drop and, with the penalty, he had to enter a game-breaking seven on his card.

Also, there is, as always, a Byron Nelson story. A golf promoter and friend of his, Eddie Lowery, was regularly being taken to the cleaners by a pair of brothers at the Santa Rosa Country Club. So Eddie asked Byron to come up and pair with him against them. He loaned Byron an old MacGregor center-shafted Spur putter (like a duffer might use) to put the brothers off-guard about his ringer. That putter, even without practice, worked for Byron like magic. Every ball dropped—12 birdies and six pars for a 12-under par 60, one of the best rounds Byron ever shot, before or since. Eddie, doubling up bets on the side with the brothers, got all his losses back and then some. In gratitude, he presented the putter to Byron. Byron used it for about a month, but couldn't make another putt with it!

a non-dominant eye." The doctor practiced what he preached and took seven strokes off his game, putting croquet style.

But, as USGA's executive director stated, "The game was becoming bizarre. It was some other game—part croquet, part shuffleboard and part the posture of Mohammedan prayer."

The shuffleboard mention was in reference to another new putter that was then on trial, the Acculine "shuffle-putter." George Thomas, pro at the Long Beach CC in Chicago,

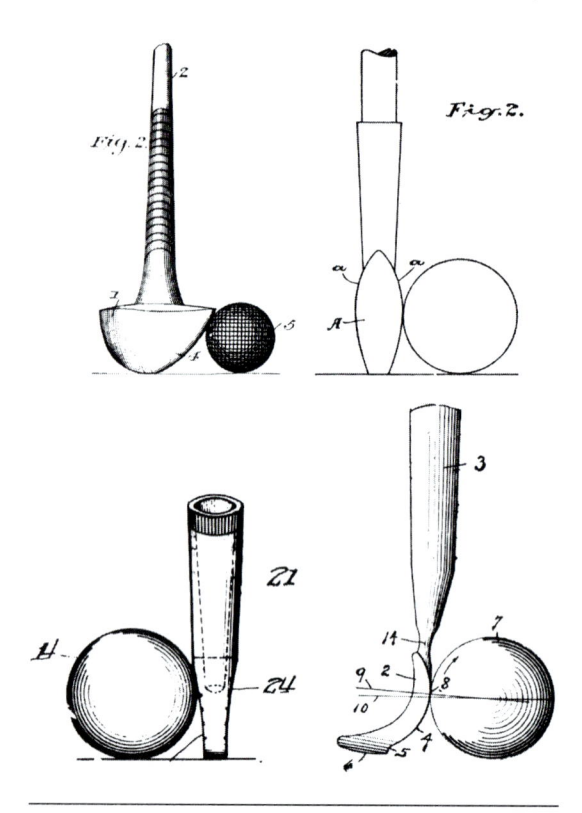

CLOCKWISE, FROM UPPER LEFT: DUNN'S DRIVER-STYLE WOOD CLUB OF 1900; PLANT'S CONVEX PUTTER FOR LEFT- (OR RIGHT-) HANDED GOLFERS; DOERR'S CONCAVE CLUB; AND LAWTON'S EXTREME CONVEX PUTTER. ALL PATENTED IN 1922.

had fashioned it out of laminated wood and brass, with a cobra-shaped head on a shaft that ran up from it at a 20-degree angle. The putter placed the clubhead behind the ball, then pushed it into the ball in a shuffleboard or vacuuming motion.

The theory behind this idea had been researched back in 1900 by William Dunn, an English billiards expert living in New York. Becoming interested in the application of billiards technique to putting, he reasoned and proved that a golf ball with a forward spinning motion would "jump small obstructions instead of being turned aside." American greens of that day were often obstructions in themselves, so the observation was important. Dunn designed and patented a wooden putter with a curved-under face "to deliver a blow which will give the ball that kind of roll which, in billiards, is known as 'follow.'" He ultimately settled on a 10-degree reverse loft, which gave the best results by far on both short and long putts. (Most putters today use only a five-degree backslope.) In 1922, three other inventors, named Plant, Lawton and Doerr, each patented putters of differing shapes, with this same goal of a forward spinning ball in mind.

In 1895, a player named Richard Peters made a more simple experiment. He showed up at the first U.S. Amateur Championship at Newport, Rhode Island with a billiard cue. He actually used it as his putter, going down on his hands and knees as though shooting pool. No rule then disallowed it.

Even the croquet stance, as odd as it seemed, was far from the most bizarre putting style the game has seen. In 1970, an Englishman named Paul Trevillion, a 33-year old 24-handicap golfer, claimed he could outputt any other golfer in the world. "Since I began using my new style three years ago," he bragged, "I haven't missed a putt of four

> IN 1895, A PLAYER NAMED RICHARD PETERS MADE A MORE SIMPLE EXPERIMENT. HE SHOWED UP AT THE FIRST U.S. AMATEUR CHAMPIONSHIP AT NEWPORT, RHODE ISLAND WITH A BILLIARD CUE.

feet or less." His method: Crouch over, with hands wide apart on the shaft, the right hand only a few inches above the clubhead and the forefinger pointing down the back of the shaft. He proposed plans for a Scottish clubmaker to manufacture a special Pencil Putter to use with his method, but it was never again heard of here in the colonies.

A BIT BEHIND IN HIS GAME: HANK EDWARDS SHOWS OFF HIS UNIQUE PUTTING STYLE.

Still more unusual was the foolproof short shot method Hank Edwards, a 52-year old Oklahoma City resident, worked out for himself in 1967. He held the putter behind his back, bent his knees slightly, stuck the putter head forward between his legs, and consistently popped the ball in from five to eight feet away. The position, he said, locked him in so that he couldn't move his head or arms and roll with the putt. "The hardest part of the shot," he grinned when reporting it, "was to have the guts to do it in public."

chapter nine

TODAY'S DUFFER HAS A MIND-BOGGLING ARRAY OF PUTTERS FROM WHICH TO CHOOSE OR BE CONFUSED!

144

putt 'er there, pardner!

THE TAPERSCOPIC PUTTER FROM 19TH HOLE PRODUCTS ADJUSTS TO VARIOUS HEIGHTS FROM ITS 15½" COMPACT SIZE.

The Long and Short of It

Still another way the golfer with putting problems can try adjusting is up and down—with a short club or a long one. Players have gone to both extremes that the USGA allows: 18 inches for the shorty and 52 inches for the longy. Neither idea is especially new, we hasten to add. A file picture from the *London News* pictures a golfer of the 1920s on Rye Golf Course in Sandwich, England, using a mini-putter that couldn't have been more than a foot and a half long.

Hardly anyone uses extreme shorties today, but let some golf pro win a tournament using one and you'll see a sudden resurgence. After all, 19th Hole Products was still advertising them just a few years back, with three Taperscopic Putters that extended to regulation length from a 15½-inch long gift package size. The center-shafted and mallet-headed putters had two-piece telescoping shafts, while the WCMH had a three-piece shaft.

PUTTERING UP

IT WAS LATE IN THE DAY SO THE GOLF PRO PUT A MIDDLE-AGED MAN AND AN ATTRACTIVE YOUNGER WOMAN INTO A TWOSOME. DURING THE ROUND THE TWO HIT IT OFF VERY WELL. WHEN THEY CAME TO THE 18TH GREEN, THEY BOTH HAD LONG PUTTS FOR PARS. THE MAN, LOOKING AT HIS BEST ROUND IN SOME TIME, SAID, "IF I MAKE THIS PUTT, I'LL TAKE YOU TO THE BEST SPOT IN TOWN FOR DINNER." THEN HE STEPPED UP AND CONFIDENTLY STROKED IT IN. THE YOUNG WOMAN, FACED WITH A 35-FOOT PUTT ON A SLANT, IN TURN, SAID—FEELING SAFE— "AND, IF I MAKE THIS PUTT, YOU CAN COME OVER TO MY PLACE **AFTER** DINNER . . . FOR DESSERT." BUT AS SHE STEPPED UP TO HER BALL THE MAN GULPED, "WAIT!" THEN HE WENT TO HIS HANDS AND KNEES, SURVEYED THE SHOT FROM ALL ANGLES, PICKED UP THE BALL AND HANDED IT TO HER, STATING, "THAT'S A GIMME IF I EVER SAW ONE."

chapter nine

With equipment nearing perfection—if there can truly be such a thing in the imperfect game of golf—the only thing left to raise the national average in putting is for the putters themselves to learn the art. Putting boils down to solving distance and direction with aim and force. But solving the correct equation is like working your way through a maze with numerous dead ends. Any one reason, or combination of reasons, can put the putter into a cul-de-sac.

Small wonder then that Jack Nicklaus takes so much time over his putts, even with people sniping at him for it. His retort has been, "It's ridiculous for anybody to tell someone else how long he should take to make a living."

Ben Hogan's classic comment on putting was: "Selecting a stroke is like selecting a wife. To each his own."

BOB PARS YET ANOTHER HOLE WITH HIS PATENTED PUTTER.

First Things First

A FOURSOME WAS PUTTING OUT ON THE 10TH HOLE AT THE DALLAS, TEXAS CEDAR CREST COURSE WHEN AN ARMED BANDIT HELD THEM UP. THEY UNHESITATINGLY HANDED OVER THEIR WALLETS, THEN WENT ON WITH THEIR GAME, PAUSING ONLY LONG ENOUGH TO DISPATCH ONE OF THE CADDIES TO THE CLUBHOUSE TO CALL THE POLICE—WHOM THEY DEIGNED TO TALK TO ONLY AFTER THEY HAD COMPLETED THEIR GAME.

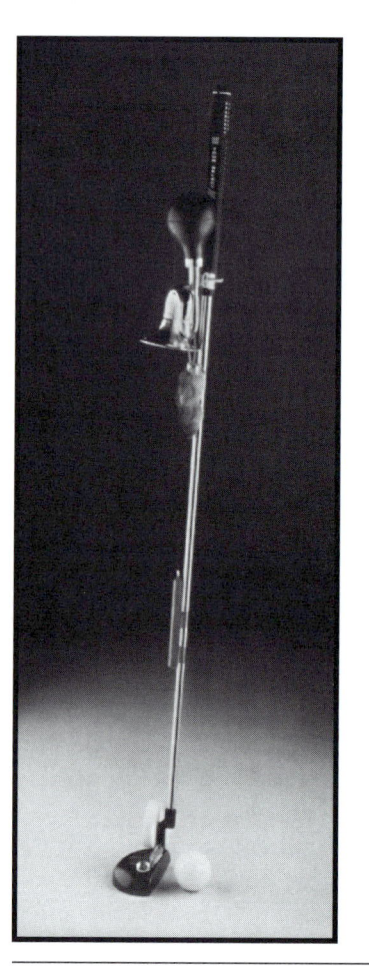

THE SCHMECKENBECKER PUTTER FEATURES A BUILT-IN COMPASS (FOR FINDING ONE'S WAY TO AND FROM THE 19TH HOLE), A CANDLE (FOR NIGHT PLAY), A RABBIT'S FOOT (RATHER USELESS, SINCE IT DIDN'T DO THE RABBIT MUCH GOOD), A CARPENTER'S LEVEL (FOR READING TILTED GREENS), A 40-INCH TAPE MEASURE (TO ELIMINATE GIMME ARGUMENTS), AND AN OLD-FASHIONED SQUEEZE-BULB HORN (TO MOVE SLOW PLAYERS ALONG). IT'S THE PERFECT PUTTER FOR THE HARPO IN ALL OF US!

Having a Ball!

chapter 10

It took a four-year apprenticeship to learn how to make the early golf balls in Scotland. They were handmade, and one efficient craftsman could produce about four or five per day. Tanned cow or horsehide was cut into strips, and softened by soaking in an alum solution. They were then stitched together and turned inside-out, leaving only a small hole through which boiled goose or chicken feathers were stuffed, using a small awl-like tool. It took a top hat full of feathers to stuff one "feathery" ball. The hole was then sewed shut, and as the ball dried, the feathers expanded and the leather shrunk, forming a hard ball. No two were exactly alike, of course, but they were surprisingly uniform, when measured by calipers.

LOOKING MORE LIKE PREHISTORIC DINOSAUR EGGS, THESE "FEATHERY BALLS" FROM THE 1700S WERE MADE FROM HIDE AND STUFFED WITH FEATHERS—NO TWO WERE ALIKE.

The first traceable shipment of Dutch leather balls to Scotland occurred in 1486. Ritsaert Clays is recorded as paying six groats to a toll station at Bergen op Zoom as export tax on one barrel of balls. In 1552, town documents of Goirlie, Holland mention a ballmaker—described as a ball "stuffer"—thus leading historians' speculation that the Gourlay family, which became famed feathery ballmakers in Scotland in the 1800s, actually came from Holland.

Douglas Gourlay and Allan Robertson were the first ballmakers to stamp their names on the balls they made, Gourlay stamping his last name and Robertson stamping his first name, for some reason. Maybe because it was a better fit on the ball.

chapter ten

VISHNU, GOD OF GOLF.

Even though a better ball—the "gutty" or gutta-percha ball—arrived in 1848, the feathery was still being used up until 1865. Some golfers had adapted to it well, like Samuel Messieux, listed as the record holder for a feathery drive at 361 yards, in 1836.

Credit for the invention of the gutta-percha ball probably belongs to the Reverend Robert A. Paterson of St. Andrews, Scotland—with a bit of help from the Hindu god Vishnu. In 1848, Reverend Paterson received a package from India. Inside was a statue of Vishnu packed in gutta-percha—essentially a milky sap that hardens when molded. Seeking a substitute for the feather-stuffed leather balls then in use, he tried molding the gutta-percha into a golf ball. But, when he tried it out, this ball went flying every which way, until it developed some nicks in it. Then it flew fairly straight. These nicks ultimately became the modern-day dimples, which create air pressure under the ball and keep it aloft. Even a modern-day ball without dimples will drop quickly after 60 to 80 yards.

Gutta-percha was soon being imported in large sheets from Malaysia. To make balls, it was then cut into pieces, softened in hot water, drawn out into ribbons, wound into a ball and pressed by hand until smooth. Then it was heated again and pressed until it was as solid as possible, before dropping it into cold water to harden. Any part that broke the water's surface tended to swell out of shape, so close watch had to be kept.

> CREDIT FOR THE INVENTION OF THE GUTTA-PERCHA BALL PROBABLY BELONGS TO THE REVEREND ROBERT A. PATERSON OF ST. ANDREWS, SCOTLAND—WITH A BIT OF HELP FROM THE HINDU GOD VISHNU.

An advantage of this ball was that scuff marks could be smoothed out by immersing the ball in warm water again and smoothing with the hands. But, later on, golfers discovered, as had the Reverend Paterson earlier, that scuff marks actually gave their balls better flight, so players started scarring *new* balls before use. Robert Forgan of St. Andrews claimed to be the first to inscribe

THE ECLIPSE BALL, THE FIRST "NEARLY INDESTRUCTIBLE" BALL, CIRCA 1877.

148

actual patterns onto balls. The first patterns were squares, mere crosshatchings. Even when dimples were introduced, they were *extruded*, not *indented*, and they were still squares. While round extrusion dimples had been tried by at least one company, Dunlop was the first to indent the square dimples. Thus, the Dunlop innovation was the true forerunner of round indented dimples.

Ball Patents

About 1870, gutta-perchas appeared with other components added—ground cork, leather, metal filings, and an adhesive liquid. Surprisingly, it was 1876 before the first patent was taken out specifically for a golf ball, by Capt. Duncan Stewart of St. Andrews. Five years before he had experimented with winding rubber thread inside a cover of gutta-percha, the basic principle followed 30 years later in the Haskell ball.

In 1877, William Currie, with the Caledonia Rubber Works in Edinburgh, got a patent for a composite ball that was molded and vulcanized. He called it the Eclipse. In it, canvas was laid inside the mold, which, later removed, left an indent or molding. Advertised to be nearly indestructible, this new ball flew very well and far, *and* ran true on the green.

It was the Silvertown gutta-percha and the Eclipse composite—the "gutty" and the "putty"—which fought it out for supremacy at the close of the 19th century. Darwin, in his *History of Golf in Britain*, stated: "I remember dimly people spoke of 27s and 28s, which were the two common sizes . . . [referring] to their weight in drachms [1.62 ounces = 27 drachms]; but the real point of controversy was between the Gutty and the Putty . . . ." The Eclipse had a brief, brilliant prime in the 1880s, and survived into the next decade as well. This was shown with a full page ad in the *Golfing Annual* for 1896-97. It was said to be "a composition of gutta-percha, vulcanized India rubber and cork."

The Eclipse was not an attractive ball, having a dull yellowish skin embossed with a St. Andrews' cross. (A solid white gutta-percha ball had been introduced sometime during the 1880s, however.) Nor did it make,

> **GOLFERS DISCOVERED THAT SCUFF MARKS ACTUALLY GAVE THEIR BALLS BETTER FLIGHT, SO PLAYERS STARTED SCARRING NEW BALLS BEFORE USE.**

when struck, the clean click sound of the Silvertown. It wasn't a great carrying ball, either, but had the advantage of keeping very low against a wind and was less susceptible to slicing and pulling. It also had a very long run on hard ground. When Horace Hutchinson won the first two Amateur Championships of 1886 and 1887 with it, others found it had more advantages. It

FROM THE RECLINER

BOB FRASER LOFTED HIS BALL A BIT ERRATICALLY ONTO THE FRONT LAWN OF A HOME BORDERING THE SAN MARCOS, CALIFORNIA COURSE. THEN HE WATCHED, FASCINATED, AS THE LADY OF THE HOUSE CAME OUT WITH A GOLF CLUB, LOOKED OVER THE LIE, WENT BACK INTO THE HOUSE TO CHANGE HER CLUB, AND CAME BACK OUT TO CALMLY STROKE THE BALL BACK TO WITHIN INCHES OF HIS FEET.

Dimple Discourse

The "dimple" marking idea to improve flight distance by making the ball fly straight was refined by an Englishman named William Taylor. He found that, if dimples are too shallow, the ball is not true; if they are too deep, they affect the distance the ball will travel. These dimple designs worked so well they soon replaced the "bramble" patterns inherent on gutta-percha covers. • England commemorated Taylor's ingenuity by erecting a plaque in the city of Leicester in 1949. The commemoration noted how, without the use of a wind tunnel, he had to observe and analyze the disturbances caused by a fast-moving sphere by blowing cigar smoke at the ball and noting the resulting eddies. • The size, shape and placing of dimples have, ever since, been the subject of much experimentation. Today's legal balls have from 318 to 552 dimples, with different sizes and depths to them. But balls have been made with as many as 812 dimples, and as few as 252. • In 1954, U.S. Rubber Company produced diamond-shaped dimples in place of the usual round or square ones, and sales manager John W. Sproul stated that company tests showed their design kept the ball in the air an extra quarter-second, thereby adding 10 yards to any golfer's drive. Uniroyal, in 1976, had a Plus-6 model ball with hexagonal-shaped dimples. And Wilson had one with a dimple it called "an inverted truncated cone shape." • Two Californians, chemist Daniel Nepela and San Jose State University physicist Fred Holmstrom, figured they could design a ball with the best features of both laminar (smooth) and turbulent (dimpled) surfaces. (Where dimples create minute turbulences that cause drag, but also provide aerodynamic lift, a smooth ball will have less drag, but develop negative lift.) The two men filled in some dimples and left others out and, after a lot of experimentation with rubberbands, plain kitchen plastic wrap and household adhesive, they produced a ball with a wide "equator" of dimples, with smooth areas at both poles. This combination, they claimed, gave the best of both possible designs. What their ball did was wiggle imperceptibly from side to side in flight, correcting itself, so to speak, whenever it started to go off-line. The result was a remarkably straight flight, with great resistance to what we know all too well as hooking and slicing. • Their ball, patent #3,819,190 in 1974, was called The Polara, but was nicknamed quickly "The Happy Non-hooker." Total cost of the experiments, according to Nepela, was $2.75. "We did our baking in the oven of Fred's kitchen," he said. The ball started selling in 1977, but was labeled illegal for USGA play in 1978. The inventors sued the USGA, and the U.S. District Court awarded them $1.47 million in damages (tripled under anti-trust laws). • The Acushnet Titleist 384 (named for the number of dimples on it) was another ball put onto the USGA hit list while it was making a big hit with tour pros. Supposedly, it "played too long and straight for the good of the game." A player was, supposedly again, able to control draw, fade and straight away hitting by the way he oriented the ball on the tee. However, there was no indication any tour player had been able to master the aerodynamic intricacies involved and so actually achieve such an advantage. Tests on Iron Byron, the USGA's own mechanical golfer, showed the ball did carry very well, but not further than the 291.2 yard limitation. • The ban was a boon for Jack Nicklaus and his MacGregor Golf Company, which produced the legal 392-dimple Muirfield ball that many pros then switched over to.

having a ball!

A SAMPLING OF INTERESTING COVER PATTERNS. THE BALL AT UPPER LEFT IS THE "ROYAL," DESIGNED BY WILLIE PARKS.

was difficult to stop on the green, but, once on, it was, according to Hutchinson, " by far the best putting ball that has ever come into being during the half century or so of golf that I have known." Though comparatively soft, it was hard to destroy, and it wasn't destructive to the faces of the wooden clubs in use.

The manufacturers wanted to make it even better, harder, and that's when they started to fail. It struggled on into the 1890s and eventually died.

Meanwhile, the A-1 brand gutta-percha ball from Silvertown—the first ball that floated—went on competing with the myriad other brands that sprang up, including Eureka, Melfort, White Brand, Henley, O.K., Ocobo, Clan, Agrippa, and Willie Park's Special Thornton. The list of balls made in the United Kingdom and the United States before 1914 actually extends for six pages in 1979's *Golf in the Making*, authored by Ian Henderson and David Strick.

Back to the Future

Today, along with the wide variety of clubs and grips to choose from, comes the tandem question of which ball to use. And that *is* a problem, because there are a *lot* to choose from. More than 1,500 different balls—made by 84 firms in 13 countries—were catalogued in 1985. In 1995, one estimable estimator reported that golf balls sold worldwide at a rate of about 2.3 million *per day*! Roughly 831.6 million for the year! Two-thirds of these were bought in the U.S—and that doesn't even include the practice balls!

IN 1995, ONE ESTIMABLE ESTIMATOR REPORTED THAT GOLF BALLS SOLD WORLDWIDE AT A RATE OF ABOUT 2.3 MILLION PER DAY! ROUGHLY 831.6 MILLION FOR THE YEAR!

chapter ten

As we have seen, ball makers have always labored to transmogrify their humble sphere. Among these imaginative toilers have been rocket scientists, who have reconstituted balls' internal organs with highly scientific (and secret) plastic stuffing. They have thickened, thinned and layered its skin. They have made its body oversize, then underweight. Its dimpled face got more lifts than an aging Hollywood star. It was tarted up with more colors than your average streetwalker. It was made mysterious and "dangerous." It was ultimately turned from a ball into a "system."

Golf balls now come in two basic varieties: three-piece, the kind that 95% of professional golfers use; and two-piece, which 86% of other golfers use.

The three-piece type has a solid or liquid center tightly wound with rubber threads. Most are covered with synthetic balata (the real stuff is made from a tropical tree sap). This is the ball that evolved from the Haskell and the later thread-wound, rubber-covered ball. It has a short life span, as it is cut easily and goes out of shape when whacked a few holes by a pro. But it has superior "feel" and "control," making it easy for a pro like Corey Pavin, who is noted for his touch on the ball, to hook, slice or add backspin whenever necessary.

The two-piece ball has a solid plastic center that looks like hardened bubblegum. It has a plastic cover, usually a Surlyn blend developed by DuPont. First sold in 1971, it has proven to go further and last longer, but is harder to control. Jack Nicklaus once likened it, in some disgust, to playing with a marble. Another virtue, though, is its lower cost of $4 or $5 per dozen.

Another ball is made by Cayman Golf Company and sold as the Desperado. The name was given to it because it is smaller and heavier then a regular ball and can be stroked farther than the rulesmakers think should be allowed. The National Golf Center in Meriden, Connecticut also came out with a no-no ball, called the "S." In 1993, the company started an unusual ad campaign, blandly admitting their ball was so good it was illegal, and offering them COD via mail order, $24.95 a dozen, white or yellow.

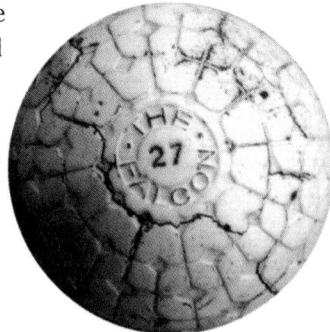

Standards adopted in 1932 state that a ball cannot weigh more than 1.62 ounces, nor be smaller than 1.68 inches in diameter, and cannot have an initial velocity off the club face of more than 250 feet per second or travel more than 280 yards on average when hit by the USGA Iron Byron or an R&A testing machine. To show how changes lag on occasion, however, the first all big-ball tournament wasn't held until 1960. The reason was that, between 1921 and 1960, the R&A decreed a smaller ball, 1.61 inches, while the USGA okayed the larger ball. So golfers had to switch back and forth if they played internationally. Of course, British golfers had been using the smaller ball ever since 1912, when the Dunlop "31" became the first small, heavy, tightly-wound ball, designed specifically for distance.

"Energized" golf balls, made at Oak Ridge, were later inventions on the American front. The B.F. Goodrich Company produced one in 1957 that was said to add 10 yards to anyone's drive. Talk had been for years that the atom was going to benefit mankind, and this looked like *it*. These balls were given two-minute exposures to gamma rays of high intensity, though this did not make them radioactive enough for a Geiger counter to click over. They did go farther, but they also lost a bit of their "atomic energy" every time they were hit. And they were so expensive to produce that BFG only experimented with them. Besides, the USGA was already

IN 1968, THE LENGTH OF THE AVERAGE DRIVE ON THE PRO TOUR WAS 258 YARDS. IN 1995, IT WAS 263 YARDS. THAT'S AN IMPROVEMENT OF ONLY FIVE YARDS IN 27 YEARS.

complaining bitterly that everyone was driving golf balls too far, so it probably would have been banned if they had produced it.

The USGA did hold one housecleaning for "hot" balls, in 1965. Several balls were found to exceed the 250 feet-per-second, the 2% tolerance in size, and/or the 1.620 ounce limitations. Banned were the Acushnet Titleist DT and DT-100, Spalding's Black Dot and BD100 Compression, and the Bristol Advisory 100. At the time, the Titleist was the country's best selling ball, while the Spalding Dot had had a major share of the market for 30 years. So the ban was as if Ford Motors and General Motors had suddenly been pulled off the roadway.

Because balls and clubs are so much better today, people get the impression golfers are hitting the ball a lot further. Frank Thomas,

A Pro's Advice on EVERY Shot

THE FRED ASTAIRE SCHOOL OF GOLF: THIS SCHEME TO IMPROVE A PLAYER'S GAME WAS SIMPLE—IMPRINT PROPER FOOT POSITIONING FOR VARIOUS SHOTS DIRECTLY ONTO THE BALL.

the USGA's technical director, debunks this, though, by quoting statistics. In 1968, the length of the average drive on the pro tour was 258 yards. In 1995, it was 263 yards. That's an improvement of only five yards in 27 years. The 1.9% difference, he thinks, results from the better shape of both fairways and golfers these days. As far as better accuracy goes, he notes that the winning score in pro tournaments is improving at a rate of only about one stroke every 25 years!

chapter ten

Tee Time

According to librarian Charles Price, the tee, that place from which you begin play on a hole, goes back to Egyptian architecture in the time of the pharaohs, where a "T" marking on building plans always designated where to begin construction.

The wooden tee was an invention patented on December 12, 1899 by an American dentist who didn't want to dirty his hands forming dirt piles as tees, as was the practice at the time. George F. Grant, an Arlington Heights, Massachusetts native, was one of the first black graduates of Harvard's dental school and went on to become a world-renowned expert on the cleft palate and inventor of the artificial palate. But he is better remembered as the inventor of the golf tee, even though he gave away the rights to it and never realized a dime from his brainstorm. Grant's tee featured a wood spike base topped with a rubber cup. "When the ball is struck," he stated in the patent, "the head will yield in the direction of the travel of the ball, offering no obstruction to its flight."

The all-wood tee didn't arrive on the golf scene until 1921. It was the innovation of another dentist, Dr. William Lowell of Maplewood, New Jersey, who also didn't like dirtying

FORE FUN and good form! Improve your game, lower your score and distract your golfing companions this sure, simple way! Body Beautiful tees are proportioned properly to focus your eyes on the ball and keep the conversation rolling. Set of 6 golden-toned metal Teezers is guaranteed to separate the duffers from the golfers. Perfect gift for fairway friends!
☐ 5577—Golf Teezer Set $1

VARIOUS VERSIONS OF "NUDIE" TEES HAVE EXISTED IN ONE FORM OR ANOTHER FOR YEARS, ALL CLAIMING TO IMPROVE YOUR GAME BY PUTTING MORE "IRON IN YOUR PUTTER." ONE WONDERS WHAT TEES THE MEMBERS OF THE LPGA ARE USING . . .

> THE ALL-WOOD TEE DIDN'T ARRIVE ON THE GOLF SCENE UNTIL 1921. IT WAS THE INNOVATION OF ANOTHER DENTIST, DR. WILLIAM LOWELL OF MAPLEWOOD, NEW JERSEY, WHO ALSO DIDN'T LIKE DIRTYING HIS HANDS IN THE TEE BOX.

his hands in the tee box. He considered the sandbox "both messy and unsanitary." His first attempt involved twisting a wire to form a circle at the top, with the straight end pushed into the ground. It worked, but it was pointed out to him that it could present a hazard if caught up in the greenskeeper's lawnmower.

So then he imagined a sharp pointed peg with a concave top made of a composition that would readily disintegrate when wet to further serve as fertilizer. Unfortunately, he was years ahead of available technology, and it wasn't until about 1990 or 1991 that that idea resurfaced, with ads in *Golf Magazine* espousing two such golf tees.

One, cleverly named the Dirt-Tee, claimed to be the first biodegradable tee that would break down into fertilizer, seed and soil. The other, called the Edem Tee, was comprised of compressed soil that dissolved when wet, and broke upon impact (and, unfortunately, also broke often when being stuck into the ground).

Actually, neither was first, though both carried the ecology theme further than the original did. The *Wall Street Journal*, prior to 1977, had carried a story about a golf tee for the ecology-minded being produced by Spectrum Marketing Company of London, Ontario, Canada. It was made of plastic and disintegrated within 90 days. The plastic was reported to contain a fertilizer that was released as the tee dissolved.

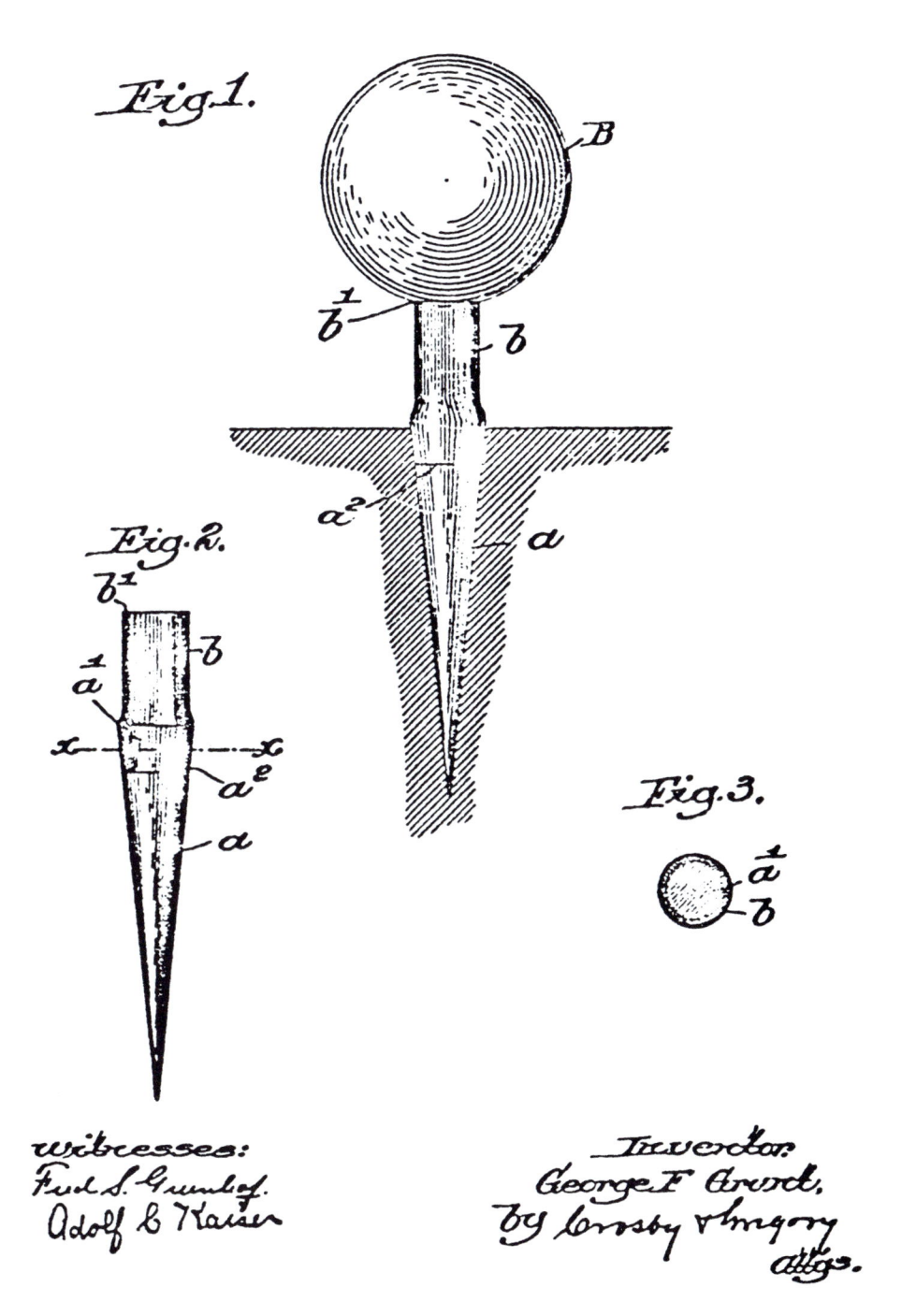

having a ball!

PATENT FOR THE FIRST GOLF TEE, INVENTED BY GEORGE F. GRANT, ONE OF THE FIRST AFRICAN-AMERICANS TO GRADUATE FROM HARVARD. HE LATER BECAME A WORLD-RENOWNED EXPERT IN THE FIELD OF DENTISTRY.

chapter ten

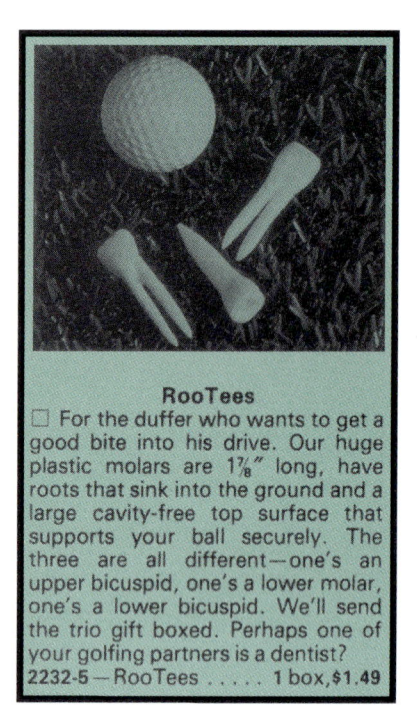

RooTees
☐ For the duffer who wants to get a good bite into his drive. Our huge plastic molars are 1⅞" long, have roots that sink into the ground and a large cavity-free top surface that supports your ball securely. The three are all different—one's an upper bicuspid, one's a lower molar, one's a lower bicuspid. We'll send the trio gift boxed. Perhaps one of your golfing partners is a dentist?
2232-5—RooTees . . . . . 1 box, $1.49

ALAS, GEORGE GRANT DID NOT POSSESS THE FORESIGHT TO TAKE HIS ORIGINAL PATENT IDEA AND COMBINE IT WITH HIS PROFESSION IN ORDER TO CREATE THIS UNQUESTIONABLE WORK OF GENIUS!

The current manufacturer of biodegradable tees is Eco Golf, based in Columbus, Indiana. The company was launched in 1994 as a recycled clothing and materials company and expanded the following year to produce the tees. Before long they were manufacturing 250,000 tees daily and shipping worldwide. They are used on some 400 U.S. courses and were the official tee at the 1996 Open, as well as the Bay Hill Invitational in February 1997.

Two types of Eco tees are made. The Magic Tee is made from a water-soluble resin that degrades within 10 hours when in contact with water. It's good for about three drives. The Tough Tee is made from a corn-based polymer, will decompose in 30 to 60 days, and is good for 10 drives. The company also makes biodegradable ball markers from the same material.

Back to Dr. Lowell. While working on his idea, his eyes happened on some still-warm gutta-percha left over from a set of false teeth he had just completed. He shaped several pointed pegs from this material, rounded out a concave shell on top with his thumb and, being an avid golfer himself, gave them a try. But they, too, proved unsatisfactory. They broke too easily, often before they could even be used. Disappointed with the composition, he was still sure he had hit upon the right design. So, one summer evening in 1921, he whittled several such pegs from the base of a small flagpole he had at his home, and the wooden tee was born.

He and his son placed an order for 5,000 such pegs to be made from white birch on a wood lathe. They were to be colored green, under the assumption they would be used only once each. Later, when they had found golfers would re-use the tees, the color was changed to red, so it could be found easier in the grass. This color gave it its eventual trademarked name, The Reddy Tee.

Surprisingly, it was not instantly successful. Lowell and his son spent almost two years traveling about eastern states handing out sample boxes of the tees and promotional literature, while another son, William, Jr. covered the Chicago area. Persistence paid off when, in 1923, Lowell contracted with Walter Hagen and Joe Kirkwood, two of the biggest names in golf at the time, to use and advertise the tees. After that, orders poured in.

But then, competing companies began to spring up. Over 200 different brands of tees were on the market in 1926, in spite of a long series of court battles by Lowell combating patent infringement. He spent $150,000 in legal fees, but New York's Court of Appeals ultimately decided that his patent was inadequate to rule infringement. So, in 1943, the Red Devil Company of Irvington, New Jersey bought rights to the Reddy Tee, and for a fraction of what had been refused in previous years.

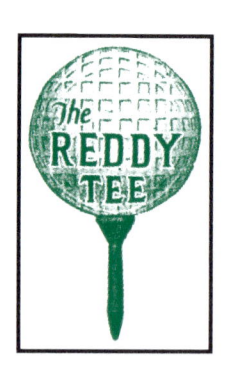

THE FIRST WOODEN TEE.

Lost Balls

The lost ball problem may be eased by adding any of a number of types of ball retrieval devices to your cart baggage. Even a pro uses five to eight balls per round, according to *Golf Magazine*, removing cut or scuffed balls and replacing balls hit into bunkers (within the rules, of course) or losing the occasional one in the drink or rough. So it stands to reason the average golfer will use more than that.

Backing up that premise is the tale behind a unique statue, "The Desert Golfer," erected by Sam Cimaroli, who lived off the sixth green of the Golf Canyon Golf Club in the foothills of Arizona's Superstition Mountains. Over the years, Sam had found literally hundreds of lost balls in the desert that edges this course. He thought it would be amusing to erect a monument to the frustrations of the desert golfer, who attempts to best the coyotes, cacti and canyons that can hide a ball forever if it strays off the narrow fairways. So his six-foot tall Desert Golfer, in perfect ball address position—right down to the left foot angled 30 degrees toward the projected target—was made from 500 lost balls.

Some courses hire swimmers with snorkel or SCUBA gear to recover balls from their water hazards, then re-sell the good balls and put the lesser ones on their driving ranges. This has proven so lucrative in some areas that clubs have had to patrol at night to keep freelancers from bottom scrounging. Other clubs sell recycling rights to people who have made a business of such salvage. Jerry Gunderson, as a kid, would roam the courses in Deerfield Beach, Florida looking for lost balls so he could sell them back to golfers for a few pennies each. As he grew older, and wiser, he capitalized on that early experience and hit a jackpot. Eventually he was paying in excess of $400,000 for the right to collect lost balls from 600 courses between Jacksonville and Atlanta, Georgia. He employed 45 divers, needing to collect 3 1/2 million balls to break even. In one year alone he exported 10 million balls and had his company on the verge of going public.

FROM THE DESERT GOLFER . . .

. . . TO THE AQUATIC GOLFER.

chapter ten

The next time her husband and his dad returned from the course, she asked how he had liked the yellow balls. "They were great until the third hole," her husband laughed, "when he hit his tee shot into a field of bright yellow dandelions."

For those intentionally hitting into water, like off the fantale of cruise ships, there are two other alternatives. Several companies, like Bob Cleveland of Norman, Oklahoma, specialize in selling "Experienced Golf Balls." They are much cheaper recycled balls. Japanese ships did this type of activity a lot, until the country's environmental protection agency appealed to naval and merchant seamen not to pollute the ocean with golf balls. The agency estimated that more than two million used balls were being consigned to the deep each year by ships' crew members.

The other alternative is a newer invention—balls made of collagen. This comes from bone, cartilage and tendon tissue and, once boiled, it turns into a gelatin. Makers of these golf balls mix it with ground citrus peel. Knocked overboard, these dissolve.

You can keep from losing balls in other ways too. Various golf ball marker kits are available via mail order from Miles Kimball of Osh Kosh, for instance. They allow a player to imprint his name, nickname or other legend of his choice on his balls before play. This doesn't keep them out of the water or the rough, of course, but does identify them if found later by honest people.

Colored balls have been offered as another means of keeping track of balls on the course. Touring pro and 1976 U.S. Open champ Jerry Pate was using an orange-colored ball in 1982. According to tests conducted by the Dunlop Sports Company, if the ball is an "optic orange" color its flight can be followed 40% farther and have a 20 to 25% better chance of being spotted if it strays from the fairway. Here's why: Orange has no equivalent in nature, except a few flowers not apt to be found around a golf course. Thus, with a fluorescent treatment of the orange color, it is four times more reflective of light than the standard white ball.

Yellow balls are pretty common now, but

NOT FOR THE FAINT OF HEART.

Put Some POP in Somebody's Swing
EXPLODING GOLF BALL

Why not? Ball explodes on impact into a harmless chalk powder. It's realistic enough to pass for a pro ball. Just sneak it onto your playing partner's tee, and watch the fireworks!

No. 7015 Exploding Ball   YOUR PRICE $2.85
Retail $3.95

not always appreciated. Carol Malfatti, for instance, tells a story about giving some of these to her father-in-law as a birthday present, thinking they would be easy for him to spot. The next time her husband and his dad returned from the course, she asked how he had liked the yellow balls. "They were great until the third hole," her husband laughed, "when he hit his tee shot into a field of bright yellow dandelions."

Col. Vincent I. Hack, who directed a color research program at Brooke Army Medical Center in San Antonio, Texas in 1966, discovered other intriguing things about color. If you tend to hit under your ball, try using a red ball, for example. Col. Hack's experiments indicated that red makes an object appear larger, thus closer than it really is. Blue, on the other hand, makes an object seem smaller and farther away. White is a neutral color and makes for accurate depth perception, which is not always a good thing. Thus, if you are hitting under a white ball, use a red one. This should make you subconsciously correct your swing. If you are topping a white ball, switch to a blue one.

Unfortunately, these colors are not commonly accessible. But the Karsten Golf Company does have what it calls Ping's Eye Balls, which are half-white and half-red. They might suffice. And, more as gag gifts than good playing balls, Leister Games sells green balls, called Losers' Balls, for obvious reasons, as well as balls that look like the 8-ball from a billiard game. And HTC International sells balls painted as rolled up money and as little baseballs, basketballs and footballs, which are, at least, conversation starters.

You can, in fact, probably get anything put on a ball. The James River Golf Club Museum recently acquired one with a photo of President Clinton on it, encircled with the slogan, "A good lie guaranteed."

New Ball, Please!

With so many balls of varied characteristics to choose from, it was little wonder touring pros started using different balls for different results in different situations. When faced, for example, with a long par-3 and a water hazard fronting the green, he could use a surlyn-covered ball which, when hit with an iron, tended to get up in the air quickly and go an inordinate distance. On the next tee he could switch to a balata-covered ball, which might not carry as far, but was easier to control. Green play could be tailored around the balls used too. A balata one-piece hits the green, takes two bounces and stops, whereas a balata two-piece hits the green, takes two bounces and rolls a few feet.

The USGA stopped all that experimentation in 1979 when it decreed a golfer would have to use balls of the same brand model and compression for the entire round that he tees off with.

Arnold Palmer was one supporter of the ruling. "I endorse it 100%," he stated. "It takes something of the skill of the game away if a guy takes a different ball out for a long water shot. I've only done it once myself, at Lancome in Paris. I was playing with Seve Ballesteros (one of the game's longest hitters). At the first hole I used one of those (high-compression) balls and outdrove Seve, then hit a monster one-iron onto the green. He laid up short, pitched on and made a putt for four. I three putted for five and threw the ball away."

chapter ten

An innovation in easily located balls might be to smear limburger cheese or garlic over them. With good olfactory senses one would never lose one of these. And it would keep wandering vampires away at the same time! (Probably everyone else, too, though.) So, better yet, secure a Stern's Company Electronic Golf Ball Set—two balls with tiny embedded transmitters and a pocket receiver to point the way to the lost ball's beeping cry for help—unless you plan to play the Royal & Ancient Club, where they banned its use in 1972, quoting Rule 37(9): "The player shall not use any artificial device which might assist him in making a stroke or in his play."

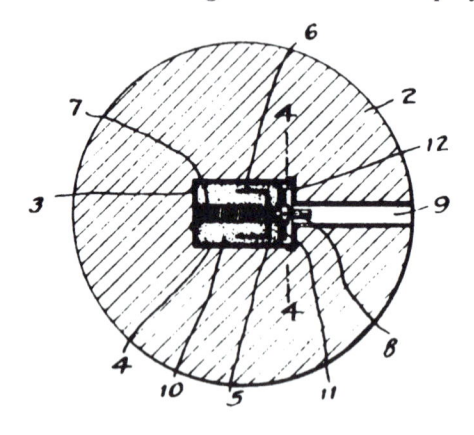

THE SOUNDING SPHERE OF 1927 HAD A WIND-UP SPRING AT ITS CORE WHICH CREATED A CLICKING SOUND TO NOTIFY THE GOLFER OF ITS HIDDEN WHEREABOUTS.

Finding a lost ball artificially, their argument went, relieves a golfer of the penalty he should have received for his bad shot.

This idea of a noisy ball was actually first invented way back in 1927. It, however, employed a wind-up spring at its core, which gave off a clicking sound for a limited time. The beeper was being worked on by a Des Moines, Iowa inventor as far back as 1962. Another early idea was to have the ball send out smoke signals upon landing. This is on record at the U.S. Patent Office, but the closest it came to fruition was a gag ball that leaves a trail of rainbow colored smoke when teed off. It serves as an innovative bit of April Foolishness when sneakily slipped onto an unsuspecting golfer's tee. Newer versions of easy-find balls have had radioactive particles implanted under their covers so they could be tracked with a portable Geiger counter.

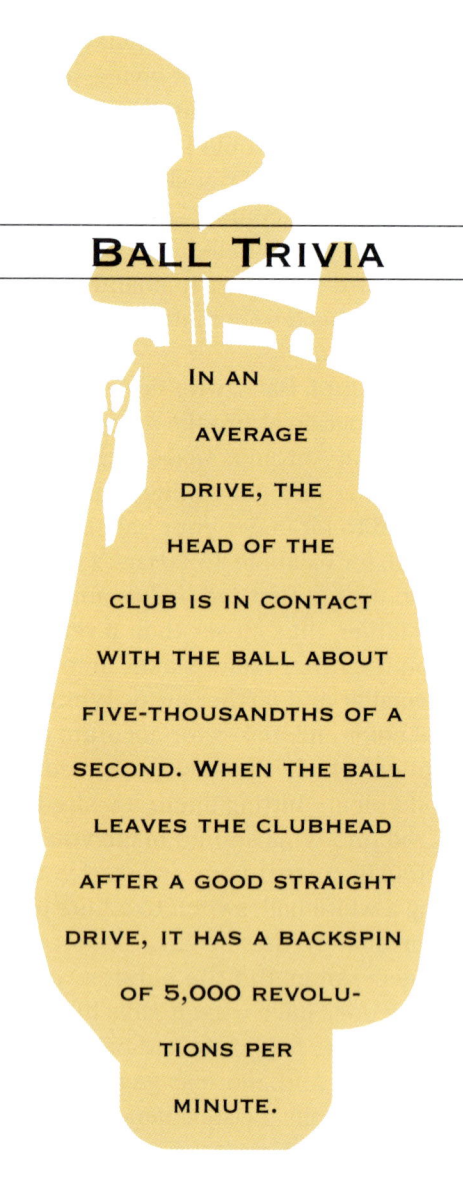

If all other methods fail in tracking and finding lost balls, a small green cardboard box with air holes punched into the sides may be your solve-ation. Produced by Laid Back Enterprises of Oklahoma City in January 1992, two golf balls—one labeled "male" and one labeled "female"—were nested inside. The box was labeled Official Golf Ball Breeder Kit. It came with care and feeding instructions, as well as how-to lessons for telling your breeders apart.

BALL TRIVIA

IN AN AVERAGE DRIVE, THE HEAD OF THE CLUB IS IN CONTACT WITH THE BALL ABOUT FIVE-THOUSANDTHS OF A SECOND. WHEN THE BALL LEAVES THE CLUBHEAD AFTER A GOOD STRAIGHT DRIVE, IT HAS A BACKSPIN OF 5,000 REVOLUTIONS PER MINUTE.

Golf
á la Cart

c h a p t e r 11

One would not ordinarily think of listing golf carts as game aids, especially since a national golf magazine once reported that walking golfers scored seven or eight strokes better than the easyriders. But with all the gear the average golfer absolutely must have along for full enjoyment of the game today—not to mention the dearth of caddies—something is needed to carry it all. And, of course, manufacturers have leaped at the chance to furnish their solutions.

For those not overly addicted to exercise, John Pirre of Stamford, Connecticut invented, back around 1968, the robot caddy. It was a little 148-pound three-wheel machine that trailed 4 to 12 feet behind the golfer at speeds up to four mph. "Maynard," the collective name given these robot units when marketed, was guided by two mini-computers working on information transmitted from a palm-sized control unit clipped to the golfer's belt. When the golfer stopped, the robot stopped, the motor turned off and the wheels locked. Powered by an auto battery, it went seven and one-half miles before requiring recharging. It retailed at about half the cost of a standard two-man riding cart.

Newer, more streamlined versions of the robot caddy are now numerous. The

chapter eleven

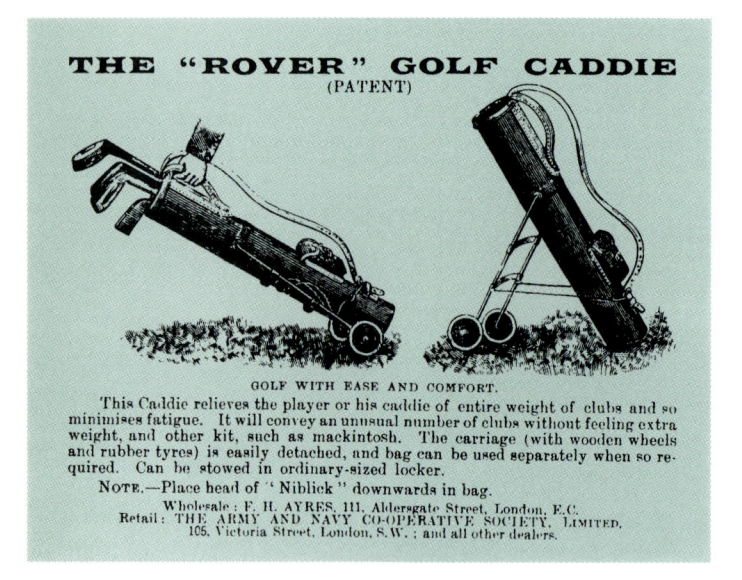

THE "ROVER" GOLF CADDIE
(PATENT)

GOLF WITH EASE AND COMFORT.

This Caddie relieves the player or his caddie of entire weight of clubs and so minimises fatigue. It will convey an unusual number of clubs without feeling extra weight, and other kit, such as mackintosh. The carriage (with wooden wheels and rubber tyres) is easily detached, and bag can be used separately when so required. Can be stowed in ordinary-sized locker.

NOTE.—Place head of "Niblick" downwards in bag.

Wholesale: F. H. AYRES, 111, Aldersgate Street, London, E.C.
Retail: THE ARMY AND NAVY CO-OPERATIVE SOCIETY, LIMITED, 105, Victoria Street, London, S.W.; and all other dealers.

AN EARLY CART BAG FROM 1899.

Kangaroo Motorcaddie, offered in three designs, features a control panel on its T-bar handle. It disassembles quickly into three parts for easy transport in the trunk of an automobile. Resting stools can be side-mounted, for those so inclined. The Lectronic Kaddy, from Lectronic Kaddy Industries, was already used in 26 countries by 1991. The Club Runner, new in 1997, is available from Golfsmith. A dial on the handle can adjust speed up to 10 mph, and its cruise control compensates for hills automatically.

Cart Blanche

Drive carts have been around for longer than most people would think. Boca Raton, Florida, for example, was famed for its golf carts from the club's establishment in the early 1920s. It was there, too, that the first actual auto was used as a golf cart! Clarence Geist, an early-day millionaire, sometimes played a few holes in a specially equipped Packard limousine.

These days, it is difficult to think of any convenience that hasn't been built-in, or gadget that hasn't been included, on carts. For real a la cart, though, it might be hard to beat the doo-dadded-up cart that singer-actor Jim Nabors gave his manager, Dick Linke. It had black fender-to-fender carpeting, chrome bumpers, leather roof, AM-FM radio, tape deck, television, cigarette lighter, ice cooler, and telephone.

Band leader Louis Prima once owned one he had fixed up with a heater for winter and air-conditioner for summer. He also included a collapsible rake for smoothing traps *as he drove through them.*

Jackie Gleason owned a $12,000 cart in 1968 when that was still a whole lot of money. Boris Becker, after winning Wimbledon's tennis championship a second time at age 18, splurged on a cart made up to resemble a Rolls Royce. And two partners in a Los Angeles Plymouth agency had carts made up copying the then-popular Plymouth Fury, tail fins, spare tire mounting and all.

ALMOST 100 YEARS LATER, THE SAME IDEA IS BROUGHT BACK IN THIS DESIGN BY HILLCREST.

golf á la cart

A whole rash of new creations were developed by custom car maker George Barris of Hollywood, designer and crafter of many of the special vehicles used in various movies over the years. One of his first was for Bob Hope, who debuted with it at his 1970 Desert Golf Classic in Palm Springs, California. It was a wildly sculptured $14,000 "Kustom Kar Kreation." It actually re-created Hope's famous toothy smile, ski slope snoot and jutting jaw. The head and face were formed from steel tubing and sheeting. The rear portion was an eight-foot simulated golf ball, while the frontal area featured shiny grillwork and running lights in the smiling mouth. Two extra wheels, with Goodyear "fats" tires, were placed in the rear to help stabilize the extra load.

TWO "MAYNARD" ROBOT CADDIES OBEDIENTLY FOLLOW THEIR MASTERS DOWN THE FAIRWAY, CONTROLLED BY BEEPERS WORN ON THE BELT.

chapter eleven

BOB HOPE'S CUSTOM-DESIGNED CART GAVE NEW MEANING TO THE TERM "HIGH PROFILE VEHICLE."

golf á la cart

> HOPE USED TO PLAY GOLF WITH PRESIDENT JERRY FORD. REGARDING FORD'S MUCH-BALLYHOOED ACCIDENT PRONENESS, HOPE QUIPPED THAT FORD'S CART OUGHT TO HAVE A RED CROSS PAINTED ON ITS ROOF.

comedian's long commercial association with that company. In the center dash was an entertainment console housing a Panasonic TV, stereo tape deck complete with record and playback capability, clock, AM-FM multiplex stereo radio, and video recorder and playback unit. A video camera, with wide angle lens, was mounted at the very rear of the cart so Hope could film his golf swing, then return to the cart for an instant replay.

ANOTHER GEORGE BARRIS CREATION, BING CROSBY'S CART SPORTED 24 COATS OF CANDY APPLE RED LACQUER & EARTH-TONE PILE CARPETING.

To illustrate the detail involved in the cart, the face was painted in combinations of pearl and candy apple red to accent Hope's dimples and broad smile. The grillwork and taillight assembly came from Chrysler, denoting the

Hope used to play golf with President Jerry Ford. Regarding Ford's much-ballyhooed accident proneness, Hope quipped that Ford's cart ought to have a red cross painted on its roof.

165

chapter eleven

Now Boarding!

The Japanese have produced a monorail system, which winds its way throughout a course carrying bags but no riders. Its cost was considered an economic hedge for the future, since rising wage scales and an expected tightening in the labor pool seemed to foretell the demise of the female caddy.

In 1980, a typical monorail setup consisted of 60 carts, each of which could carry four bags of clubs. The carts rode on an I-beam rail that skirted the roughs and passed behind the greens, with the rail almost always out of view, covered by landscaping and gardening. Most systems were battery powered, though a few operated on electric current in the rail, like subway trains. In some cases the carts were operated by on-board push buttons, though remote-control systems were growing in popularity. Tiny control panels that had a signal range of 150 meters could fit inside a breast pocket.

The monorails have received mixed reactions. Some golfers grumble about walking to and from a cart for practically every shot. And, except at switching points, carts can't pass each other. But the monorails proved to be economical for customers, as well as for course owners. And some golfers have admitted they are glad to give up human caddies, sparing themselves embarrassment.

The Crosby Cart

Bing Crosby, Hope's compadre in a raft of "road comedies," also had one of the "personality profile" carts created by Barris. It re-created his everpresent pipe and favorite pork-pie hat—complete with a feather in the band—on the roof. Bing's eyes were hand-painted on the plexiglass windshield, and the exterior finish was done in 24 coats of candy apple red lacquer, coordinated with pleated interior done in earth tones accented

THE BOMBARDIER IS ADVERTISED AS A HIGH-TECH NEIGHBORHOOD ELECTRIC VEHICLE (NEV) DESIGNED FOR USE ON AND OFF THE COURSE.

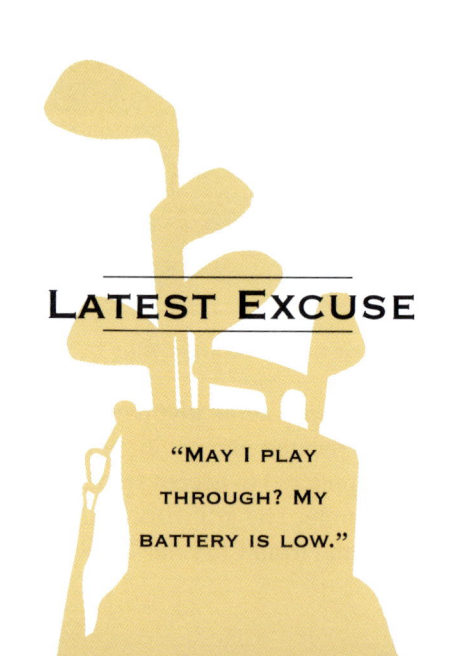

LATEST EXCUSE

"MAY I PLAY THROUGH? MY BATTERY IS LOW."

by deep-cut pile carpeting. The entertainment console, which included a 12-inch TV, AM-FM stereo and cassette tape deck was handmade in Brazilian walnut. A special feature was a musical horn that played the Crosby "ba-ba-ba-boo" musical trademark.

Barris also produced the Kandy Orange Kart special for Frank Sinatra, and the Good Times Buggy for singer Glenn Campbell. Comedian Flip Wilson, when Bob Hope appeared on his 1975 TV show, compared carts with Hope. Flip's $18,000 customized job included color TV, refreshment bar, quadraphonic AM-FM eight-track tape deck, a loudspeaker amplifier and three chrome Italian horns which sounded off in harmony. The seats were done in gold metal plate, with his name spelled out in blue metal flakes.

The most famous cart of all was probably the one given to Dwight Eisenhower, when he was President of the United States. Because he brought the city so much attention

CLASSIC GOLF CAR COMPANY MAKES A NUMBER OF CARTS BASED ON SPORTS AND TOURING CARS OF THE 1930s.

chapter eleven

THIS "MERCEDES-ESQUE" CART FROM RE/NEW AU IS HIGH ON STYLE.

when he vacationed and played there, all of the Palm Springs country clubs got together and presented him with a Turf Rider IV, a $1,385 fiberglass cart considered the Cadillac of (assembly line) golf carts at the time.

So many of these special creations existed in the movie and entertainment colony which vacationed around the eight California desert resorts of Palm Springs, Rancho Mirage, La Quinta, Indio, Indian Wells, Desert Hot Springs, Cathedral City and Palm Desert, that Palm Desert eventually started an annual Golf Cart

golf á la cart

TWO WOMEN WHO DROVE THEIR CART OFF A COURSE WERE CHARGED WITH OPERATING A VEHICLE WITHOUT TAILLIGHTS OR STOPLIGHTS, NO TURN SIGNALS, NO HORN, NO REARVIEW MIRRORS, NO WINDSHIELD WIPERS, NO WINDSHIELD, NO REGISTRATION AND NO INSURANCE.

THE "2+2" FROM TEK CART IS GOLF'S ANSWER TO THE STRETCH LIMO.

Truth of the Lie

A HIGH SCHOOL TEACHER, WHO IS QUESTIONING A STUDENT'S EXCUSE AS TO WHY HIS ASSIGNMENT IS LATE: "DO YOU KNOW WHAT HAPPENS TO YOUNG MEN WHO TELL LIES?" STUDENT: "YEP. THEY ATTRACT THE ATTENTION OF BIG SHOTS AND, AS A RESULT, CAN MAKE A LOT OF MONEY." TEACHER: "YOU SEEM TO BE QUITE A CYNIC." STUDENT: "NOPE, I'M A CADDY."

Parade, the first Sunday in November. After all, they had 90 golf courses in the immediate vicinity to draw from!

Sunday Golfers

People, it seems, have gotten so comfortable in their golf carts that they often use them outside the courses. You see them all over retirement centers and mobile home parks, going for the mail, and so forth. You occasionally see one used as a handicap vehicle in a supermarket. Occasionally a country club even finds one of theirs missing. There was an example of this in Lawrence, Kansas a few years back. A couple of young women, each in a cart, were playing golf on a Sunday afternoon at the Alvamar Orchards

chapter eleven

CURRENTLY BREAKING ALL SPEED RECORDS ON THE COURSE IS THIS LAMBOURGHINI-STYLED CART COURTESY OF LUXURY CARTS OF HAWAII.

course there. Late in the afternoon, a maintenance man reported seeing the two carts being driven way out-of-bounds near the fifth hole. Since these vehicles were valued at about $3,000 apiece and the club had already had some wandering carts damaged, course officials rushed to corral them, without success. So the police were called. They finally found the carts about a half-mile from the course, parked behind Becerros, a Mexican restaurant. The two women were inside having a snack and drinking margaritas. They explained that, after playing two holes very badly, they were hot, tired and thirsty. They fully intended to return the carts when finished. The ladies were charged with operating a vehicle without taillights or stoplights, no turn signals, no horn, no rearview mirrors, no windshield wipers, no windshield, no registration and no insurance.

AT HOME ON THE OPEN RANGE OR THE DRIVING RANGE, THE '36 STEPSIDE FROM CLASSIC GOLF CAR COMPANY SPORTS A SOLID OAK TAILGATE.

Hole in One Helter-Skelter

chapter 12

Does a hole in one take luck or skill? "To tell you the truth, when I made my hole in one, I had six highballs and I could hardly see the ball," reported one golfer who didn't wish his name to be printed. Then there was C.C. Graves of New Haven, Connecticut, who bought a set of clubs on Monday, took his first lesson on Tuesday, and scored an ace on Wednesday. And Carl Sodi, playing the first game of his life, scored a 156 on a par-70 course, but had a hole in one. Henry Poli of Salem, Massachusetts carded a 150-yard ace *using a putter*!

A short time after losing his right arm in an industrial accident and learning how to play the game left-handed, Art Baird hit an ace at the Roadhaven Resort course in Apache Junction, Arizona (March 1991). In 1969, there was a news report of a right-handed golfer who tried

> **HENRY POLI OF SALEM, MASSACHUSETTS CARDED A 150-YARD ACE USING A PUTTER!**

chapter twelve

JOE KIRKWOOD HAD 26 HOLES IN ONE DURING HIS CAREER, INCLUDING ONE PLAYED OFF THE CRYSTAL OF A WATCH.

swinging lefty just for the fun of it and, on the first swing, made a hole in one.

Going them one-up was John W. Moore, who, in 1961, shot a hole in one from his wheelchair. He used a three-wood on the 110-yard 7th hole at Sunken Gardens course near San Jose, California. Four years earlier he had started swinging sawed-off clubs one-handed from the right side of his wheelchair just for exercise.

Margaret Waldron, 74 and legally blind, used a seven-iron and an old golf ball she had found to make holes in one on the same hole on consecutive days. It happened in March 1990 on the 87-yard 7th hole at the Long Point course at Amelia Island Plantation, Florida.

So you judge whether a hole in one takes skill or luck!

Easy as Pie

Sometimes, holes in one can drop with surprising ease. For instance, Pullman, Washington Golf Club manager Bill Stroup once decided to declare himself ineligible to compete in their hole in one tournament. In a moment of sublimely painful irony, he stepped up during a lull in play to hit a bag of balls for the fun of it—and dropped three into the cup!

hole in one helter-skelter

Golf Vocabulary: A Quiz

Can't make a hole in one? Well, at least you can learn to talk the talk.

1. Apron
2. Backdoor
3. Banana Ball
4. Bingle-Bangle-Bungle
5. Birdie
6. Bisque
7. Borrow
8. Bunker
9. Buzzard
10. Chili-Dip
11. Dormie
12. Duck Hook
13. Eagle
14. Explosion
15. Fluffy
16. Flush
17. Four Ball
18. Frog Hair
19. Fried Egg
20. Gimme
21. Hole Out
22. Honor
23. Hosel
24. Island
25. Jungle
26. Match Play
27. Medal Play
28. Muff
29. Mulligan
30. Nassau
31. 19th Hole
32. Punch Shot
33. Rain Maker
34. Sclaffing
35. Scratch Player
36. Shagging
37. Shank
38. Skin
39. Snake
40. Stick
41. Stony
42. Stroke Play
43. Stymie
44. Sweet Spot
45. Texas Wedge
46. Waggle
47. Wet Tee
48. Whiff
49. Wormburner
50. Yips

Answers:

1. Moderately mowed area immediately surrounding the greens.
2. When the ball rims the cup, then falls in from the backside.
3. A slice shot that starts out to the left, then fades right.
4. A gambling game that has three payoffs for each hole: ball reaching the green first, ball nearest the cup after all players reach the green, and first ball into the cup.
5. Making a hole one under par.
6. A handicap stroke that may be used on any hole.
7. Compensation figured in line of putt when putting over slanting section of green.
8. Sand trap.
9. A score for a hole made in two strokes over par.
10. Hitting the ground with your club before you hit the ball, thus producing a weakly lofted shot.
11. In match play, when a player or side is up by as many holes as remain to be played.
12. Right-to-left curve shot with the ball hooking or veering and rapidly dropping.
13. Hole made two strokes under par.
14. Blast shot out of a sand trap.
15. A ball that is sitting high up in the grass.
16. Full-swing hit flush on the center of the clubface.
17. Play in which partners count only their best ball strokes on each hole.
18. Short grass around the edge of the greens.
19. A ball that is half-buried in the sand.
20. Putt close enough to the hole to be considered unmissable.
21. Finish putting.
22. Privilege of driving off first, usually decided by lowest score on the preceding hole.
23. The hollow part of a club head into which the shaft is placed.
24. Floating green or one reached over a bridge.
25. Heavy rough.
26. Two-sided competition by holes.
27. Play in which the winner is determined by stroke play (total of hole-by-hole score).
28. To mis-hit a shot.
29. Courtesy second shot given after a poor first one.
30. Play with points given for each of nine holes and the 18.
31. The bar.
32. Striking down at the ball so it will fly low to the green.
33. Very high shot.
34. Scraping the clubhead along the ground before hitting the ball.
35. Player with no established handicap.
36. Picking up golf balls from a driving range.
37. A shot that, when struck by the club's hosel, travels to the right of the intended target.
38. A prearranged bet, with winner of each hole collecting a "skin" from each player.
39. Long putt where the green slopes in more than one direction between ball and hole.
40. Golf club.
41. To hit a ball close to the flagstick.
42. Same as Medal Play.
43. Ball on the green between hole and opponent's ball. No longer in use, since ball marking became official.
44. Spot on club, or ball, that provides maximum power.
45. What the putter is called when it is used from off of the green. Also any shot attempted off the green with the putter.
46. Practice swings before hitting ball.
47. A dangerous water hole.
48. To swing and completely miss the ball.
49. A ball hit with decent distance that stays close to the ground.
50. Shakiness or nervousness when attempting a shot (particularly a putt).

Scoring:

45-50—PGA Champion
35-44—Club Champion
25-34—Amateur
0-24—Duffer

chapter twelve

There was also the time a freshman at Hamilton College in New York was trying out for the golf team. He went up to the first tee and scored a hole in one. He, of course, made the team.

A relaxed demeanor may be the secret to the hole in one. Two elderly men were playing the Worthington Golf Course in Massachusetts, one down on the ninth hole. "I guess we need to birdie," joked Art Rolland, 72, looking at the flag 145 yards away. "In that case," returned George Torrey, 75, "I reckon I'll have to get a hole in one." He selected a six-iron, addressed the ball and swung. The ball bounced once on the green and plopped into the cup.

"That takes all the pressure off me," grinned Rolland as he teed up. He swung, the ball hit the edge of the green and, again, incredibly, fell into the cup.

Los Angeles, as a city, showed the whole rest of the country, back in May 1966, how easy holes in one are. In a seven-day period, the city's courses reported 14 of them. Only 11 had been made the preceding *year* on the *professional golf tour*! During the rest of the year, inexplicably, Angelenos only scored seven more.

Champ of Aces

Former Masters champion Art Wall, Jr. was often credited as the pro with the best all-time hole in one record, with 42. However, the 1988 *Guinness Book of World Records* gave amateur Scott Palmer of San Diego, California credit for "the greatest number of holes in one in one career at 98," and Palmer added two more a short time later. He was also written up in *Ripley's Believe It or Not* (1984): "Between Feb. 17, 1983 and March 6, 1984, Scott Palmer made 24 holes in one—17 with the same ball." In case you are wondering, Scott is not related to Arnold Palmer.

You made it, now display it!
Save that ace with this solid redwood plaque, and personalize it with your name, date, course, hole number, yardage and club used. Specify: 3 lines/38 chars. per line. USA.

HOLE-in-ONE TROPHY

THIS PAGE: A VARIETY OF HOLE IN ONE MEMORABILIA.

174

Longest Odds

Arnold Palmer, a week away from his 57th birthday, executed a shot sequence that has been computed at 10 million to 1 by statisticians. Using a five-iron on the 187-yard par-3 hole at the Tournament Players Club in Potomac, Maryland, Palmer made a hole in one, *the second one in two consecutive days on the same hole!*

Again, however, the odds maker is guessing, for records show that even this feat is not unique. Floyd Foreman of San Clemente, California once aced the par-3 140-yard 18th hole at his hometown course, then came back 17 days later to use the same four-iron and same ball to ace the same hole.

A somewhat similar happenstance involved Phyllis Campbell in Honiton, England, where she fired an ace on the sixth hole in 1965—the same hole at the same club she had aced ten years earlier.

Yvonne Leslie hit an ace on the 112-yard par-3 seventh hole at the Sea Island, Georgia Golf Course, then duplicated the feat a month later, on the same hole using the same four-iron.

Joe Vitullo probably holds the record for the most aces on the same hole. He made 10 on the 130-yard par-3 16th at Hubbard, Ohio.

Beyond these accomplishments research starts to get into the "Believe-It-or-Nots" of golfdom.

Dr. W.C. Bradbury made a hole in one at Bel Aire's 130-yard 5th hole every year for three years running.

Englishman John Hudson, as a 25-year old assistant pro competing in a Martini International tournament in Norwich, England, aced the 195-yard par-3 11th hole, then followed it with another ace on the 311-yard par-4 12th hole. W. Wheaton Morin, of Ottawa, Canada, at age 17, fired consecutive aces on holes of 220 and 155 yards.

The two-in-one holes in one, where a player in the same foursome trumps another's ace, turns out to be too common an occurrence, surprisingly, to include among our believe-it-or-nots. Quick research uncovered six cases in all.

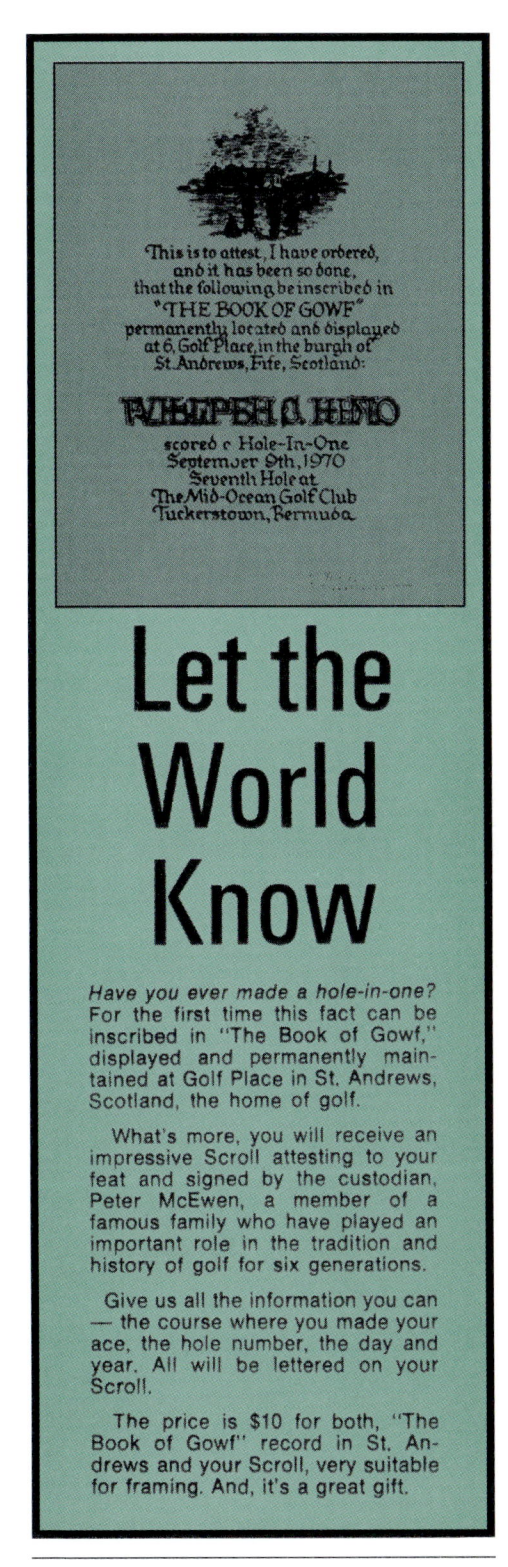

Let the World Know

Have you ever made a hole-in-one? For the first time this fact can be inscribed in "The Book of Gowf," displayed and permanently maintained at Golf Place in St. Andrews, Scotland, the home of golf.

What's more, you will receive an impressive Scroll attesting to your feat and signed by the custodian, Peter McEwen, a member of a famous family who have played an important role in the tradition and history of golf for six generations.

Give us all the information you can — the course where you made your ace, the hole number, the day and year. All will be lettered on your Scroll.

The price is $10 for both, "The Book of Gowf" record in St. Andrews and your Scroll, very suitable for framing. And, it's a great gift.

MAKE A HOLE IN ONE? PLACE YOUR FEAT IN THE ANNALS OF GOLF HISTORY!

chapter twelve

Longest Holes in One

The longest hole in one, by a female, is recorded at 393 yards, by Marie Robie of Wollaston, Massachusetts in 1949. Longest by a male is 480 yards, by Larry Bruce of Hope, Arizona in 1962. But it was a dogleg hole. The longest on a straightaway is 444 yards, by 5 foot, 6 inch, 165-pound Robert Mitera of Omaha, Nebraska in 1965, when he was a 21-year old Creighton University student. His tee shot, at the Miracle Hills Golf Course, was picked up by a 50-mph wind,

> THE LONGEST HOLE IN ONE, BY A FEMALE, IS RECORDED AT 393 YARDS, BY MARIE ROBIE OF WOLLASTON, MASSACHUSETTS IN 1949. LONGEST BY A MALE IS 480 YARDS, BY LARRY BRUCE OF HOPE, ARIZONA IN 1962.

carried over a high hill, and plopped down onto the green where it trickled into the cup. It was witnessed by a nearby foursome.

The youngest girl to score an ace was Rebecca Ann Chase, 8, who made the hole in one on the first hole she ever played, the 125-yard par-3 5th at Oak Knoll in Dallas, Oregon with a three wood. Youngest boy: Coby Orr, also playing his first round of golf, aced the 103-yard 5th hole with a five-iron at San Antonio's Riverside course in 1975, at age five.

The most prolific pre-teen would be Mancil Davis, 12. In 1966, he made five aces from January through August, the longest being a 205-yarder in Odessa, Texas. His total was eight, though he didn't like counting two of them, he said, one of which was on a par-3 course (though 167 yards) and one that hit a tree and a water sprinkler before going into the hole. By 1988, as a Texas club pro, he had been credited with 48.

The oldest female in this informal Ace High Club would be Mrs. Lily Parry. After Lily searched the rough and finally found her ball in the cup for her third career ace, fellow members claimed a world record for her. She was 81 years, 11 months old at the time (1971).

The oldest male to turn the trick is Otto Bucher of La Manga, Spain, who, at age 99, aced a 130-yard hole on his home course (1985).

Another ace of aces is Norman Manley. From 1963 to 1988, on 40 regulation courses, he shot 59 holes in one. *The Guinness Book of World Records* gives the title, though, to Scott Palmer, mentioned earlier, with his 100.

GROOVY THREADS, REBECCA!

Two Aces, Same Hole, Same Day

It is a relative rarity to have two aces on the same hole in the same day, but, still, not impossible. Lu Gilman and Mike Dougherty both used seven irons an hour apart to ace the 135-yard third hole at the Bel Aire, California Country Club, in 1962. And Dick McLeod and Mrs. Martha Baker did it just 20 minutes apart on the 195-yard 16th hole at the Springfield, Ohio Country Club. Still more unusual was Grant Anderson and his wife, Mary, doing the same thing while playing together in Portland, Oregon in 1975. They shot toward a partially hidden green of a 145-yard par-3 hole, then couldn't find either ball when they reached the green. "Goodness, you don't suppose they both went into the hole?" joked Mary. But they had. And the same thing

APRIL FOOL

WE WERE PLAYING A ROUND ON APRIL 1. WE WERE ON THE GREEN, A SHORT PAR-3, BUT LOCATED AROUND A BEND IN THE FAIRWAY, WHEN A BALL OFF A HIGH, BLIND TRAJECTORY DROPPED AT OUR FEET. DECIDING TO HAVE A LITTLE APRIL FOOL FUN AND, AT THE SAME TIME, GIVE THE UNKNOWN PLAYER A BIT OF A THRILL, I BOOTED THE BALL INTO THE CUP. THEN WE WAITED AROUND UNTIL AN ELDERLY GENTLEMAN CAME HUFFING AROUND THE BEND AND ASKED IF I HAD SEEN A BALL LAND. WHEN I TOLD HIM IT HAD GONE RIGHT INTO THE CUP, HE TURNED AND SHOUTED BACK TO HIS BUDDY, "HEY, JOE, YOU GOT AN EIGHT."

A Record Four Holes-In-One at the 6th Hole

How The Balls Bounced

Pate's ball landed about 7 feet past the pin, then rolled back.

Weaver's shot hit on the hill about 18 feet from the pin, then rolled back down.

Wiebe's shot landed about 9 feet to the left of the cup, then spun in.

Price's ball hit about 8 feet from the pin, jumped forward, then rolled back and in.

FURTHER PROOF THAT THE MILLENNIUM IS UPON US.

happened to George and Margaret Gordon while playing the Turnberry Golf Course in Scotland in 1963. In fact, according to *Golf Digest*, *seven* husbands and wives had scored aces on the same hole in the same round as of October 1988.

To have *four* players ace the same hole on the same day seems unbelievable! But it, too, happened, in a span of less than two hours on the 167-yard 6th hole at Oak Hill Country Club in Rochester, New York. Doug Weaver, Mark Weibe, Jerry Pate and Nick Price used seven-irons and each spun the ball back into the cup (1989).

On the subject of "all-in-the-family aces,"

chapter twelve

"THE WONDERFUL THING ABOUT TIGERS, IS TIGERS ARE WONDERFUL THINGS. THEY'RE CERTAINLY VERY GOOD PUTTERS, AND THEIR DRIVES ARE AS GOOD AS THEIR SWINGS. THEY'RE READY STEADY, LIKELY NIKE AND FULL OF HOLES IN ONE—BUT THE MOST WONDERFUL THING ABOUT TIGERS IS, THEY'LL BE #1." TIGER WOODS HAD A HOLE IN ONE IN THE FINAL ROUND OF HIS FIRST PROFESSIONAL TOURNAMENT.

three members of the Don Dugan family of Brockport, New York each shot an ace in less than a month, and four members of the Needham family of Palo Alto, California turned the trick in a seven month period.

Insurance, Anyone?

The worst thing about holes in one for a golfer (and the best thing for the liquor industry) is the hoary tradition that the lucky individual is expected to buy drinks for everyone in the clubhouse. Some wise-guy years back tried an end run around this custom by petitioning the USGA to declare his an unplayable lie instead of a hole in one, but his petition was denied. After his third hole in one, Tom Breen of Circencester, England, took out insurance against any more. This was a new thought at the time. But today companies like CGA, Inc. of Mishawaka, Indiana, American Hole 'N One in Buford, Georgia and Hole in One International in Reno, Nevada make big business of such insurance. But their insurance is for tournament sponsors, not for individuals looking to save an astronomical bar bill. And, as sports writer Jim Murray once put it, "insurance companies are crapshooters who bring their own dice and pay only house odds."

Lloyd's of London insured a Palm Springs, California tournament against a hole in one, charging $4,000 against an advertised $50,000 payoff. And they crapped out. A golfer named

Joe Campbell made one. The next year the cost of the premium went up to $12,000. And pro Don January made one. It was never admitted that any underwriters at Lloyd's were fired, but when Palm Springs wanted insurance the following year again, the company said, "That will be $68,000, please."

Gift From Heaven

The elderly minister was probably among the world's worst golfers. However, one day on a fairly long, straight hole, he uncorked a whopping drive right in line with the pin. The ball bounced off the hard turf and began a fast roll. As though drawn by a magnet, it continued to roll—over an apron, across the front of the green, on and on right at the flag. It teasingly slowed, but had just enough momentum to drop into the cup. The astounded clergyman, turning his eyes toward heaven, testily remarked, "Father, please, I'd rather do it myself!"

Golf Is...

- ...flog spelled backwards.
- ...always played with your worst enemy—you.
- ...a game few people play, but many work at.
- ...a game in which a ball 1½ inches in diameter is placed on another ball 8,000 miles in diameter, with the object being to miss the big ball and hit the little one.
- ...a compromise of what your ego wants you to do, what experience tells you to do, and what your nerve lets you do.
- ...a game where a player blames fate for accidents, but feels personally responsible if he makes a hole in one.
- ...like taxes. You drive hard to get to the green, then end up in the hole.
- ...a lot of walking broken up by disappointments and bad arithmetic.
- ...a game where a player yells "Fore," takes six and puts down five.
- ...a game where a lot of guys chase a golf ball because they're too old to chase anything else.
- ...a game in which you claim the privileges of age and retain the playthings of childhood.
- ...a game some play religiously—every Sunday.
- ...like a love affair. If you don't take it seriously, it is no fun. But, if you do, it breaks your heart.
- ...a sport in which the ball usually lies poorly, but the player well.
- ...different from most sports in that it has no defense. No matter how well a golfer plays, he can't prevent another golfer from playing better.
- ...after all is said and done, not a matter of life or death. It's much more important than that!

Resources

Association of Disabled American Golfers
7200 East Dry Creek
Suite G-102
Englewood, CO 80112
(303) 220-0921

Bad Dog Press
P.O. Box 130066
Roseville, MN 55113
(612) 482-0700   fax: (612) 482-0404
website: www.octane.com

Ban Products, Inc.
1156 Berwick Ln.
So. Euclid, OH 44121
(216) 381-6189

Barris Kustom Industries, Inc.
10811 Riverside Dr.
North Hollywood, CA 91602
(213) 877-2352

Classic Golf Car Company, Inc.
12535 320th Ave
Princeton, MN 55371-3374
(800) 950-4351   (612) 389-9139   fax: (612) 389-2417

C.N. Is Believing
NITELITE® Golf
P.O. Box 1200
Wolfeboro Falls, NH 03896
(603) 569-1533   fax: (603) 569-5752

Coeur d'Alene Resort
P.O. Box 7200
Coeur d'Alene, ID 83816
(208) 765-4000   fax: (208) 664-7276
website: www.cdaresort.com

The Cow Pasture Open
Big Hole Tourism
Box 193
Wisdom, MT 59761
(406) 689-3254

Dennis Walters Golf Show
8991 S.W. Eighth Street
Plantation, FL 33324
(954) 474-3350
fax: (954) 236-6766

Divot the Clown
Trick Shot Exhibition
5883 S.E. Riverboat Drive
Stuart, FL 34997
(561) 283-1240

Douglas Keister Photography
1550 Marin Avenue
Albany, CA 94706
(510) 558-9909
fax: (510) 527-8679
e-mail: keister@pacbell.net

Eddie Elias Enterprises, Inc.
1720 Merriman Rd.
Box 5118
Akron, OH 44313
(800) 331-2953

Frank Zega, Jr.
130 Eastfield Drive
Fairfield, CT 06432
(203) 372-2443
(203) 261-6262

Golf Collector's Society
P.O. Box 241042
Cleveland, OH 44124
(216) 861-1615
fax: (216) 861-1630

Golf Nuts Society of America
P.O. Box 1226
Carefree, AZ 85377
(602) 488-0401
(602) 595-0114
e-mail: headnut@golfweb.com

Golfsmith International, L.P.
11000 North IH-35
Austin, TX 78753
(512) 837-8810
fax: (512) 837-9347

GolfTek
0201 First St.
Lewiston, ID 83501
(208) 743-9037
fax: (208) 746-3559

resources

Gorilla Sports, Inc.
P.O. Box 1334
Tacoma, WA 98401
(253) 272-7684

Grand Haven/Spring Lake Area Visitors Bureau
One South Harbor Drive
Grand Haven, MI 49417
(800) 303-4097   (616) 842-4499
fax: (616) 842-0379
website: www.grandhavenchamber.org
e-mail: events@grandhavenchamber.org

Paul Hahn, Jr.
Trick Shot and Exhibiton Clinic
309 Mariner Cove Club
Hilton Head Island, S.C. 29926
(800) 742-4069
(803) 681-6767
fax: (803) 681-6760
website: www.golftrickshots.com

Hammacher Schlemmer
Operations Center
9180 Le Saint Drive
Fairfield, OH 45104-5475
www.hammacher.com
orders: (800) 543-3366
fax: (800) 440-4020

The Homestead 1766
P.O. Box 2000
Hot Springs, VA 24445
800-838-1766
fax: (540) 839-7782
website: www.thehomestead.com

Houston Designs
P.O. Box 849
Eagar, AZ 85925-0849
(800) 776-1594
(520) 333-5162

HTC International, Inc.
5405 Morehouse Dr.
Suite 230
San Diego, CA 92121-4725
(800) 437-5999
(619) 626-2800
fax: (619) 626-2808

James River Country Club Museum
1500 Country Club Rd.
Newport News, VA 23606
(757) 595-3327   (757) 596-4772

Joey "O"
P.O. Box 1196
Cedar Rapids, IA 52406-1196
(319) 365-7546 ext. 302

Karsten Manufacturing Corporation
2201 West Desert Cove
P.O. Box 9990
Phoenix, AZ 85068
(602) 870-5000
fax: (602) 678-1641

Laid Back Gifts
4020 Will Rogers Pkwy. #700
Oklahoma City, OK 73108
(405) 948-8555
fax: (405) 948-1784

Leister Game Company
511 Sumner St.
Toledo, OH 43609

Luxury Carts of Hawaii
98-1277 Kaahumanu St.
Suite #152
Aiea, HI 96701
(808) 625-9890
website: www.luxurycarts.com

Matzie Golf
43-695 Jackson St.
Indio, CA 92201
(800) 722-7125

Mike Calbot Golf Exhibitions
12520 Woodtimber Lane
Ft. Myers, FL 33913
(800) 298-9223
fax: (941) 561-3701

Nicklaus Golf Equipment
7830 Byron Dr.
W. Palm Beach, FL 33401
(561) 881-7981
(800) 322-1872
fax: (561) 881-8214

Oak Knoll Golf Club
6335 Highway 22
Independence, OR 97351
(503) 378-0344

Oldsmobile Scramble Golf Tournament
127 Industrial Ave.
Coldwater, MI 49036
(800) 582-1908

Palm Desert News Bureau
P.O. Box 11655
Palm Desert, CA 92255
(760) 776-0020

Par T Golf Marketing Co.
7310 Smoke Ranch Road
Suite H
Las Vegas, NV 89128
(800) 350-7277
(702) 243-6811
fax: (702) 243-6801

The Peter Longo Golf Show
Box 27283
Tempe, AZ 85285

The Pilcher Company
P.O. Box 1456
Hellendale, CA 92342

Ralph Maltby's GolfWorks
4820 Jacksontown Rd.
Newark, OH 43055
(800) 800-3290
(740) 328-4193
e-mail: golfworks@nextek.net

Renaissance Golf Design, Inc.
12719 S.W. Bayshore Dr.
Suite 10
Traverse City, MI 49684
(616) 941-7499
fax: (616) 941-2114

RE/NEW AU
2650 Whitfield Avenue
Sarasota, FL 34243
(941) 739-CARS (2277)
fax: (941) 751-0906

Ron Kirkwood Photography
1114 N.W. 55 St.
Oklahoma, OK 73118-4002
(405) 840-2744

Sizzle NEV
4215 Westerville Road
Columbus, OH 43224
(800) 433-BAJA   (614) 478-4072
fax: (614) 478-4099

Speed Golf
World Speed Golf Association
P.O. Box 99518
San Diego, CA 92126
(619) 581-0905
fax: (619) 581-0906
e-mail: jlarson@adnc.com

SportsHealth
527 W. Windsor Rd.
Glendale, CA 91204
(800) 289-7889

TEK Cart
1750 Mojave View Circle
Corona, CA 91720
(909) 371-3334
fax: (909) 371-2459

True Temper Sports
8275 Tournament Dr., Suite 200
Memphis, TN 38125
(901) 746-2000

USGA Museum and Library
P.O. Box 706
Far Hills, NJ 07931
(908) 234-2300

Wedgy Winchester
728 E. Rose Ln.
Phoenix, AZ 85014
(602) 274-4145
fax: (602) 279-4108

Wildcat Golf
P.O. Box 805
Kent, WA 98035
(888) 794-5322   (253) 850-8002
fax: (253) 850-8140

Acknowledgments

The following individuals, organizations, and companies have furnished ideas, information, photographs, illustrations, catalogs and comments. We thank them wholeheartedly.

Ace Golf Cars, Robin Denise

Ada Mark, Inc., Robert C. Stewart, Grand Rapids, MI

Ajay Enterprises, Delavan, WI

Aldila, San Diego, CA

Align-A-Putt, Dale Nephew, Snohomish, WA

American Golf Unlimited, Inc., Jerry Gunderson, Pres., Deerfield Beach, FL

AP/Wide World Photos, Holly Jones & Ann Perkins, Los Angeles, CA

Archive Photos, New York, NY

Association of Disabled American Golfers, L. Gregory Jones, Exec. Director, Englewood, CO

Australian Golf Club, Ltd., Jim Grant, Rosebery, New South Wales

Bad Dog Press, Tim Nyberg, Roseville, MN

Ban Products, Inc., Thomas E. Ban, Pres., So. Euclid, OH

Barber, Jerry, Los Angeles, CA

Barris Kustom Industries, George Barris, North Hollywood, CA

Bell Products, Napa, CA

Beta Engineering, Pineville, LA

Big Hole Tourism, Barb & Wayne Challoner, Wisdom, MT

Bobby Grace Golf Design, Inc., Scott Halleran, Marketing/ Media Director, St. Petersburg, FL

Bodleian Library, Christine Mason, Principal Library Asst., University of Oxford, Oxford, England

British Library, Head of Informational Services, London, England

Brue, Bob, Shorewood, WI

Bushnell Sports Optics, Overland Park, KS

C&D Sports, Las Vegas, NV

Classic Golf Car Company, Inc., John Herou, Princeton, MN

C.N. is Believing/NITELITE® Golf, Corky Newcomb, Wolfeboro Falls, NH

Coeur d'Alene Golf Resort, Mike DeLong, Coeur d'Alene, ID

Colton Golf Products, Roland J. Colton, Port Washington, NY

Competitive Edge Golf. New York, NY

Corbis-Bettman Archives, Norman Currie, New York, NY

Course Non-Sense, Joyce Schmidt, Owner, Powell, OH

Creative Sports Group, Sally Tanos, VP Sales/Marketing, Fullerton, CA

Cushman Motor Sales, Tom Jarrett, Santa Fe Springs, CA

Davis Home & Away Products, Frederick W. Davis, Medfield, MA

Delhi Golf Club, Col. R.S. Brar (Ret), New Delhi, India

Dennis Dawson Products, Dennis Dawson, Pres./CEO, Moorpark, CA

Dennis Walters Golf Show, Dennis Walters, Plantation, FL

DeVac, Inc., Northbrook, IL

"Divot the Clown," Kevin Compare, Stuart, FL

DME, Costa Mesa, CA

Douglas Keister Photography, Doug Keister, Albany, CA

Druid Hills Golf Club, David Paulsen, Gen. Mgr., Atlanta, GA

Eastern Golf Corp., Stephen Kohuth, VP Sales, Hamlin, PA

Eco Golf, Scot Marsella, Sales Mgr., Columbus, IN

Eddie Elias Enterprises, Eric McClenaghan, Akron, OH

Edwin L. Holt Company, Edwin L. Holt, Boynton Beach, FL

Eldorado Products, Inc., H. D. Meyer, Pres., Newport Beach, CA

Embassy of Japan, Japan Information & Cultural Center, Washington, DC

Embassy of Sweden, Ann-Marie Brisbois, Washington, DC

Enticements, Mt. Vernon, NY

First Flight, Belleville, IL

Florida Golf Warehouse, Orlando, FL

FM Precision Golf Corp. (formerly Brunswick), Torrington, CT

Fort St. John Golf Course, Jack Musson, Fort St. John, BC, Canada

Full Swing Golf, Inc., Scott Werbelow, VP Sales, San Diego, CA

GAB Enterprises, Inc., Frederick W. Davis, Phoenix, AZ

acknowledgments

Game Room, Spencer Howell, Washington, DC

Golden Shine, Inc., Mei Lee, Mgr., Anaheim, CA

Golf Around the World, Inc., Gary Wiren, CEO, Dane M. Wiren, President, Lake Park, FL

Golf Collector's Society, Tom Kuhl, Dayton, OH

Golfcraft Company, Bill Glasson, Engineer; Ralph L. Kolle, Sales Coordinator, Bakersfield, CA

Golfmaster, Houston, TX

Golf Nuts Society of America, Ron Garland, Carefree, AZ

Golfomat Division, EMC, Daniel J. Creveling, Natl. Marketing Mgr., Alexandria, VA

Golf Pride Company, John Lancaster, Laurinburg, NC

Golf Rite Products, Houston, TX

Golfsmith International, L.P., Barry Rinke, Marketing Dir., Austin, TX

GolfTek, Bud Davison, Lewiston, ID

Gorilla Sports, Inc., Tom Tuell, Tacoma, WA

Grand Haven/Spring Lake Area Visitors Bureau, Heather Johnson, Grand Haven

Hammacher Schlemmer, Sabrina Balthazar-Vlcek, Chicago, IL

Hardison, Frank, Laguna Beach, CA

Haverhill's, San Francisco, CA

Head Freezer, Jackson, MI

Head Trainer, Mesa, AZ

Heavy Hitter Golf, Tina Brandell, Orlando, FL

Henricus, Inc., John Green, VP Sales, Walnut, CA

Hole in One International, Zak Woodhead, Sales Mgr., Reno, NV

Holland Area Convention & Visitors Bureau, Holland, MI

Home Health Services, Becky Keshen, Admin. Asst., Colfax, WA

The Homestead 1766, Mary Brady Sanders, Hot Springs, VA

Hope, Bob and Dolores

Hope, Guy and Nancy, Phoenix, OR

Horvat, Edward J., Littleton, CO

Houston Designs, Kristi and Russell Houston, Eagar, AZ

HTC International, Inc., Leanne Michael, San Diego, CA

Huntington Leisure Products, Tamar International, Inc., John Gear, Huntington, NY

Huxley, R.C., Administrator & President One Boat Golf Club, Ascension Island, South Atlantic

James River Country Club & Museum, Weymouth B. Crumpler, Curator, Newport News, VA

Joey "O," Cedar Rapids, IA

John Lambert Associates, Venice, CA

Jones & Relfe Company, Charlie Jones, Montgomery, AL

JOP Enterprises, No. Bergen, NJ

Jornel, Inc., E.W. Jorgensen, Pres., Spokane, WA

Kangaroo Motorcaddies, Columbus, NC

Karsten Manufacturing Corp., Pete Samuels, Adv. Mgr., Phoenix, AZ

Katy Parsons Golf Course, Parsons, KS

Kerdad, Inc., Alamo, CA

Lady Pro, Julie Neumann, VP Sales/Marketing, Zion, IL

Laid Back Gifts, Max Colclasure, Oklahoma City, OK

Las Vegas Discount Golf, Las Vegas, NV

Leister Game Company, Nancy Leister, Toledo, OH

Links of Scotland, David Piwko, VP Corp. Sales, Woburn, MA

Long Ball Sports, Inc., Brent Lewis Offerman, Englewood, CO

Los Angeles Supply Company, Richard R. Austin, Pres., Los Angeles, CA

Luxury Carts of Hawaii, Michael Hruby, Aiea, HI

Marksman Manufacturing, John M. Hart, Chula Vista, CA

Matzie Golf Company, Randy Bose, VP, Indio, CA

Mayor's Office, Mims, FL

Medicus, Tracy Lehnecker, Dir. Marketing/Sales, Brunswick, OH

Michigan Travel Bureau and Michigan Jobs Commission, Livonia, MI

Mike Calbot Golf Exhibitions, Mike Calbot, Ft. Myers, FL

Mitsubishi Electric Sales, Inc., Cypress, CA

Muscle Matic Company, James Brown, Sales, St. Petersburg, FL

National Golf Foundation, Jupiter, FL

National Library of Scotland, Jane Rose, Asst. Reference Services; J. McFarlane, Head, Reference Services; Mrs. O.M. Geddes, Sr. Research Asst., Edinburgh, Scotland

acknowledgments

Natural Golf, Chip Woods, Sales Dir., Hoffman Estates, IL

Netik Enterprises, Monterey, CA

News of the North, Mary Jenkins, Yellowknife, NWT, Canada

Nicklaus Golf Equipment, Andrew W. York, Dir. Marketing, W. Palm Beach, FL

Northern Golf Ball Company, Chicago, IL

Northern Transportation Company, George Inglis, Edmonton, Canada

Nunn, Henry L., LaJolla, CA

Oak Knoll Golf Club, Joe Barnes, Manager, Independence, OR

Ofer Custom Clubs, Canton, OH

Oldsmobile Scramble Golf Tournament, Brent Whitcomb, Coldwater, MI

Palm Desert News Bureau, Kristy Kneidling, Palm Desert, CA

Palm Springs Desert Resorts Convention & Visitors Bureau, Laurie Armstrong, VP Communications, and Pamela Lee Henry, Communications Manager, Rancho Mirage, CA

Par Aide Products, St. Paul, MN

Par Buster Company, Tulsa, OK

Par Buster, Inc., F.J. Petrowski, VP, Parma, OH

Par-Phernaliia Golf Products, San Diego, CA

Par T Golf Marketing Co., Tom Bowerman, Las Vegas, NV

Paul Hahn, Jr. Golf Exhibitions, Tom Thomas, Dir. Sales, Hilton Head Island, SC

The Peter Longo Golf Show, Peter Longo, Tempe, AZ

PGA of America, Jess D. Taylor, Manager Golf Services, Atlanta, GA

Pilcher Company, Pug Pilcher, Helendale, CA

Powakaddy Corp., Rockport, MA

Ralph Maltby's GolfWorks, Ralph Maltby, Pres.; Sandy Ramey, Staff Photog.; Steve Gilligan, Marketing Mgr., Newark, OH

Ralph W. Miller Golf Library & Museum, Marge Dewey, Mgr., City of Industry, CA

Ranging, Inc., J. Michael Murray, Pres., Rochester, NY

Renaissance Golf Design, Inc., Tom Doak, Traverse City, MI

RE/NEW AU, Sarasota, FL

Right Touch Company, Craig foster, Owner, Olympia, WA

Ron Kirkwood Photography, Ron Kirkwood, Oklahoma, OK

Ryobi-Toski Corp., James J. Shea, Newark, OH

Sasse Golf, Inc., Howard A. Sasse, Southern Pines, NC

Saugatuck/Douglas Convention & Visitors Bureau, Saugatuck, MI

Scorecard Plus, John Ryan, VP Adv. Sales, Canton, OH

Select A Putt, Inc., Ernest R. Andis, Racine, WI

SGD, Norm Schmidt, VP Marketing/Sales, Akron, OH

Sharper Image, San Francisco, CA

Shepherd's Pack, Ltd., Allenhurst, NJ

Sizzle NEV, Bruce Rutherford, Columbus, OH

Smith, Fred, Palm Desert, CA

Smith, Mel, Glen Ellen, CA

Soft-Tee Enterprises, Kent, WA

Speed Golf, Jay Larson, Solana Beach, CA

SportsHealth, Bill Cox, Glendale, CA

Sports Marketing & Management Group, Joe Sweeney, President, Milwaukee, WI

Swing-O-Meter, Englewood, NJ

Tee-Off Company, Jim Laabs, Madison, WI

TEK Cart, Corona, CA

Thorner, Jeff, San Anselmo, CA

Titleist & Foot Joy Worldwide, David E. Overmeyer, VP Marketing, New Bedford, MA

TJZ Enterprises, D. Granelli, San Francisco, CA

True Temper Company, Charles D. Barker, VP, Memphis, TN

UCLA, Nanette McIntrye, Prof. Raymond A. Snyder, Human Performance Lab, Westwood, CA

USGA, Bill Anderson, Communications Asst., Far Hills, NJ

USGA Museum and Library, Andy Mutch, Far Hills, NJ

Vedoro, Ltd., Roland Warden, Gen. Mgr., Wichita, KS

Vent Sign Company, Burbank, CA

Vistatronics, Inc., Minneapolis, MN

Voit Sports, Los Angeles, CA

Wedgy Winchester, Phoenix, AZ

Wham-O Manufacturing, Chino, CA

Wildcat Golf, Melody K. Brown, President, Kent, WA

Wood Wand Corp., Southern Pines, NC

Wright Weight Corp., Ludlow, MA

Zega, Jr., Frank, Fairfield, CT

Permissions

While every effort has been made to contact manufacturers, companies and individuals, some sources of certain photographs and illustrations were impossible to track down. Any uncredited image brought to our attention by its owner will be credited in future editions.

Frank Hardison: 9, 21, 124, 137, 147 (all), 148 (middle), 151, 152 (all)

James River Country Club Museum: 10, 159 (lower left)

Fred Smith: 11 (bottom), 18 (lower right))

Corbis-Bettmann Archives: 11 (upper right), 12, 68, 141

The Homestead 1766: 15 (lower left)

Tom Kuhl: 15 (right), 16, 123, 148 (lower right), 156 (lower right), 162 (upper left)

Wedgy Winchester: 23, 64,

Archive Photos: 26

Eddie Elias Enterprises, Inc.: 29

Houston Designs: 31, 67

Golf Nuts Society of America: 32, 35 (all),

Douglas Keister Photography: 33, 56-57, 58, 72,

Lois Schwartz Photography: 36

C.N. Is Believing/NITELITE® Golf: 38

Jeff Thorner: 39, 40 (both)

Grand Haven/Spring Lake Area Visitors Bureau: 42 (both)

Laid Back Gifts: 43 (bottom), 157 (right)

Bad Dog Press: 44 (all), 45, 46

Association of Disabled American Golfers: 47, 48 (both)

Big Hole Tourism: 52, 53

Oldsmobile Scramble Golf Tournament: 54, 75

Ron Kirkwood: 59, 60, 76, 77, 134, 172

Paul Hahn, Jr.: 61, 62 (upper left)

Dennis Walters Golf Show: 62 (bottom)

Mike Calbot Golf Exhibitions: 63 (upper right)

Joey "O": 63 (lower left)

Kevin Compare: 65

Gorilla Sports, Inc.: 66 (upper right)

Peter Longo: 66 (bottom)

Tom Doak: 73

permissions

Coeur d'Alene Resort: 80

True Temper Sports: 81, 83

Ralph Maltby's GolfWorks: 86, 105, 117, 144

GolfTek: 87, 92, 94

Par T Golf Marketing Co.: 93

SportsHealth: 97

Golfsmith International, L.P.: 99 (lower left), 128 (left), 158, 174 (all)

Hammacher Schlemmer: 101 (both), 133, 146 (lower right)

Ban Products, Inc.: 102 (middle, right)

Leister Game Company: 118 (middle, bottom), 138

Frank Zega, Jr.: 121

Nicklaus Golf Equipment: 126, 129

Karsten Manufacturing Corporation: 127

USGA: 130 (bottom)

The Pilcher Company: 139

Matzie Golf: 140

Wildcat Golf: 146 (upper right)

HTC International, Inc.: 159 (upper right)

Classic Golf Car Company, Inc.: 167, 170 (lower right)

Barris Kustom Industries, Inc.: 164, 165

Sizzle NEV: 166 (right)

RE/NEW AU: 168

TEK Cart: 169

Luxury Carts of Hawaii: 161, 170 (upper left)

Oak Knoll Golf Club: 176

AP/Wide World Photos: 178

Books Available From Santa Monica Press

Offbeat Golf
A Swingin' Guide to a Worldwide Obsession
BY BOB LOEFFELBEIN
192 pages $17.95

Offbeat Museums
The Curators and Collections of America's Most Unusual Museums
BY SAUL RUBIN
240 pages $17.95

What's Buggin' You?
Michael Bohdan's Guide to Home Pest Control
BY MICHAEL BOHDAN
256 pages $12.95

Letter Writing Made Easy! Volume 2
Featuring More Sample Letters for Hundreds of Common Occasions
BY MARGARET MCCARTHY
224 pages $12.95

The Book of Good Habits
Simple and Creative Ways to Enrich Your Life
BY DIRK MATHISON
224 pages $9.95

Health Care Handbook
A Consumer's Guide to the American Health Care System
BY MARK CROMER
256 pages $12.95

Letter Writing Made Easy!
Featuring Sample Letters for Hundreds of Common Occasions
BY MARGARET MCCARTHY
224 pages $12.95

How to Win Lotteries, Sweepstakes, and Contests
BY STEVE LEDOUX
224 pages $12.95

How to Find Your Family Roots
The Complete Guide to Searching for Your Ancestors
BY WILLIAM LATHAM
224 pages $12.95

Helpful Household Hints
BY JUNE KING
224 pages $12.95

Order Form

1-800-784-9553

	Quantity	Amount
OFFBEAT GOLF ($17.95)	_____	_____
OFFBEAT MUSEUMS ($17.95)	_____	_____
WHAT'S BUGGIN' YOU? ($12.95)	_____	_____
LETTER WRITING MADE EASY! VOLUME 2 ($12.95)	_____	_____
THE BOOK OF GOOD HABITS ($9.95)	_____	_____
HEALTH CARE HANDBOOK ($12.95)	_____	_____
LETTER WRITING MADE EASY! ($12.95)	_____	_____
HOW TO WIN LOTTERIES, SWEEPSTAKES . . . ($12.95)	_____	_____
HOW TO FIND YOUR FAMILY ROOTS ($12.95)	_____	_____
HELPFUL HOUSEHOLD HINTS ($12.95)	_____	_____

Shipping & Handling:
- 1 book $3.00
- 2-3 books $4.00
- Each additional book is $ .50

Subtotal _____
Shipping and Handling (see left) _____
CA residents add 8.25% sales tax _____
TOTAL _____

Name _____

Address _____

City _____ State _____ ZIP _____

❏ Visa   ❏ MasterCard   Card Number _____

Signature _____

❏ Enclosed is my check or money order payable to:

Santa Monica Press LLC
P.O. Box 1076
Dept. 1027
Santa Monica, CA 90406
www.santamonicapress.com
smpress@pacificnet.net

1-800-784-9553

About the Author

Bob Loeffelbein has had several careers. He started as a physical education teacher at Stanford University, followed by stints at the University of Southern California and the University of the Seven Seas—a shipboard college sailing around the world. Mr. Loeffelbein later switched to teaching journalism at St. Mary's College of Maryland.

He served with the U.S. Navy's Amphibious Landing Forces in the World War II battles of Iwo Jima and Okinawa, and was aboard one of the first ships taking occupation troops into Nagasaki, Japan. After the atomic bombing in Nagasaki, he was aboard the armada's flagship in Tokyo Bay as the armistice was being signed. As such, Mr. Loeffelbein is probably the only person to follow the atom bomb from beginning to end, having worked as a public relations specialist with General Electric Company at the Hanford Atomic Products Operation, where plutonium for the bombs was made, and then seen first-hand the bomb's result ashore at Nagasaki. He was also recalled for the Korean War.

After taking a Master's Degree in Recreation Management at the University of Oregon, Mr. Loeffelbein served as superintendent of Parks & Recreation at River Road, Oregon and Twentynine Palms, California. He then became dean of the Navy Department's Special Services Training Facility for five years.

Since 1979, Mr. Loeffelbein has been a full-time freelance writer, with over 3,500 articles appearing in some 734 different publications in the U.S. and abroad. He has also had 12 books published, including: The Doodler's Dictionary (a humorous sketch book); Physical Education Teaching & Grading Manual; How to Goof-Proof Your Golf Game (about golfing gadgets); The Playground Summer Game Book; Knight Times: Jousting in the United States (a historical reference on the official state sport of Maryland); Script Tease: The Treasury of Surprise Endings (a short story collection); A Pack of Lies (a tall tale collection); Putting Your Best Feats Forward (a self-help book on job hunting skills); The Recreation Handbook (with over 500 new games described); The United States Flag Book: Everything About Old Glory; and Offbeat Golf.

He currently lives in the small town of Clarkston, Washington.